MUHLENBERG COLLEGE LIBRARY
ALLENTOWN, PA 18104-55

W9-DBY-782

WITHDRAWN

WITHDRAWN

Designing the
Green Economy

Designing the Green Economy

The Postindustrial Alternative
to Corporate Globalization

Brian Milani

ROWMAN & LITTLEFIELD PUBLISHERS, INC.
Lanham • Boulder • New York • Oxford

ROWMAN & LITTLEFIELD PUBLISHERS, INC.

Published in the United States of America
by Rowman & Littlefield Publishers, Inc.
4720 Boston Way, Lanham, Maryland 20706
http://www.rowmanlittlefield.com

12 Hid's Copse Road
Cumnor Hill, Oxford OX2 9JJ, England

Copyright © 2000 by Brian Milani

A Dream Like Mine words by Bruce Cockburn © 1991 Golden Mountain Music Corp. Used by permission.

All rights reserved. No part of this publication may be reproduced,
stored in a retrieval system, or transmitted in any form or by any
means, electronic, mechanical, photocopying, recording, or otherwise,
without the prior permission of the publisher.

British Library Cataloguing in Publication Information Available

Library of Congress Cataloging-in-Publication Data

Milani, Brian, 1948–
    Designing the green economy : the postindustrial alternative to corporate
globalization / Brian Milani.
        p.   cm.
    Includes bibliographical references and index.
    ISBN 0-8476-9189-6 (alk. paper)—ISBN 0-8476-9190-X (pbk. : alk. paper)
        1. Sustainable development. 2. Environmental economics. 3. Competition,
International. I. Title.

HC79.E5 M469 2000
338.9—dc21

00-029081

Printed in the United States of America

∞™ The paper used in this publication meets the minimum requirements of American
National Standard for Information Sciences—Permanence of Paper for Printed Library
Materials, ANSI/NISO Z39.48-1992.

Contents

Green Building
Power, Money, and Built-Form
Strategic Opportunities in the Built-Environment

Historical Trends: From Quantity to Quality
Decentralization, Integration, and the Landscape
Renewable Energy and Distributed Generation
End-Use and Dematerialization
Deregulation: Competition for What?
The Green Municipal Utility
Elements of Green Energy Strategy

Scale, Craft, and Community
The New Industrial Eco-Structure
The Closed-Loop Economy
Product Design and Product Stewardship
Beyond Petrochemicals: Benign Materials and the
     Carbohydrate Economy
Community Consumerism and Sharing
Advanced Technology and the Information Economy
Eco-Infostructure: Gaia's Nervous System

Scarcity, Power, and Commodity-Money
Going Local
Money as Information
LETS: Storing Value in Community
Money, Value, and Production
Indicators: Vital Signs of Real Wealth
Regenerative Finance and Community Self-Regulation

Green Community Self-Regulation
Scale and Accountability
Participatory Planning and Green Municipalism
New Rules and Regulation
Designing Markets for Regenerative Exchange
Ecological Tax Reform

Knowledge and Self-Regulation
Beyond the Bioregion: Planetary Transformation
Business, Labor, and the State
Economic Conversion and (R)Evolutionary Strategy

Foreword

Thomas Berry

As we look out over the world about us we see a magnificent diversity of geological formations and living forms caught up into a single community of existence. Even beyond the Earth, this community includes the sun that shines upon us in the day and the moon and stars that we see at night. We ourselves come into being as one of the components of this community. To be integral members of this vast and lovely world is to experience an inner exaltation that makes life meaningful.

Each mode of being has its own unique rights and functions. So too each, as species and as individual, is able to contribute something that no other being can contribute to the integral functioning of the planet. We are so related that the wellbeing of each member of the community depends on the wellbeing of the other members of the community. This law of the integral functioning of the Earth constitutes what might be considered an ontological covenant bonding the universe into a single manifestation of the wonders of existence. This unity finds one of its highest expressions in the ever-renewing cycle of the biosystems of the planet.

The difficulty that western civilization is experiencing in the opening years of the twenty-first century is the consequence of violating this ever-renewing process. While this violation has a history that would take us back to earlier moments in our cultural development, the most severe form of our present difficulties found expression in the last two decades of the nineteenth century. This was the period when we moved from a land-based organic ever-renewing economy to an extractive industrial non-renewing economy.

Within two brief decades at the end of the nineteenth century the industrial foundations of twentieth-century America—and indeed of the modern world—were established. The five main petroleum corporations, including Standard Oil, were formed. So too the public utilities: General Electric, Westinghouse, American Telephone and Telegraph; the great steel corporations: United States Steel, Jones and Loughlin; the pharmaceutical companies: Johnson and Johnson, Clinton which later became Merck; the lumbering companies: International Paper, Scott Paper, and Weyerhauser—all these were founded in the late nineteenth century. A few years later, in 1903, Ford Motor Company was founded, then General Motors in 1908. The paving of the roads began. The industrial establishments assumed the mandate to take over the continent and all its resources.

Such an economy we might consider terminal, since a program based on extracting non-renewing resources from the Earth and even exhausting renewable resources cannot long survive, especially when the amount of extraction is so great in its volume and the industrial establishment is so relentless in its demands. In such an economy the basic resources cannot be renewed. An industrial economy causes immense devastation, creates extensive toxicity, and leaves a vast amount of non-disposable waste.

Because of this exploitation of the planet, a large proportion of the natural world has been destroyed. As regards the living world, such knowledgeable scholars as E. O. Wilson, Peter Raven, and Norman Myers tell us that no extinction so extensive has occurred since some 65 million years ago at the end of the Mesozoic and the beginning of the Cenozoic period. We seem not to realize that the pattern of living and being is so woven together that the entire fabric of life is weakened and tends to fall apart when even a few threads are removed or when the natural setting is disturbed in some manner.

When this outer world is disturbed so profoundly, the inner world of the human experiences corresponding difficulties, for the outer world of nature and the inner psychic world are two dimensions of a single reality. If an economy devastates the natural world then neither the psychic nor the physical structure of the human component of the Earth community can function in any satisfying manner.

The need for the surrounding wonders of the planet Earth is one of the main reasons why humans could not come into being until the late Cenozoic when the Earth blossomed in a brilliant phase of its life expression. We needed such a setting for our existence as humans. We can understand this when we consider that if we lived on the moon our imagination would be as empty as the moon, our emotions would be as desolate, our minds would be retarded, our sense of the divine would reflect the lunar landscape.

As the industrial world reduces Earth to a lunar condition, we lose the sublimity of our inner lives. The real reason why we cannot live on Mars is not exactly our inability to establish the physical conditions for life there. The real reason is that we would die in our inner world.

From these observations, we can see that a viable economy cannot be constructed simply by mitigating the consequences of the industrial world while keeping such an exploitative attitude. A new mentality, a new mystique, is needed, a new way of being present to the world around us. Already by referring to the materials of the natural world as "resources," we bring them into a context that has reduced the relationship that should exist between ourselves and the world about us.

We need to understand the entire world as primarily a communion of subjects, not as a collection of objects. This relationship I refer to as that of *intimacy*. The entire universe is caught up in this intimacy of all things with each other. We need an economy born of this intimacy with a world that we commune with, not out of a world of "natural resources" that we exploit. Both the natural world about us and we ourselves would prosper in this understanding of ourselves and our universe.

What we are proposing here is not a scientific or technological iconoclasm. We are simply proposing that our human technologies be in accord with, not subversive of, nature's technologies. In an amazing engineering achievement nature is constantly drawing up an immense amount of water from the oceans, raining it down over the continents to nourish the forests and grasslands, then drawing it into the great rivers where it flows back into the seas. While this great hydrological cycle is such a remarkable technological accomplishment, it is in the service of the organic world of flowering plants and all the wild creatures that swim in the rivers, roam over the land, and fly through the air.

We need simply to integrate our own technologies into this process, drawing off what is appropriate for ourselves, yet remembering always that we must not deny other modes of being the fulfillment of their own needs. Any viable economic program must be a planetary economy, an economy that finds a place for every member of the great Earth community. For every being has the right to be, the right to habitat, and the right to fulfill its role in the ever-renewing processes of nature.

Before we build a dam on any river we must consider the consequences throughout the region. Before we build our railroads or highways along riverbanks we must consider the need other animals have for access to the river. Before we build our automobiles and highways we must consider how these affect the atmosphere, the forests, and all the other living forms. Before we pour poisonous pesticides over our cultivated fields, we need to be clear about the larger consequences. It is especially wrong to dam the rivers in such a manner that we deny the fish access to their spawning grounds.

Yet we need all the biological insight and technological skills we are capable of to obtain the nourishment and energy we require for our own survival and well-being. In the end we will have established a viable scientific understanding and practice of an organic economy. If such an economy is often severe, it is a creative rather than a destructive economy. However demanding, it offers a fulfillment beyond anything we can obtain in our present industrial economy.

The Earth will feed us, clothe us, shelter us, heal us and bring us to fulfillment of our deepest aspirations if only we abandon our present predatory attitude. The natural world and ourselves, we are not enemies. We arise from a common origin. We have a common destiny. We should find our fulfillment in each other and in the larger universe that infolds us.

Acknowledgments

When a book is a synthesis of a lifetime's thinking and activism, one feels indebted to an enormous number of people. It is impossible here to express my gratitude to all those who have supported or inspired my thinking over the years. That said, my partner in life, Angela Miles, stands out—as my biggest supporter, critic, counsellor, influence, and inspiration—a feminist with a joy in theory and practice.

My thinking has always been inspired by practical needs for social change, and therefore it has been influenced considerably by the environmental, feminist, social justice, labor, and community movements. In recent years, Toronto's Coalition for a Green Economy has been my main reference group and greatest source of environmental inspiration. It has given me the opportunity to meet, discuss, and even conspire with some of the most innovative pioneers of green alternative development—from Wayne Roberts, Susan Brandum and Stephen Hall to Greg Allen, Martin Liefhebber, and Ed Lowans, to name only a few.

Thanks must also go to the Metro Labour Education Centre, headed by Trish Stovel, which has given me the opportunity to marry my commitments to the labor and environmental movements, and to theory and practice, by teaching the *Green Economy* course there—and to feature exciting guest speakers from every green field. Thanks must also go to my co-conspirators at the Transformative Learning Centre (TLC) of the Ontario Institute for Studies in Education (OISE/UT) where I teach the material in this book. In particular, Prof. Edmund O'Sullivan has been a supporter, inspiration, promoter, and nagging critic. At York University's Faculty of Environmental Studies (FES), Ellie Perkins leads the list of those who have gone out of their way to support my research and teaching in radical green political-economy.

Besides the feedback I have received from Angie, Wayne, Ed, and Ellie, a number of others have offered very useful comments on this manuscript at some stage in its development—including Maria Mies, Terry Fowler, Richard Douthwaite, and Wolfgang Sachs. Special thanks must go to Father Tom Berry for his comments and wonderful foreword. There were also some excellent insights from a couple of anonymous reviewers contracted by my publisher. I would be remiss to forget that in previous decades, endless hours of discussion with other good friends—Bob Cole, Milton Freeman, Frank Smalls, Linda Hale, Tony Miles, Mike McConkey, Mike Welton, Marie Welton, Rick and Charo Shepherd— spawned the basic "Marxist-Taoist" intellectual framework upon which this book has been built.

Speaking of building, I must acknowledge the patience and inspiration of fellow construction colleagues who have put up with my political and theoretical preoccupations primarily because they've had powerful social visions of their own. They can attest to the fact that we didn't get into this for the money. Most significant is my former partner in Green City Construction and the Carpenters Union Environment Committee, Gilles Arseneault, whose battle back from a near-fatal disabling injury has been another kind of inspiration. But there is also Green City carpenter Peter Shepherd, and project manager Doug Webber, both committed to making ideals work in practice.

Finally I must thank my editors and contacts at Rowman & Littlefield, especially Dean Birkenkamp, for their support, criticism, and patience. Making such a comprehensive yet concise book work is a challenge for everyone, and they've shown a real commitment to do it.

Introduction: Dimensions of Green Economics

When you know, even for a moment, that it's your time, then you can walk with the power of a thousand generations.

—Bruce Cockburn, *A Dream Like Mine*

WEALTH VS. ILLTH

This book is about wealth, or rather the battle between two concepts of wealth, old and new. The old concept is wealth as money and things—quantitative wealth. It concentrates power and drives an economy that today destroys more than it creates. The new concept is wealth as *regeneration*—qualitative wealth—the (inner) development of people, the (social) development of community, and the restoration of all living systems. It is the wealth that defines the goals and strategies of green economics.

Green economics is commonly associated with "clean up," new markets, and new technologies. Like environmentalism, it is often equated with environmental protection. Environmental protection is an important concern, but it is actually a small part of real ecological economics, and it can even be a major distraction from dealing with fundamental problems. Environmental protection assumes a basic conflict between humanity and nature. It presumes an intrinsically destructive human economy from which nonhuman nature must always be shielded.

But must the human economy be so intrinsically destructive, or do we possess the capacity to adapt and fit benignly within natural processes? Does our preoccupation with limiting and controlling brown industry divert our attention from redesigning and implementing sustainable, and even regenerative, agricultural, energy, and manufacturing systems? Throughout this book, I will argue that there are great and growing potentials for human and ecological regeneration that mainstream proposals for economic reform often obscure. My position is that the success of our social change strategies depends on tapping these positive potentials, which involve all aspects of human development.

The possibility of positive qualitative development throws new light on the debate about "sustainability." Like mainstream concerns about environmental protection, most notions of sustainability assume all economic development must be *quantitative* development. It follows that the aim of sustainability is to reduce economic activity to a level that destroys nature no faster than nature can regenerate itself. This attitude, as Paul Hawken (1993) notes, treats sustainability as a gray area, where humanity is neither helping nor hurting nature appreciably. But belief in such a realm is probably a delusion. And it is certainly a delusion to believe we might reach this gray area simply by limiting or restricting the industrial economy.

In practice, our choice is between destruction or restoration; we must base our economy on one or the other. Either we are consciously implementing economic activities that *regenerate* communities and ecosystems, or we will destroy them. Quantitative development, driven by the profit motive, is today destructive economics. The key to the future is not limiting development, but transforming it.

The focus of this book therefore is not how to mitigate environmental destruction but how to *eliminate* it with a whole new kind of development that is not simply environmental but social and spiritual as well. It is the kind of holistic "development" that Herman Daly (1996) distinguishes from "growth," or what I call quantitative development.

There are two underlying assumptions to this book. One is that fundamental change is necessary; the other is that it's possible. It's often suggested that the left and social change movements have failed to transform society because they have been too radical and insufficiently pragmatic. Supposedly, they haven't been willing enough to compromise and find common ground. I argue precisely the reverse: that we have *underestimated the degree of qualitative change necessary* for us just to survive as a species. One powerful example is the calculation of Germany's prestigious Wuppertal Institute that basic sustainability in the developed countries requires a 90-percent (or "factor ten") reduction in resource use. Such efficiency is well beyond the capacity of existing industrial production and regulation. Something fundamental must change.

My second assumption is that not only must things change but they *can* change, radically. Our social, economic, and environmental crises are not simply the result of a destructive system run amuck; they exist because this system is suppressing and distorting qualitative development. These cultural, political, and technological potentials have been building over the past century. They have been partially expressed and largely suppressed by our industrial economies, and they go far deeper than the so-called information revolution. They revolve around a special role for human creativity and result from *a new relationship of culture to the economy.* The new productive forces (or NPFs) based in human culture are the product of economic development. They have been used by industrial capitalism as a means of accumulating capital. But these forces of human development cry out to be an end in themselves, and making this happen is what progressive social activism is all about today.

The economic possibilities for humanity to establish direct democracy, harmonize our activities with nature, and meet everyone's basic needs are actually growing. Such a green economy is the historically appropriate expression of our level of technological and economic development. Why this seems such a utopian project is not because it is not possible, but because the existing industrial system is mobilized so completely against these possibilities—and against the primary productive forces of our era. This situation suggests that the most efficient and painless way of dealing with our practical problems today may be acting on a fairly ecotopian agenda.

Redirecting economic development, however, does depend somewhat on understanding how the industrial system suppresses or channels emerging human potentials. Relationships of domination and exploitation have been largely compatible with quantitative industrial development. But they are absolutely incompatible with development geared to, and based on, human cultural development. For this reason, these emerging human potentials represent a threat to class society and all forms of domination. For competitive reasons, capitalism must continue to employ and channel the new productive forces. But it can never unleash them without undermining its primary structures and values.

Corporate globalization is turning opportunities for individual self-actualization, community self-reliance, direct democracy, equality, and integration with nature into their opposites: extreme forms of cultural decay and dependence, community decline, powerlessness, and environmental destruction. The irrationality of the dominant forms of development is matched only by their hypocrisy. The notion of "efficiency" is used to justify the most ludicrously wasteful forms of production, consumption, and competition. What is efficient for accumulating money today is most often destructive to real wealth and efficiency. Similarly, fears about public debt are used to create support for austerity programs designed partly to increase the economy's dependence on private debt. It is no accident that a new breed of social critics has resurrected Ruskin's term "illth" to describe the main output of today's economy (Cobb, Halstead, and Rowe, 1995). A number of these critics identify our era as the "cancer stage of capitalism" (McMurtry, 1999; Korten, 1999).

The cure to this dis-ease will not come primarily by cutting out the cancerous growth. Rather, it will come by starving the cancer, by unblocking and transmuting the repressed regenerative energy and redirecting this energy to healing activity. The prescription calls for a diverse mix of positive grassroots action, guided by a new paradigm of holistic development.

This book is a contribution to the discussion about this new paradigm. It is an attempt (in part 1) to situate the green economy in a historical context as the only authentic form of postindustrialism: the forms of production, consumption, and organization appropriate to a new stage of human development. It also tries (in part 2) to clarify the principles of this new paradigm as expressed in different areas of the economy. Thus, while it is a work of theory, it is also intended to be of practical significance in suggesting some general ways forward.

Covering so much in such a short space, it is clearly far from exhaustive. The intention, however, is to provide a concise work of synthesis that can spur debate and action.

FROM QUANTITY TO QUALITY

The contrast between concepts of wealth is intended to highlight green economics as a holistic paradigm of evolutionary development. Such historical perspectives are not exactly in intellectual fashion. Many thinkers on the left apparently feel burned by the left's past association with mechanistic forms of Marxism or failed experiments with state socialism. Others in the academy seem to be reacting in fear to the emergence of spiritual tendencies in the social movements, dismissing any large historical vision as "essentialism." Understanding the economy from a historical perspective should, of course, be the strong suit of Marxists. But unfortunately, few Marxists have gone beyond the application of mechanistic categories, tangentially related to nineteenth-century capitalism. Very few have attempted to look at qualitative changes in the nature of productive forces over time.

This work takes off from the traditional Marxist notion that the (old) "relations of production" become fetters on the (new) "forces of production," that is, the old social institutions hold back the developing productive forces (Marx, 1859). It attempts to build on the insights about historical changes in the productive forces offered by Radovan Richta, Fred Block, Larry Hirschhorn, and others. Their perspectives form the basis for my argument concerning qualitative/regenerative modes of development.

Although quantitative and qualitative aspects of any process always interact, as paradigms of development they are mutually exclusive. They have radically different forms, contents, *and* driving forces. Accumulation, however reengineered, will never be an appropriate means of creating regenerative wealth. Money and matter will have to be put in their place as simply means to an end. We now need new kinds of incentives for those things that communities decide represent real wealth for them. Those attributes of wealth are necessarily different for every community, even if many of the methods we use to monitor and account for them may be similar. Every community and region needs to design its own forms of valuation as well as the range of incentives it uses to build real wealth creation into everyday life. Most of the conventional methods of economic growth and accounting will be useless for this task.

One of the biggest factors obscuring the developmental potential of the new productive forces has been that they have been somewhat disguised by their gradual and piecemeal emergence. Another factor is how the threat they pose to the industrial order has been expressed in a wide variety of social, economic and political phenomena. Since the most obvious breakdown of the old industrial market system—in the Great Depression—measures have been instituted that have had the effect of spreading the impacts. This has made capitalism less vulnerable to acute economic crisis, but it has also deepened the negative effects.

The fact that these NPFs have been channelled or suppressed has made it very difficult to see their basic character. Mainstream writing on postindustrialism—including the work of Alvin Toffler (1980) and John Naisbitt (1982)—while often brilliantly insightful about certain things, has often failed to distinguish between actual postindustrial potentials and the decadent reactive tendencies of capitalism. Ecology has also had little or no role to play in these accounts.

The position of this book is unequivocal: authentic postindustrialism would be postmaterialist. Materialism is not simply the philosophy of industrial society but its driving force, structured into its markets and forms of regulation. Industrialism defines wealth as money and matter, and the goal is the accumulation of as much of each as possible. Money, the main goal of capitalistic economic activity, is essentially abstracted matter, pure quantity. Use-value (the service function of a good, which is shaped by social need) is always subordinate to exchange-value; it is a by-product, spin-off, or trickle-down of the competition for money.

Closely connected to this subordination of use-value is the relationship of scarcity to class, accumulation, and waste. A great irony of a quantitative system like industrialism is that it needs material scarcity to exist. As will be discussed later, all class societies are based on scarcity, both material and cultural. At a certain point, because of its very productiveness, industrialization begins to undermine this scarcity, threatening the existence of capitalism. For this reason, after reaching a certain historical threshold, roughly around the Great Depression, industrialism has had to artificially maintain scarcity in order to perpetuate itself. Waste has been the primary means by which material scarcity has been reproduced, and debt is the means by which monetary scarcity has been reinforced.

This perspective, which argues that our current environmental (and social) problems are basically problems of scarcity, runs counter to the mainstream environmental movement position that they are problems of abundance and affluence. Environmentalists would be right, however, to argue that the source of our problems is materialism because, in the industrial world, materialism and scarcity are inextricably connected. By contrast, real abundance—what Dane Rudhyar (1974) called "plenitude"—is qualitative, not quantitative. A postscarcity society would use less material, not more, both because it would center production directly on human and environmental regeneration, and because it would have the technical capacity to satisfy these needs with minimal resources. One of the most important tendencies of real economic development is dematerialization, the practical significance of which for green economic sectors I will discuss in part 2. Industrial society, based as it is on quantitative development, cannot allow any appreciable dematerialization. For this reason, truly ecological economics must be considered a subversive influence.

POSTINDUSTRIALISM AND ECOLOGY

The idea of qualitative wealth suggests two important elements of green vision that have major implications for social change strategy. One is the connection between individual and social change. The other is the possibility of a symbiosis between humanity and nature.

At the core of postindustrial productive forces is human self-development—what I call "people-production" and what Marxists have called the reproduction of labor-power. Whatever one calls this new importance of culture and creativity, the fact remains: the kind of people we become is crucial to the fate of society. *Regenerative development demands not just a new natural and social ecology but a new ecology of mind.* Our current industrial system is premised on various forms of mental slavery, addiction, and dependence that constantly distract us from what we really are and can be. Even social change organizations fall victim to unhealthy relationships among individuals acting out needs for recognition, acceptance, power, escape, and so on. New forms of ecological development are based on human creativity, but in most cases they also require new social skills and an authentic attitude of service, both to the community and to the planet. This is easier said than done because real consciousness change is not simply a matter of changing our values or beliefs. It also means changing habitual patterns of perception and reawakening or spawning deeper forms of awareness. This task can take many forms, but the point is that it can no longer remain the exclusive preserve of isolated artists or mystics. Furthermore, this psychological/spiritual project cannot be separated from social change, something that feminists have stressed most persistently.

The other important dimension of green vision is the identity of interests between human and nonhuman nature. The possibility of qualitative wealth throws important light on the debate between social ecologists and deep ecologists and on the supposed conflict between human and biospheric interests. This book will argue that, while conflict between human and nonhuman nature certainly does exist, it shouldn't—*if* human beings are acting in their own *deepest* interest. Acting from our deeper interest is no easy task, of course, but it is becoming increasingly clear that we are shooting ourselves in the foot (or head!) by pursuing a more narrow, short-term self-interest. The feedback loops for our ignorance are becoming tighter and tighter. At the same time, we are becoming aware of a deeper sense of identity that is both humbling and awe inspiring.

Although this book puts some emphasis on the ontological interrelationship between personal, social, and environmental change, my main concern is to highlight how our historical/evolutionary situation puts such a special focus on these connections. One of our current historical tasks—and opportunities—is to eliminate domination. This task is simply another way of expressing our quest to liberate repressed human potentials. While it is essential that the struggle against each form of domination be waged in its own terms—and not reduce one form to another or lump them all together—the practical conditions of establishing alternatives in every area will require making important connections.

Male supremacy, racism, and the exploitation of nature certainly existed to some degree in primitive societies. But the *institutionalization* of domination as we know it—of both people and nature—had its roots in civilization. Unravelling that oppressive institutionalization is our main task today. Suppressing nature required the suppression of much of the natural in ourselves and the creation of unhealthy forms of social dependency. By the same token, reestablishing regenerative relationships with nature will require human self-development.

This task has a spiritual side, but it also has a technical dimension. Ecological forms of production and organization depend on substituting human intelligence and creativity for nature's materials and energy. To do this, humans must stop being cogs in the megamachine and systematically develop their knowledge and holistic sensibilities. Human development and ecological regeneration depend on each other. While green economic design and ecological restoration depend on human creativity, so also do ecological production and consumption in turn provide the decentralized economic basis for direct democracy and social equality.

Postindustrial production is necessarily ecological production. In fact, economics should be seen as simply the human side of ecology, the study of how we survive by interaction with nature. By implementing economic processes that consciously work as subsystems of nature, we can produce at much higher levels of efficiency than even the best of conventional industrial production. Eco-production is geared to produce the most with the least. It does this partly by directly targeting social and environmental need. But it is so efficient also because it mimics the elegance of natural systems. Wherever possible it is integrated into the natural productivity of the landscape, as in the case of eco-infrastructure. In other cases, such as eco-industrial parks, it works by imitating the multifunctionality of ecosystems in human-made organization.

Some of the biggest "advances" of the green economy would involve simply recovering a heritage of ecological wisdom embodied in aboriginal and other traditional cultures. But humanity can also benefit from an enlightened use of scientific knowledge, which can help us "do more with less" while aiding nature to restore its own systems. Our use of enzymes and plant-based chemistry, for instance, can contribute to an environmentally benign "carbohydrate economy," which displaces the use of petrochemicals and even much renewable matter. Similarly, our knowledge of ecology can allow us to build "living machines," mini-wetlands and greenhouses that can purify water without chemicals or nonrenewable energy inputs.

Producing ecologically is also the answer to the crisis of unemployment. One reason is simply that eco-production is intrinsically people-intensive because it functions to replace materials and energy with human intelligence. It can reverse the industrial tendency to displace people with machinery and materials. It also overcomes unemployment by focusing attention on the need to properly remunerate important work that takes place outside the paid formal sector. In actual fact, there is no crisis of unemployment because there is no shortage of useful work to be done. The crisis is in how to remunerate this work or share out the wealth created. Eco-production takes place everywhere—in residential buildings, back yards, parks, back alleys, on rooftops—and in many cases the food, energy, water, feedstocks, and services provided can act as direct forms of remuneration. But, as we will see in part 2, there is a need for other mechanisms, such as community currencies and basic income plans, to support essential forms of eco-production and realize opportunities for gainful employment.

FROM OPPOSITION TO ALTERNATIVES: THE STRATEGY OF DESIGN

The emergence of more qualitative productive forces changes politics as much as it changes economics. Besides the fact that conscious planning becomes more important, the form and content of politics are transformed. Because the new productive forces are everywhere, everyday life becomes the key field of political action. Establishing fundamental alternatives does not require prior control of the state, a situation that changes the longstanding relationship between opposition and alternatives in social movement strategy: the direct creation of positive social and economic alternatives becomes the top priority of social change.

The possibility of such direct action indicates that, in an important sense, we have history on our side. The key trends of development are toward decentralization, participation, equality, and the direct satisfaction of need. In contrast to nineteenth-century industrialism, where capitalism's priorities of exploitation and domination were in sync with maturing industrial productive forces, today's class society has to resist and distort the new productive forces. The institutionalized forces of domination are still incredibly powerful and in many ways are growing even stronger. But the growth of liberating potentials nevertheless endows a distinct fragility to the current system, and the crucial political factor of the next several decades will likely be how quickly and comprehensively the social movements can create parallel power based on qualitative alternatives and vision.

Similar to the way that ecology has become an important productive force, which can help us establish regenerative development, so have the new, more culturally defined movements—feminist, environmental, first peoples, peace, human potential, and others—become forces of people-production. They have challenged every form of domination embedded in civilization, and they have questioned not just the distribution of wealth but the "what" and "why" of industrial production. In recent years, these movements not only have found ever more common ground with one another but also have put increasing emphasis on developing concrete alternatives.

The central importance of alternatives in social change strategy reflects a basic change in the appropriate role of the state in a postindustrial society. On one hand, human cultural and technological powers demand much greater levels of popular participation and direct democracy. Postindustrial production, based on human development and ecological integration, requires unprecedented levels of conscious planning. But this planning must be generated at the grassroots level and must be incredibly flexible. Both the unconscious market forces and the cumbersome bureaucratic hierarchies of industrialism are inadequate in the new situation. New network structures of participation and coordination are necessary. Ecological production in itself demands great participation—the high "eyes to acres" ratio that can make the most of every microclimate.

A new role for the state is also implied by our current social and environmental crises. Green economist Paul Hawken (1993) has argued that these crises are not primarily crises of *management* but of *design.* It will not help simply to replace our political leaders or bolster our regulatory apparatuses. We must fundamentally redesign the economy—in its content, its structure, and its driving forces.

Changing economic goals or driving forces is particularly crucial in making a transition from quantitative to qualitative development. In class societies, the state has always had a contradictory dual role: to support and reinforce exploitation as well as to protect the system from its own aggressive energies. Today, the state can no longer succeed in its "guardian" status (Jacobs, 1992) by curbing the excesses of accumulation and exploitation. It must be a part of changing those driving forces altogether by implementing *new rules* for the economic game.

Perhaps the most important aspect of these new rules is redefining the outputs of the economy in terms of their service qualities. Some industrial ecologists call this type of economy an "ecological service economy." Such an economy would be created through incentives for providing service and disincentives for the use of materials and energy. Green design would encourage access or mobility, rather than cars; heat and light, rather than electricity; nutrition, rather than food commodities; entertainment, rather than VCRs; clean clothes (or laundry services), rather than washing machines. New rules would encourage these needs to be satisfied in the most comprehensive, efficient, and elegant ways. This type of economy would, of course, entail radical new forms of producer liability and product stewardship that would challenge industrialism's long-standing emphasis on commodity production.

Various advocates of "green capitalism," including Hawken, feel that the profit motive and monetary accumulation can be left intact—and can even propel positive changes—as long as markets fully reflect real social and environmental costs. I will argue against this position even as I recognize that the struggle to make real costs visible is an important one, because I hope to show that a transformation to qualitative development must ultimately be driven by new kinds of values—and not simply quantitative ones like money. It is crucial that money and matter both be returned to the status of means to an end.

Part 2 will demonstrate how the principles of end-use and ecological design can be practically applied to the creation of postindustrial community-based economies. I hope to show that a truly knowledge-based economy is an economy of service and one that is well within our capacities. First, however, in part 1, I want to put these possibilities in historical perspective, to demonstrate the historical connection between money and matter in the development of industrialism, and to highlight some of the larger relationships defining current struggles.

I

Beyond Materialism: The Postindustrial Redefinition of Wealth

Economists must now change their models and assumptions to conform to the new reality: "inputs" to production are energy, resources and knowledge and the "output" must be more fully-human beings.

—Hazel Henderson, *Paradigms in Progress*

1

Industrialism and Quantitative Development

One of the most important debates in the environmental movement concerns economic growth. In the mainstream are discussions about how state regulation can limit economic growth enough to allow nature to rebound, and how enough prosperity can be generated to allow society to "afford" environmental protection. The introduction suggests why these discussions pose the wrong questions. On one hand, simply restricting development without redefining it will be hopelessly inadequate. On the other hand, the preoccupation with affordability implies we can finance the protection of nature by its destruction, which is ludicrous. Clearly something more qualitative is required than new forms of management, or environmental protection, or add-on markets.

A couple other perspectives on growth, however, should be mentioned. One is the apparently radical environmental argument against economic growth per se. The second is the position of "green capitalist" advocates like Amory Lovins and Paul Hawken, who feel that production can be transformed enough to disconnect monetary from material accumulation. That is, the profit motive can be used not only to encourage resource-efficiency but to actually shrink the physical economy while increasing the quality of life.

The anti-growth position is quite realistic in the sense that it acknowledges the connection between monetary and material accumulation (which I try to clarify in this book) and sees the need to put an end to growth, period. Its flaw, however, is that, like other "environmental protection" perspectives, it does not question the industrial definition of economics and wealth. It doesn't see that economic activity might be transformed completely to be regenerative and disaccumulative, or that, in Daly's (1996) terms, "development" can be differentiated from "growth." It overlooks that humans have a responsibility to actualize their potentials in service to the planet, and that this can and should be our economic activity.

The green capitalist position, influenced by industrial ecology, understands that disaccumulation and dematerialization are possible, and that production can be transformed. But it underestimates the connection between environmental and social domination as well as the qualitative changes that would have to take place in the driving forces of the economy. While we can certainly make use of a reshaped profit motive in the transition, in the long run the primacy of monetary accumulation is antithetical to an economy based on end-use, real need, and quality.

A third position, which so far as I know has not been explicitly articulated in these terms, is being promoted in different ways by writers like Richard Douthwaite (1999, 1996), David Korten (1999), Murray Bookchin (1989, 1991, 1995), and Barbara Brandt (1995). It constitutes a radical critique of quantitative growth and capitalist market relationships and yet posits a qualitative alternative that is quite different from traditional state socialism.

This book is, in a sense, an articulation of this third position, but from a postindustrial historical perspective. It argues that industrialism and capitalism are intrinsically systems of quantitative growth, and that our survival depends on a fundamental transformation of the means and ends of economic life to prioritize social and environmental need. In other words, growth and development are based on two radically different conceptions of wealth, on quite distinct driving forces, and even on completely different organizational forms. The next three chapters will be devoted to exploring the dynamics of quantitative growth.

INDUSTRIALISM AND CAPITALISM

The materialism of industrial society has its roots in the earliest class societies, or civilization, and is the culmination of tendencies that had been building for millennia. By *civilization* is meant those societies with a permanent economic surplus, classes, cities, the state, large-scale agriculture, patriarchy, and independent crafts. As a stage of human development, civilization can be seen as a massive *control project.* Control of nature has been its ecological nexus, but external control of other people and of certain aspects of the human psyche has been a crucial part. The structure of civilization is, therefore, based in interrelated forms of domination, where the hegemony of humans over nature, of imperialist over imperialized nations, of ruling over working classes, and of men over women all reinforce one another. The human capacities civilization has developed — individualism, materialism, rationalism, and historical consciousness — have been closely connected with this project of external control. While these capacities have blossomed with industrialism, their evolutions have been crucial elements in the development of civilization. As Lewis Mumford (1967) wrote decades ago, the very first civilizations anticipated industrial machine organization in their "megamachine" social structures, in which most people were strictly cogs in the social machine.

Contrary to popular notions of preindustrial civilization as static, economic growth has been a long-term trend of the development of civilization. Preindustrial material development, however, tended to move in long cycles and was limited by a complex of social and technological factors (Snooks, 1994). Civilization represented a major break of the human ego from what Marx called the "tyranny of Nature" and from the collectivistic ethos of primitive society. But until industrialization, open-ended economic growth could never be the single-minded focus of the human economy. The materialism of preindustrial civilization, therefore, was somewhat constrained and limited to certain strata of society. It is only with industrial capitalism that the ego's aggressive individualistic and self-aggrandizing energies could be completely unleashed to operate as the ruling principles of society.

Industrialism and capitalism are not exactly the same thing, but historically they seem to have required each other to attain their full development. Each has involved certain kinds of alienation and objectification. Industrialism involves a particular use of energy, materials, and cog-labor. It is driven by the ever greater use of physical resources and simple labor-power, where the worker is simply a cog in the machine. It is preoccupied with the production of *things*. It is the material or technological side of economics.

Capitalism is the financial or monetary side. It makes things (and people and processes) into commodities: items for sale. It is essentially a means of unequal exchange: money making money in the process of exchange. For centuries it took place on the fringes, in external trade and circulation, and was not seen as productive activity. But the gradual penetration of market relationships into economic life in the centuries before the industrial revolution was an essential prelude to industrialization. When the means of production became forms of capital, the motor force for constant technological revolution was established. The expansion of production became almost synonymous with the accumulation of capital. Capitalism's tendency to objectify and commodify people financially—on the labor market—complemented industrialism's tendency to depersonalize people as cogs in the machine.

While capitalism's profit motive supplied the driving force for industrialism's constant technological revolution, capitalism needed industrialism's technological power to commodify the whole of social and economic life. Such breakthroughs as steam power and especially the use of fossil fuels like coal were essential to go beyond the natural limits of agricultural productivity and photosynthesis and so institutionalize constant growth.

In one sense, industrialism is simply the extension of capitalism into actual production, which is basically how Marx saw it. But noncapitalist forms of industrial society did emerge in the twentieth century, primarily in reaction to imperialism and underdevelopment, at a time when planning became more necessary to industrial development. These forms did not, however, except perhaps for brief periods, institutionalize substantial qualitative alternatives to the quantitative regime of industrial capitalism. In some cases, they may have distributed wealth more fairly, but they did not attempt to redefine wealth. State-socialist regimes, while modifying or suppressing market forces within their boundaries, acted in essence like giant corporations in the world economy, treating their workers accordingly (Wallerstein, 1979).

The labels we use to name an economy, however—be they capitalist, industrialist, state-socialist, or state-capitalist—are less important than understanding the forces at work. What this book emphasizes is the relationship between the monetary and material dimensions of a regime of narrowly quantitative development. In the next few sections, I want to look at both these aspects and their relationship to political-economic organization.

THE INDUSTRIAL DEFINITION OF WEALTH: MATTER

The technological key to early industrialization was the application of vast amounts of energy to production. It was this application that made possible the transfer of power from owners of land to owners of machinery. For centuries, even where a rigorous division of labor was achieved, energy was ultimately a limiting factor. Even the classical economists Malthus, Ricardo, and Smith, who lived during the industrial revolution, refused to believe in the concept of continual economic growth because they felt that the productivity of the land provided a long-term limit to such growth. They did not foresee that a shift to the stored solar energy concentrated in fossil fuels could take the economy beyond the limits of photosynthetic energy for more than two centuries (Wrigley, 1994). This new role of stored energy involved a great centralization of production and the transfer of prime productivity from the landscape to machinery.

Technologically, the key elements of industrial production have been routine labor (or what Marxists would call simple labor-power) and physical capital—or massive amounts of natural resources. While it is usually presumed that industrial technology is highly efficient, it is really quite the opposite. What has made industrialization so powerful is its unprecedented capacity to process vast amounts of raw materials. Industrial notions of productivity have, by and large, referred to *labor* productivity—the ability to produce ever greater numbers of products with ever less labor. But real productivity must also include *resource* productivity; from this perspective, industrial technology is quite inefficient. In fact, Patrick Geddes (1915) referred to the industrial period as the "Paleotechnic Era" because of the crudeness of industrial processes. What has made industrial technology profitable is primarily its ability to process large volumes of unpriced or drastically undervalued natural resources.

As we will see, capitalist markets are subsidized by essential processes and substances that are made invisible by these markets. Unpaid domestic labor is one of these processes. The undervalued materials of nature, the value of which is reduced simply to their cost of processing, are another example. Even more invisible are the complex services nature provides through the provision of water, air, soil, and so on by acting as a sink for the absorption of humanity's wastes, and more generally through the complex self-regulation of the ecological balance and diversity that makes life possible. Industrial development has presumed it could use, or even disrupt, these services for free.

The industrial economy has been one of production for production's sake, where consumption has never been taken seriously. For people, this has meant that real human need has largely been ignored, while for nature and people, it has meant that the role of consumption in reproducing life has been disregarded. The theoretical models of economists might have money circulating continuously, but in the material world the industrial economy is a linear path from extraction to disposal, with little or no recycling or reuse. Industrial production has thus been premised not only on a fundamental separation between production and consumption but also on a restricted definition of production that has dismissed both the inherent productivity of nature and of unwaged household and community-based work.

The satisfaction of human need has always been a spin-off or a by-product of industrial development focused on production. In early industrialization, one reason human consumption could be taken for granted is that at that time the economy's main end-uses were geared to primary needs for food, shelter, clothing, and basic infrastructure. This is why progressive working-class struggle at this time did not seriously contest the *content* of wealth production, but rather its *distribution*. One could hardly argue with the material focus of production, and material production can be standardized to a much greater level than production for nonmaterial needs.

The focus on production for primary needs was reflected in the emphasis early industrialization put on products of the food and clothing industries—the first place that mass demand arose (Hoffman, 1958: 38). Textiles in particular played an important role because most early industrial countries had a thriving cottage textile sector before industrialization, and expenditure for clothing was the most important expenditure after food and shelter had been taken care of (Pollard, 1990). Capital goods production and production of the necessary infrastructure (such as railroads) followed quickly.

Because primary/material human needs can be standardized, early capitalist market mechanisms could function to spin off a greater level of authentic use-value than do today's markets. They could legitimately take consumption for granted. Although the markets of the early industrial period were exploitative and inequitable, they did function for a certain time to allocate resources and drive a fantastic accumulation of productive forces, primarily because of the overwhelmingly material character of early industrialization.

THE INDUSTRIAL DEFINITION OF WEALTH: MONEY

Markets driven by the profit motive function by abstracting the value of labor, materials or any other entity into pure quantitative value, that is, into money. Money is abstract quantity, and its reification as the ultimate goal of economic activity, through capitalism, is a perfect fit with the unbridled power of industrialism to produce lots of stuff.

Of course, there are different kinds of money, and money is not necessarily a bad thing. It facilitates useful exchanges. The problem emerges when money becomes an *end* of economic activity and not simply a *means*. This alienation or objectification of economic activity is precisely what capitalism does. A critique of this alienation was at the core of Karl Marx's work. He built his analysis of capitalism on the commodity relationship, that is, on how the exchange circuit commodity-money-commodity (C-M-C', with money simply a means of exchange) gets changed to money-commodity-money (or M-C-M', with commodity a means to increase money). Worse still, is M-M', where money simply invests in making money (Marx, 1887). In industrial capitalism, the satisfaction of social need—the use-value or "utility" produced by the accumulation of capital—has always been a by-product, a side effect, a spin-off, of the accumulation of money. Exchange-value always takes precedence over use-value. Industrialism's real wealth is money.

The strength and weakness of money is its impersonality and abstractness. It helps people go beyond the limits of direct barter in both time and space. Before money, reciprocity helped people in villages give and take in complementary ways; their exchanges didn't need to be one-on-one, and the "give" and the "take" could be separated in time. But this was possible because people knew one another and could trust in the group. By contrast, money allows transactions with complete strangers from far away. Polanyi (1968) in fact stresses the origins of money for exchange in external trade. Money basically conveys information about work a person has done in the past; it expresses a debt society owes the person.

This impersonality can take on a totalitarian character, however, when money becomes a thing-in-itself rather than simply a means of facilitating useful exchanges. The standard textbooks usually cite several characteristics of money; they are all generally connected in some way with two principal aspects of money: it is (1) a means of exchange, and (2) a store of value. Money as a means of exchange is primarily connected with its informational function, described above. It's the role of money as a store of value that is the source of the problems of money as an end-in-itself. As a store of value, money tends to become a thing-in-itself, a commodity, which allows money to become a means of social control and domination of the powerless by the powerful. Power can be exerted by those who control the money supply. Money can be hoarded by those who have more than they need, and they can attract more money to themselves by their control. Class power is based in the control of scarce resources by a minority; the control of money, and the ability of some to create money-scarcity for others, reinforces class power.

It is essential to understand that since its inception, money has evolved in tandem with economic development, and that this evolution is continuing. Down through history, money has always been some combination of a means of exchange and a store of value, but the relationship has changed over time because of the needs of increasingly complex trade. The store-of-value and social-control functions of money tend to get in the way of money as a socially useful instrument.

The simplest way value is stored in money is by having money that is worth something in itself. The original forms of money included cattle and bushels of grain. Precious metals also became a handy form of money. Money as a store of value has long been connected with money as a thing-in-itself, such as grain or gold. In other words, it is a "commodity-money." This has been a way to help keep money from losing its value. Exchange with commodity-money is really a form of indirect barter, adding another commodity (money) to the exchange (Galbraith, 1975; Mandel, 1962).

But there are real problems with commodity-money. First, as mentioned above, there are questions of social justice: commodity-money can be monopolized by a few against the many. The scarcity of money has been a powerful tool to force people to do things they wouldn't freely choose to do on their own. Also, important work might not happen because of a lack of money to facilitate it. Even in today's capitalist token-money or credit-money systems, money that is created out of nothing is treated as a thing-in-itself and is kept scarce through interest charges.

In addition to these social justice questions, there are other functional problems with commodity-money. It is subject to variations in availability that have nothing to do with the need for money for exchanges. The ideal amount of money is that which is just enough to facilitate all the necessary exchanges in an economy. But down through the ages, events like new discoveries of gold or silver have created rapid inflation by causing an oversupply of money. Periods of rapid trade expansion have sometimes been held back by a shortage of currency to carry on exchanges. In short, commodity-money lacks the flexibility needed for complex economies (Mandel, 1962).

The response by governments and traders has been to create token-money, or credit-money, which only represents value; it isn't valuable in itself. And there have been combinations of commodity-money and token-money—like metallic coins. By and large, there has been a tendency for money to evolve from being a commodity-money, or store of value, to being a token-money, or means of exchange. This is a tendency toward the dematerialization of money, that is, money becoming less and less a thing-in-itself. From crops and metals, to metallic coins, to public and private fiduciary currencies, to "fractional reserve" banking on the gold standard, to a semi-gold standard with single dominant currency, to today's floating exchange rates and computer currencies—there has been an increasing

movement away from commodity-money in order to facilitate increasingly sophisticated trading systems (Mandel, 1962).

This shift has been somewhat of a dilemma because a class society like industrial capitalism cannot dispense with the social-control functions of money. Exchange systems require trust, and the solid value-in-itself nature of commodity-
money has always been the main substitute for personal connections in attaining
this trust. A competitive, aggressive economy like capitalism seems incapable of
establishing the necessary trust to convey value in any way other than a com-
modity-base (Guttman, 1994; Mandel, 1962). In addition, as I will elaborate later,
class society is based on scarcity, and the money-scarcity that commodity-money
can enforce.

The creation of various forms of debt-money is the primary way that the totalitarian functions of money have been maintained while providing more flexibility than that provided by conventional commodity-money. Today, the monetary
system is based on debt—money, which is treated more than ever as a commodity or a thing-in-itself but has none of the positive attributes of commodity-money
because it does not have value in itself and cannot store real economic value.
What it actually stores is power, since its function is to keep people chained to a
rat race of mindless and typically useless production. This emergence of debt-
money has been necessary for capitalism because economic development itself
would begin to undermine the fit between money and material accumulation.

The potentially destructive implications of the pursuit of money on the social
fabric was recognized almost universally by preindustrial societies through the
restrictions they put on markets and money. Markets for people ("labor") and nature ("land") were long banned or restricted by most preindustrial societies. The
penetration of monetary relationships into domestic economic life helped pave
the way for industrialization, but it was only with industrialization that market society came into its own.

The open-ended character of industrialization was made possible by technology but driven by money. In early industrialization, the accumulation of money
and matter would work together in near total harmony. As noted in the last section, however, industrialization was not only fuelled by material inputs but
shaped by the material character of human need—primary needs for food, shelter, clothing, and basic infrastructure. While workers might object to the power
of money and the horrible conditions of exploitation, they had little objection to
the material focus of the economy. In this sense, despite the brutality and inequality of nineteenth-century industrialization, there was ultimately a closer fit
between the accumulation of exchange-value and the spin-off of use-value for society as a whole. Quantitative development met real human needs—primary
needs that could be standardized and abstracted by the accumulation process and
the profit motive.

For this reason, despite the drastic fluctuations of the business cycle, alternat-
ing boom and bust, the "invisible hand" of markets could function to guide this

massive economic upheaval. These markets worked reasonably efficiently in a situation where both the inputs and outputs were material and quantitative in character.

This situation would not last long, however. As industrialization progressed, both the inputs and outputs of the process tended to become more nonmaterial. Real development needed to take on a more qualitative character, and production-for-production's sake became more destructive than creative. The Great Depression marked the last gasp of conventional market mechanisms, as new productive forces based in human creativity began to make an impact on society. These essentially nonmaterial productive forces signal the necessity of completing the evolution of money from a store of value to a pure means of exchange. That is, the dematerialization of production demands the dematerialization of money. This has been reflected in the increasing obsolescence of conventional commodity-money and the growing importance of money as information. Emerging postindustrial potentials, however, would begin to challenge not just the material character of development and the status of money as a thing-in-itself but also the basic structure of industrial society.

This structure is shaped by fundamental divisions between production and consumption and between politics, economics, and culture. Before looking at this new situation, we should look more closely at the organization of quantitative development.

THE DIVIDED ECONOMY: SUBORDINATING REPRODUCTION

Perhaps the most obvious fact of industrialization was the pulling of production out of, and away from, the home—in craft production and agriculture—and its centralization in large factories and offices. This shift established a "public" sphere of paid work and political power and a "private" sphere of unpaid domestic labor and family life. This paid/unpaid division has been the basis for industrialism's sexual division of labor. The public formal economy became the domain of men, the home the sphere of women (Matthaei, 1982).

While women have played an important role in paid production, their position there has been affected by gender-role stereotypes and responsibilities that identify their "real" sphere as the home. Since industrialization does not stop, it has continued to pull various forms of production out of the home, in a "socialization of labor" process. This process has affected the nature of relationships between men and women in the economy as well as the relationship of both sexes to the whole system (Kessler-Harris, 1982).

The cash, or formal, sphere has been the domain of quantitative development, and, until recently, both conventional and Marxist economists have treated this sector as if it were the entire economy. At best, the domestic economy has been considered the sphere of (largely passive) consumption, or (to Marxists) the reproduction of labor-power, which could generally take care of itself if wages were adequate in the formal sector. In fact, this officially invisible domestic sphere has always comprised a substantial portion of society's production and has constituted a continual subsidy to production in the formal sphere (Seccombe, 1993; Brandt, 1995). It is the sphere of "people-production," the site of qualitative forms of service production that would become increasingly important throughout the twentieth century.

This subordination of people-production (or the reproduction or self-production of human beings) has been just as essential to quantitative development as the super-exploitation of nature. And like the exploitation of nature, it has been increasingly difficult in recent decades to completely overlook. Feminist researchers, in particular, have documented the subsidy of domestic labor to capitalist enterprise (Armstrong and Armstrong, 1990), as well as dollar equivalencies for various types of housework and the quantities of unpaid time women have contributed to the economy (Cowan, 1983). This work, along with other unpaid services and skills in the economy, has been conceptualized as "social capital," just as many of nature's undervalued resources and services have been identified as "natural capital." Such recognition has, however, remained largely academic and has meant very little in practical economic policy terms.

Because the divided economy has been the basis for industrialism's sexual division of labor, this very division has contributed to a negative form of people-production, that is, it helps produce gender identities and sex-roles. Men and women are supposed to have complementary personalities, in the same way that their respective work is supposedly complementary. Similarly, the idealized "family wage" for the male worker supposedly provided for the material needs of his spouse as well. In this sense, the real "individual" of industrialism has been the family. Men and women were molded to be dependent half-persons: men needed to be competitive selfish breadwinners, women selfless nurturers and home workers. Both needed each other and gained in cooperation (Matthaei, 1982). However, the system's need for new kinds of workers has tended to undermine these gender identities, just as women's challenges to them threaten some fundamental economic divisions.

Quantitative development must continue to serve new markets and new needs, even if it has to invent these needs. Therefore, the socialization of labor—pulling production from the home—continues. After goods production (such as clothing), education and health care were among the first services to be socialized. Today, the trend continues with child care and fast foods. But as industrialization moves from goods to cultural production and becomes more dependent on scientific knowledge and education, some inevitable contradictions arise. The economy necessarily becomes more concerned with people-production, consumption, and the reproduction of labor-power, and as we'll see, this focus threatens some of the basic priorities and structures of industrialism.

Many feminists have had a vision of a very different kind of socialization of labor, one that would prioritize autonomous human development. By and large, conventional economic development has seen the "male" sphere gobble up parts of the "female" sphere. The "material feminists" of the nineteenth century, however, called for a decompartmentalization of urban space through such means as housing co-ops, community kitchens and laundry services, and district heating. Through spatial redesign of development, women could maintain control of the socialization of their own work. Instead of women's work being commodified in the male sphere, public space would be reintegrated into the women's sphere (Hayden, 1981).

Despite the often brilliant designs of the material feminists, such an endeavor was, at that moment, a virtually impossible dream, since the whole thrust of industrial development (including mainstream socialist alternatives) worked against such integration. This was the same wave that swamped the experiments of the utopian socialists and other communitarians. Today, however, the capitalist socialization of labor has gone virtually as far as it can go without having the opposite overall effect of undermining the commodity economy and quantitative development. The marketization of new household services continues, but new productive forces have begun to reverse the trend in significant areas, with more and more production taking place in the informal economy, in the home and community, outside the bounds of the formal economy (Burns, 1975; Henderson, 1978).

Qualitative development, however, entails much more than the expansion of informal economic activity. It involves a reintegration of the Divided Economy, and of production and consumption generally, to harness the natural productivity of both the community and natural systems. This kind of reorganization, however, also means going beyond the dominant form of labor in the formal sector, cog-labor. Now we'll look more closely at cog-labor's crucial role in the industrial system and its organizational implications.

COG-LABOR AND THE MEGAMACHINE

Central to quantitative industrial development, and to the suppression of human potential, is cog-labor. If money and matter are industrialism's concept of wealth, cog-labor is its concept of human beings. That said, the dependent individuality that accompanied the generalization of industrial labor was something of a historical step forward for working people. This is because, before capitalism, individuality of any sort (and formal equality) was not available to the working masses. For the average human being, industrialism would be a mixed blessing, increasing regimentation of daily life while according a legalistic equality to more and more sectors of the population, at least in the developed world. For many it would accord, after a brutal decline of conditions during early industrialization, a chance to increase their material standard of living. Increasingly through the twentieth century, however, cog-labor has been perpetuated artificially as a means of suppressing human potential and maintaining social class relationships.

As Lewis Mumford (1967) pointed out, the machine organization of industrial production was anticipated in the earliest civilizations. The difference was that these early "megamachines" were completely social in character and lacked technological hardware. The production machines that built the pyramids were comprised completely of human cogs. And, in fact, the whole of class society was based on a kind of machine principle in that the common people were considered simply cogs in the social machine run by the ruling elite.

In industrial society, however, the megamachine principle took a decidedly technical form in an ever more rigorous division of labor in the machine system. Unlike preindustrial craft production, where the tool was an extension of the worker, in industrial organization the worker is literally a cog within the production system. And whereas the peasants had to know their places in the social order, they had more control over their hour-to-hour work rhythms and day-to-day lives. Taylorism—or the "scientific management of production"—has attempted to break down labor functions into their simplest and most routine elements—not simply to increase productivity, but to keep workers under control (Noble, 1977; Braverman, 1974).

In response to the brutal conditions of early industrialization, organized labor emerged to defend the interests of the worker-as-cog. The purposes of the labor movement were to uphold the dignity of the worker and the worker's labor and also to minimize exploitation by getting as big a share of the wealth produced as possible.

Over time, organized labor had to respond to the revolutionizing of production, as new technologies were brought in to either increase productivity or increase management control (Dubofsky, 1987; Gordon, Edwards, and Reich, 1982). Usually these two things went hand in hand. Management has always taken the opportunity technological change provided to get an edge on the workers, even if it has meant compromising productivity. Again, in the formal economy, it is profits and paper wealth that really count, not material goods or services.

The labor movement has consistently had to reorganize itself in response to technological change. Each sector of the movement had to have an organizational form that could effectively defend its interests. Workers' success in organizing and achieving gains also helped shape production and set general living standards for the entire population.

Workers' movements were hard-pressed to constantly respond to Taylorist methods of work simplification. The rise of mass production industries, for instance, reduced the power of skilled workers by the creation of vast numbers of semiskilled assembly-line jobs. Workers' bargaining power could no longer be based on their superior knowledge, because Taylorism increasingly concentrated such knowledge in management.

But the labor movement responded to new forms of exploitation in mass production with a completely different form of unionism: industrial unionism, exemplified by the Congress of Industrial Organizations (CIO) in North America (Dubofsky, 1987; Brody, 1980). This was a new form that compensated for decreased skill with broader social solidarity, covering entire industries. Industrial unionism was more political, more socially conscious, and it was the peak of power within production for the worker-as-cog. It was as far as worker organization *within production* could go because industrial society itself would be forced by emerging productive forces to go far beyond the organization of commodity production.

Progressive working-class organization in the future would have to involve community organization and more qualitative demands—or risk a decline in labor's power. Essentially, the forces of cultural production, placing primary importance on human development, make cog-labor obsolete, or at least anachronistic. Later in part 1, we'll look at how the new social movements of the 1950s, 1960s, and 1970s expressed a new working-class rebellion against cog-labor and related industrial values. In doing so, they raised qualitative perspectives on development and pointed toward new horizons for popular struggle.

The future for labor, and the struggle to transcend cog-labor, goes well beyond a new political and economic vision. Corresponding to a new notion of wealth, it demands a completely new definition of politics and economics. Politics in the industrial order was conditioned by the need for cog-labor. By the same token, possibilities for going beyond cog-labor are limited by the very existence of politics as we know it. Qualitative development demands a new relationship between politics, economics, and culture than the relationship that has shaped industrial life.

THE SEPARATION OF POLITICS, ECONOMICS, AND CULTURE

Industrialism's narrow materialistic conception of economics shaped the restricted function of industrial politics. Politics would largely be the struggle to oversee quantitative economic growth, primarily through the state, and to divide up the spoils of such growth. Closely connected to industrialism's primary separation of production and consumption is its separation of the spheres of economics, politics, and culture—in just this descending order of importance. The perpetuation of inequality and domination within industrial society has depended upon maintaining this separation of spheres. The very progress of economic development earlier this century, however, began to undermine these crucial divisions as industrialization intruded into the realm of culture and began to lay the basis for the politicization of everyday life.

The prevailing notion of politics as what Bookchin (1989) calls "statecraft," or more generally as oppositional activity, is conditioned by the narrow industrial conception of economics. In its most extreme form, that of classical market capitalism, the "invisible hand" of the market was premised on the subordination of consumption and reproduction to production-for-production's sake, since conscious consideration of consumption requires some sort of planning. This subordination of end-use to production, therefore, meant a subordination of politics. This was reinforced by the difficulties for political participation presented by most people's immersion in (paid or unpaid) cog-labor.

As most people recognize intuitively, the ideology of free markets is an attempt to isolate the economic realm from political inference. As Polanyi (1968: 30) wrote, "A self-regulating market demands nothing less than the institutional separation of society into an economic and political sphere." The ideology of self-regulating markets has, of course, always been something of a myth, as shown by writers like Polanyi, Seabrook (1991), and McMurtry (1998). But to the degree that there was any truth concerning the efficiency of (profit-driven) markets, it was because of the material character of industrial development. As we will see, the very logic of economic development, moving in nonmaterial directions, would demand a greater planning of consumption as well as production and so would impose an increasing degree of political and economic integration. In this context, particularly after the Great Depression, the separation between politics and economics would have to be artificially maintained to guarantee the existence of the system.

Not only has the role of cog-labor been a factor in the creation of a separate political realm, but the creation of cog-labor has been a means of artificially maintaining this separation. The kind of labor the workers had to be involved in meant that they had neither the time nor the appropriate skills to manage society. Industrialization did, however, open up new political possibilities for the common people. In almost all previous class societies, the workers had no say whatsoever in running society. Because of the new importance of constantly increasing production, industrial society brought a new dignity to labor. And because these constantly expanding economies were like runaway locomotives with no one at the controls, ruling classes found that forms of representative democracy could be useful as feedback mechanisms, generating more stability (Toffler, 1972). Suffrage was something that had to be fought for by working people, but it could be granted without jeopardizing basic class relationships in society, as long as politics and economics were separate.

Industrial society was, therefore, a mixed blessing for the common people. On one hand, workers gained a new footing on the political stage of history. On the other hand, industrial organization chopped up the more integrated lifestyle of agriculture and craft, subjecting daily life to new disciplines. And workers' new political power was severely circumscribed because, in the new capitalist economies, real power was centered in the economy, and political intervention was somewhat limited by rules of the free market game. As David Montgomery (1993: 2) describes nineteenth-century America: "The more that active participation in government was opened to the propertyless strata of society, the less capacity elected officials seemed to have to shape the basic contours of social life." The United States was the most extreme example of such market-driven fragmentation, but differences from other contemporary capitalisms were of degree, not of quality.

Really substantial change—revolutionary change—required a dual strategy for workers: (1) organization at the workplace, geared to "seizing the means of production"; and (2) political organization, through a Labor, Socialist, or Democratic party, to get control of the state. Only then could real alternatives be implemented.

Workers could organize themselves through their unions at the point of production, but they were dependent on others to represent them in the political structure. The historic role of the organized left—typically, sympathetic intellectuals and advanced workers—was to act as the proverbial "head on the working class body," to be the workers' "shadow state." The submergence of the workers in cog-labor made this dependence necessary.

The legitimate concerns of the workers' movements were primarily those of equality and fairness. Workers wanted better working conditions, of course; they struggled against various forms of regimentation. And they wanted time for their self-improvement and limits on their exploitation—as expressed in the struggle for shorter hours. But their strategic focus was on a fair *distribution* of society's wealth, not on the content of this wealth (Paehlke, 1989). Who can argue with production for primary needs?

Classical industrial society was a cohesive package: thing-production for primary needs; driven by the struggle for money; fueled by raw materials and cog-labor; supported by unpaid domestic labor and nature's services; structuring cultural, political and gender dependence. This was the framework for quantitative development. These dependencies, and the very existence of class, would increasingly be threatened by new productive forces based in cultural production and human self-development. The history of the past several decades—particularly in the developed countries—is the story of how such threats have been suppressed or postponed by the manipulation or repression of those productive forces.

2

Crisis and Waste: Fordism and the Effluent Society

THE GREAT DEPRESSION AND THE THREAT OF ABUNDANCE

Quantitative development, to paraphrase Marx, sows the seeds of its own destruction. One reason for this is that the positive benefit to society of material growth reaches a limit. As Daly (1996), Rees (1995), and others have argued, the economy is a subsystem of the biosphere, and anyone who thinks a physical organism or entity can keep growing indefinitely and remain healthy is either a madman or an economist.

To these intrinsic biophysical limits, we must add a related inherent contradiction of industrial capitalism owing to the fact that it is a class society. As Marx noted, permanent technological revolution tends to eventually undermine class society because all class societies are based in scarcity, which will eventually be eliminated by constant quantitative growth (Mandel, 1962).

Primitive societies, based in hunting and gathering or the simplest agriculture, had no permanent economic surpluses to support the growth of ruling groups to control that surplus. *Absolute* scarcity tends to encourage cooperation and reciprocity; individual survival is closely bound up with tribal survival. By contrast, the *relative* scarcity of civilization, with its cities, states, and independent crafts, keeps most people working but allows the emergence of leisure classes, or ruling classes.

Absolute *abundance,* on the other hand, totally undermines class rule, because people aren't so likely to work for others against their will when all their basic needs are taken care of. Ruling classes exist by virtue of their control over "scarce resources." When these resources are no longer scarce, people do what they want.

In most of the first industrial capitalist nations, the market system had worked reasonably well, if unfairly. Karl Polanyi (1957) showed that this system was a conscious creation of ruling groups, and that state intervention supplied essential help to all these economies, particularly ones that began industrialization later.

Poverty, inequality, and oppression thrived. But the market as a mode of regulation and distribution functioned more or less effectively, in tandem with the state, which defined property rights. It worked in a situation of relative scarcity geared to production of material commodities to satisfy primary needs and related infrastructure. It worked in a situation where consumption could take care of itself, where not much conscious collective decision was necessary, and where vast quantities of cog-labor and physical capital were the main inputs to production. It worked for a stage of development where economics could be kept separate from politics and culture.

Periodic crises are endemic to capitalism. The early business cycles of industrialism were temporary crises of overproduction (By this is meant, of course, not the production of more goods than people can use but more goods than they currently have money to buy). This overproduction caused great social misery, but the deflation wiped out much bad investment and usually laid the basis for vigorous recovery.

The Great Depression of the 1930s was something else altogether. It was a *structural* crisis of overproduction—a spontaneous system shutdown in reaction to the threat of abundance. Fantastic increases in productivity resulted from the technological advances following World War I, during the Roaring Twenties. For the first time in history, gross quantities of labor actually declined, even as output multiplied (Sklar, 1969; Block and Hirschhorn, 1979). The wages of working people did not, therefore, keep up with this vast production, making for a shortage of purchasing power. In the United States, explicit concern about the threat of overproduction emerged into public awareness and political discussion in the 1920s, prompting various proposals to share work or create new consumer demand (Hunnicutt, 1988). When the speculative bubble eventually burst and the market crashed, a normal recovery did not take place. Capitalists lacked sufficient "business confidence" to reinvest because they didn't feel that workers could supply enough "effective demand" to buy vast numbers of commodities (Guttmann, 1994).

Human consumption would no longer take care of itself to keep markets functioning; consumption would now have to be planned, the same as production, to keep the system going. But this opened up a whole new can of worms involving both state intervention into the economy and the redistribution of income. The redistribution of income to give workers more buying power seemed the only solution to the crisis of effective demand. The struggles of workers to organize themselves in the new mass-production industries added more pressure for redistribution. But how this could be done without jeopardizing class power and industrial structures was a dilemma. The basic divisions between production and consumption, and between politics, economics, and culture, were threatened. Planning for consumption means essentially planning for end-use, for use-value, for human needs. This is a fundamental threat to the hegemony of money and exchange-value.

FORDIST CAPITALISM AND THE
REINTEGRATION OF POLITICS AND ECONOMICS

Despite the bold initiatives of the New Deal in the United States, it was World War II that finally ended the Great Depression. Much of the industrial elite fully expected that the capitalist economies would return to depression after the war (Block, 1977). Wartime reconstruction—which guaranteed plenty of "effective demand"—delayed this concern for much of the developed world. But in North America, fears of renewed depression were great. Industrial capitalism needed some kind of income redistribution and some kind of consumption planning that would not undermine market mechanisms, the primacy of production, or the labor discipline enforced by scarcity.

Part of the solution lay in new social contracts that gave working people and the poor new levels of security and protection. Workers' rights to join unions and bargain collectively were guaranteed by law, and the creation of the welfare state gave the poor some safety nets. These gains, while real (more real in some countries than in others), were nevertheless ambiguous. Corporate employers gained much more stability in their production-planning, as the labor contract essentially turned unions into instruments of labor management. Predictable, and (in some sectors) high, wages—along with state welfare spending—also provided much effective demand for corporate production (O'Connor, 1973; Brody, 1980; Dubofsky, 1987; Montgomery, 1979).

"Fordism"—named after mass production pioneer Henry Ford—is the term given to the postwar initiatives at reorganizing capitalism both within and beyond the factory gates. It included a new role for the state in society and a greater importance of planning per se. In a sense, it was the natural accompaniment to Taylorism, the so-called "scientific organization of production. "Like Taylorism in production, Fordism concentrated decision making above. The very nature of technology was forcing a reintegration of politics and economics; the genius of Fordism was how it could accomplish this integration at the top while maintaining ever more fragmentation at the base.

Political intervention in the economy was not, of course, a completely new phenomenon. The state helped create markets and specified various limits and conditions. It helped protect weak sectors, especially in countries trying to "catch up" with the leading industrial powers. By the turn of the century, as corporate business organization grew in prominence, various reform movements grew to mitigate some of the worst abuses of industrialization and also to place some limits on monopoly power. The "progressive era" in the United States had its parallels in social reform movements elsewhere. Nevertheless, a general separation between the state and markets remained pervasive until the Depression.

Industrial society has maintained a facade of having separate "political" and "economic" institutions. But by the end of World War II, all developed capitalist states had become planned economic sectors. Modern corporations, for their part, had become, in David Bazelon's words, "industrial governments." Their taxing powers were their growing power to administer prices. Private bureaucracies, many with revenues greater than most countries, their deal-making had come to more closely resemble diplomacy or backroom politics than classical capitalist entrepreneurialism (Bazelon, 1963). According to Alfred Chandler (1977: 1):

> In many sectors of the economy the visible hand of management replaced what Adam Smith referred to as the invisible hand of market forces. The market remained the generator of demand for goods and services, but modern business enterprise took over the functions of coordinating flows of goods through existing processes of production and distribution, and of allocating funds and personnel for future production and distribution. . . . The rise of modern business enterprise in the United States, therefore, brought with it managerial capitalism.

Even trade unions had become integrated political-economic institutions. Their real power—their lobbying power—was exercised in the national capitals by their leaders. At the grassroots level, however, the union contract generally restricted bargaining issues to narrow economic "bread and butter" issues (Dubofsky, 1987; Henderson, 1981).

The various developed industrial countries exhibited important differences in the shape of their Fordist compromises, but the overall pattern was dictated by threatening crisis and by growing productive potentials, which had to be simultaneously suppressed and employed. The new forms of political-economic management and control were to a large degree made possible by the growing role of culture in the economy. The new bureaucracies were hierarchies of mental labor, of white-collar cog-labor. Bureaucracies handled the immense information flows necessary to administer mass production and distribution, and increasingly complex political systems. The industrialization of culture accomplished a depersonalization of rule on an unprecedented scale.

This objectification of class power is part of industrialism's tendency to alienate: to turn human powers and capacities into external things. Contrary to conventional wisdom, classes in industrial society do not evaporate; they just become depersonalized, like everything else in society. The power once claimed by a Rockefeller or Massey or Morgan has been objectified in giant bureaucracies staffed by workers whose job it is to identify with the organization. Whether this organization is "public" or "private" is sometimes just a matter of semantics. The organization still functions to reinforce class relationships.

The postwar Fordist reorganization—with political-economic decision making concentrated at the top and daily life ever more fragmented at the base—expressed the prevailing potentials for social control. This kind of organization, dominated by bureaucracy, began to fall apart by the late 1970s under pressure from technological change, competitive pressures, and growing social costs.

THE PRODUCTION OF MONETARY SCARCITY:
KEYNESIANISM, DEBT, AND THE PAPER ECONOMY

Preserving industrial capitalism required much more than new forms of regulation and control. In the face of growing potentials for qualitative or nonmaterial development, industrialism also had to reinforce the industrial definitions of wealth, based in matter and money. And in doing this, it had to reproduce scarcity in order to maintain social class relationships.

Somehow, industrialism would have to continue quantitative development while maintaining scarcity. The primary means by which Fordism would reproduce *material* scarcity while reinforcing production for production's sake was *waste production*. The key means by which *monetary* scarcity could be maintained without undermining economic growth was *debt*. I will look at the monetary aspect first.

The popular image of postwar Keynesian and welfare state reforms is of major redistribution of wealth and greater equality in society. But the facts show that there wasn't much real redistribution of wealth. Postwar expansion made possible continual growth and real gains in the standard of living for substantial numbers. But the relative shares of wealth between classes changed little (Teeple, 1995). Processes were also instituted by which some gains by working people could be recaptured for the corporations. Worker power in production, and the crisis of overproduction, forced the elite to find other ways to extract the economic surplus than simple exploitation at the point of production. Those new means were fiscal and monetary.

The fiscal means have involved the growing role for the state in the economy. It runs many unprofitable but necessary industries and services. It provides investment in physical infrastructure, in education, in research and development—most of which benefit the corporate sector. And it raises taxes for its activities, which can slide back to the corporations via infrastructure, or subsidy or tax breaks. In addition, in many industrialized nations, the military and a quasi-public arms production sector serve to provide jobs and economic stimulation.

The monetary means used to regulate the economy were planned inflation and creation of money, credit, and debt. The institutionalization of unions essentially tied wages to productivity gains in the mass production industries. Coupled with the "downward rigidity" of prices due to the planning powers of the modern corporation, and the upward price pressure exerted by pervasive debt (Rowbotham, 1998), this linking of wages and productivity structured permanent inflation into the new capitalist economy. Monopoly price regulation therefore increased the stability of the system, but it required inflation and the continual devaluation of money (Guttmann, 1994).

Inflation was used to redistribute income back to business to compensate for wage gains. It became an increasingly important mechanism in the United States as the productivity of American industry flagged and as other sectors where productivity is not so easily increased (or even measured)—such as services—became unionized.

This pattern also applies to Europe, where the left and trade unions were even more restive. As Fred Block (1977: 78) describes the postwar situation:

> The demands for social reforms and for redistribution of income in favour of the working class made inflation a more or less conscious strategy of the employers. . . . To resist wage demands strenuously, for example, would have invited a further radicalization of the working class and raised the spectre of revolution. Instead, the employers would concede large wage increases and then compensate by increasing prices. Or if taxes were increased, the employers could pass the cost of the taxes along through higher prices for consumers. In this way, the effort of the working class to increase its share of real wealth could be continually undermined by a rising cost of living.

The cooperation of state policy makers was necessary for this strategy to work, and for this reason, inflation must be seen as a deliberate means of extracting the surplus (Rowthorn, 1980).

Inflation was not the only monetary means of social control and demand creation, because inflation was premised on an even more fundamental transformation—the creation of a debt-based economy. The inflationary re-redistribution of income depended on a continual growth of the money supply. This growth depended on new forms of credit and debt, as did the government deficit-spending, which was used to affect aggregate demand, and, in the United States, a growing role for the dollar in the world economy. (This international monetary dimension will be discussed later). Debt—both public and private—would become the key monetary means of creating scarcity, while reinforcing cog-labor and production for production's sake.

Since the beginning of capitalism, the creation of various forms of debt-money had been necessary to compensate for the inflexibility of commodity-money like gold and silver. After World War II, however, new forms of money had also to compensate for the chronic lack of purchasing power that had caused the Great Depression. Debt took on a qualitatively new role. It would be the primary means of creating money while simultaneously reinforcing monetary scarcity and economic dependence, and it would do this in a milieu of potential abundance. The use of debt in the Keynesian Paper Economy would also begin a process of financialization of the industrial economy, which would establish a growing disconnection between real and financial wealth.

As discussed above, the intentional growth of the money supply was a means of providing effective demand (and labor peace) that could be recouped by corporate rises in price. But the expansion of the money supply did not take place by the government's simply "printing money." Most of this money derived from private bank credit, which created private and commercial debt. Bank loans would be used not simply to provide capital for particular projects but also many times over as new money. Henceforth, government-created money would become an increasingly minute percentage of the total money stock, and a vicious cycle of indebtedness would be created by every growth of the money supply.

As writers like Rowbotham (1998), Greco (1994), and Kennedy (1995) have shown, this means of money creation guaranteed a continuing situation of money-shortage and a perpetual dearth of purchasing power, since there would never be enough money in the system to purchase all the existing goods. If all debts could be suddenly paid off, almost no money would exist. In fact, money-shortage was such that not all debts *could* be paid off; debt-based money means inevitably that some people are losers. Ultimate reckoning could be delayed, however, by continual borrowing. People mortgaged their futures, as Bazelon wrote more than thirty years ago in *The Paper Economy* (1963), by paying for current consumption with "gold-tomorrow."

Besides keeping people chained to cog-labor in (as we will see) increasingly destructive jobs, debt also aggravated some of the worst tendencies of capitalism. As Rowbotham has described, systemic lack of domestic purchasing power has fuelled export warfare and the wasteful use of long-distance transport to seek adequate markets for growing mass production. Competition for scarce money and markets has also discouraged quality production and favored mass production of cheap products whose limited durability would help expand demand.

The new situation of credit-based development has typically been portrayed as "people living beyond their means" and as spending exceeding income. This is true only in an environmental sense, in that the wasteful Fordist economy resisted paying the full costs of development. As Rowbotham points out, however, the debt-based economy is an accounting mechanism that has kept people on a treadmill where day-to-day living would always be "beyond the means" of most people.

The negative implications of inflation and the debt economy was disguised at this time by the incredible economic growth in developed countries during the Fordist era. As long as productivity could grow as fast as the money supply, and material production and consumption could keep expanding, the unhealthy forms of economic dependence would largely be overlooked. The material standard of living increased for substantial sections of the population in these countries. This situation could not last, however, because it was ultimately based on both the super-exploitation of nature and environmental costs that would eventually have to be paid.

The accounting procedures of the debt-economy also could not be expected to be effective indefinitely. They would create a financial house of cards that would eventually have to crumble. The Keynesian/Fordist Paper Economy could serve as a temporary solution for capitalist crises because it was new. It was successful also because of a number of political and economic circumstances, such as the undisputed political and economic dominance of the United States at that time.

This helped the Bretton Woods international monetary system to enjoy a temporary reprieve from some of the inherent contradictions between international trade and domestic economic management.

The postwar credit-money economy was a further step in the long-run evolution of money away from being a store of value in itself (a commodity-money) and toward being flexible information-money. But, through debt, the credit-money economy was designed to maintain the totalitarian social-control aspects of commodity-money. The Keynesian Paper Economy also established the beginnings of a fundamental disjunction between monetary and real wealth. But because it was based on a "gold-exchange standard" and on growing consumption levels by the working class, it maintained a tenuous connection between financial and material life. Of course, this connection would eventually have to be paid for, since it was based on waste production and intensifying the exploitation of nature. Waste would be the crucial means by which Fordism could create scarcity that looked like abundance.

THE PRODUCTION OF MATERIAL SCARCITY: THE WASTE ECONOMY

The crisis of overproduction and effective demand could not be solved simply by new forms of income distribution and redistribution, credit, or funny money. New forms of consumption were required that somehow wouldn't undermine the coercive power of scarcity. The logical solution, waste, has been the most important means of perpetuating quantitative growth as a mode of development. It is also the single most important concept we can use in understanding not just Fordism but our *current* social, political, economic, environmental, and even spiritual problems. In this sense, post-Fordism has simply taken waste to a greater extreme, while purging Fordism's concerns with working-class consumption.

Our problems of deficits, unemployment, productivity, pollution, social decay, and psychological malaise are all directly connected to waste. Even seemingly unrelated problems of inequality, oppression, and exploitation are today inextricably connected to waste, since waste has been used to reinforce scarcity and class relationships. By "waste," I mean in the normal sense of needless squandering of material resources and energy. But I also mean it in the sense of the waste of human creative potentials, which are the nexus of real postindustrialism. They are our capacities to develop ourselves, individually and collectively, and they affect our ability to live in harmony with one another and with nonhuman nature.

Waste has been the systematic means used to prevent recognition and implementation of a basic change in the nature of human wealth brought by developing productive forces. Waste production and waste consumption—from weapons to cars to toxic chemicals to junk food to pornography—have suppressed and diverted growing human potentials for self- and community-development, for greater levels of democracy, and for reintegration with nature. Waste has been the "solution" to the major market failure of the Great Depression, providing "effective demand" for capitalist production. It was the essence of Fordist capitalism and the long twenty-five-year economic expansion, which dominated the globe's political-economy after World War II until being thrown back into crisis again, beginning in the 1970s.

It is common for economists and environmentalists to look at our environmental crisis simply in terms of an overblown, overdeveloped human economy outgrowing its ecological limits. But this book looks at waste as the essence of postwar capitalism, which has been as crucial to the suppression of social progress, working-class autonomy, and individual freedom as it has been destructive to the environment. Waste has been a means of maintaining alienated economic structures that are inextricable from industrial forms of wealth, based in money and material.

This interpretation of Fordism may sound overly conspiratorial to some readers. It is certainly true that, in many instances, corporate and government policy makers were quite conscious of the choices they were making. But the Waste Economy was also a logical *systemic* response of capitalism to a fundamental crisis of profitability and growth. The possibility of increased free time and developmental social services was not foreign to many social visionaries, including left New Dealers, earlier in the century. But for mainstream capitalists, any means to perpetuate production for production's sake that would not impinge on the freedom of private business was appropriate. Choices for resource-intensity, for chaotic development, for useless commodities, didn't have to be completely conscious choices for waste in order for this new regime of accumulation to be established.

The Waste Economy was expressed in both the form and the content of Fordist production and consumption. In the next sections, I will review aspects of the Waste Economy, especially in North America, expressed in its two key elements: (1) the War Economy, and (2) the privatized Consumer Economy based in the auto/oil/suburb complex.

MILITARY KEYNESIANISM: THE MILITARY-INDUSTRIAL COMPLEX

It was not the New Deal, but the Second World War, that ended the Great Depression. This fact was not lost on policy makers of the U.S. government in the years following the war. There was a pervasive fear of a return to depression conditions following the exhaustion of the postwar pent-up demand. Among left New Dealers, wartime mobilization offered a different model for postwar economic organization than the one eventually taken. The idea was to direct the massive mobilization for war to peaceful purposes after the war. Planning to mobilize resources to fight poverty, supply housing and needed services, and so on might supply the "effective demand" to solve the crisis of overproduction. As feminist

Delores Hayden (1984) has documented, wartime planned communities, replete with community services like childcare, offered models of sensible urban development for the future. Under Truman, however, the right wing eventually triumphed, primarily because corporate America felt threatened by this social-industrial complex. Another war-inspired version won out: the Cold War model of the military-industrial complex (Block, 1977; Arrighi, 1994).

Most discussion of Keynesianism focuses on its redistributive fiscal and monetary policies. But, as Fred Block (1977) has shown, the U.S. State Department under Acheson and Nitze saw U.S. and European rearmament as a cornerstone of a larger economic policy. Domestic rearmament would sustain demand, while European military aid would help keep Europe open, militarily and economically, to U.S. interests, even after the Marshall Plan expired.

The Cold War was a boon to weapons producers. Perhaps a quarter of the U.S. economy could be tied to the "defense" sector in some way or another. Risk-free superprofits of defense contractors are legendary. Research and development in the United States was dominated by the military. Seymour Melman (1987) has done extensive exploration of the impact of war production on the U.S. economy and found it an efficiency drag on the entire economy—not simply in terms of waste of otherwise productive capital but in terms of shaping the character of the many client industries. With annual defense budgets exceeding the net profits of all U.S. corporations combined, criteria of cost-effectiveness went right out the window, and client industries—from electronics to machine tools—all suffered competitively to Japanese and European firms as a result.

SPACE TO CONSUME: THE AUTO/SUBURB COMPLEX

The privatized Consumer Economy has been the other half of the Waste Economy. It has many dimensions, but perhaps its most important is spatial: the land use patterns intrinsic to the auto/suburb complex that have fuelled individual consumption beyond all social and ecological reason. As will be discussed later, spatial design and the built environment play an especially important role in a postindustrial society. The auto/suburb complex is a negative example of how design can be used to create efficiencies or inefficiencies. Referring to the United States, Knox and Agnew (1989: 99) write:

> The Housing Act of 1949 locked the federal government into a massive stimulus of the U.S. economy through a transformation of the American landscape. Suburbanization by means of housing subsidies and highway construction funds served both as a fiscal regulator and a massive stimulus to the relocation of industry and other economic activities [including agriculture].

The suburban sprawl of isolated nuclear family homes on subdivided plots facilitated the super-consumption of virtually every commodity. Workplaces were increasingly separated from homes. In many areas, existing mass transit systems were rooted out to increase dependence on cars. Community laundry services became a thing of the past, and even milk and bread delivery services evaporated. Every household required at least one car, a washing machine, a dryer, televisions, and more. Developed shopping centers and malls began to replace town squares and public gardens, bringing the death of true public space. This development was not necessarily a fully conscious strategy of urban growth, but it was, according to David Harvey (Fowler, 1992: 148), since the late 1930s, a "de facto urban policy" intended to stave off a return to depression conditions.

The abandonment of experiments in intelligently planned communities in favor of deliberately chaotic private development essentially prostituted the planning and design professions to big capital. Zoning that was originally developed to protect communities from the ravages of industrial production was now employed mainly to maximize individualized consumption by irrationally segmenting communities. So, too, architects drew up monuments to their own and corporate egos, even as they sought to concentrate design expertise within their professional domain. To the degree the design professions monopolized design, they lost all sense of the spiritual influence of design in creating community and communion. Buildings became machines to live in, or amenities to consume, or ways to make external "visual statements." The built environment became a crucial means of discouraging depth of feeling and personal connection.

THE SYNTHETIC ECONOMY: OIL AND MATERIALS

The blood of the wasteful new infrastructure was oil. Not only did this highly mobile fossil fuel power the internal combustion engines that moved people and goods over greater expanses, but it also became the basic feedstock for a new breed of materials that become problematic for the health of both humans and ecosystems. Petrochemicals displaced more benign plant-based materials in industry almost completely by the end of World War II. New kinds of synthetic products were developed that would completely remake the immediate environments of most people in the industrialized world. Petrochemical production was used to reinforce the capitalist preference for materials-intensive, labor-displacing development. According to John Bellamy Foster (1994: 123):

> For instance, since World War II, plastics have increasingly displaced leather in the production of such items as purses and shoes. To produce the same value of output, the plastics industry uses only a quarter of the amount of labor used by leather man-

ufacture, but it uses ten times as much capital and thirty times as much energy. The substitution of plastics for leather in the production of these items has therefore meant less demand for labor, more demand for capital and energy, and greater environmental pollution.

The use of petrochemical plastics in packaging has been rationalized in terms of convenience, health, and safety. Recently, McCain, the Canadian agribusiness giant, has even argued that its tetrapaks save energy compared to glass bottles. In fact, such savings could only happen within production-consumption loops that are nonecologically large in both time and space. Agribusiness needs foods that can be stored over long time periods and shipped over vast distances. The "throw-away" society is also a society of preservatives, "fat-foods," and chemical-intensive factory-farming. The application of petrochemicals in packaging and in agriculture has made possible the destruction of local economies and organic food systems—intensifying materials throughput, destroying soil, polluting water, and undermining human and environmental health.

It is ironic that, at a time when, historically, human wealth could begin to be defined less materially—through information, services, quality of life, and so on—conditions of scarcity would be reproduced by massive material production. The growing power of science and information in the economy logically should have effected a displacement of both cog-labor and materials from production. Instead, materials consumption skyrocketed. Between the end of the war and the mid-1970s, for example, U.S. paper and mineral consumption more than tripled, metal consumption more than doubled, and plastics use grew thirty-five times over (Young and Sachs, 1994). Other industrialized countries experienced similar increases. The new productive forces were repressed by defining production and consumption in a strictly material way.

The Waste Economy served all the basic requirements of reinforcing a dysfunctional industrial order. It maintained and even extended the separation of production and consumption at a time when they should have become ever more integrated. It reinforced thing-production through its capital-intensive development, and although new superficial needs were created through advertising, people still had to work hard to satisfy primary needs. Finally, waste production extended cog-labor, stifling potentials for the release of labor for more creative work.

FORDISM AND ALIENATED LABOR

The attitude of the left, labor, and social change movements to Fordism is understandably ambivalent. Despite the waste and bureaucratic character of Fordist organization, postwar capitalism consolidated real material benefits for many sections of the working class. Collective bargaining was institutionalized for many.

Wages in the mass production and related sectors were linked to productivity. A social safety net was established, and a greater role for the state provided some measure of political input for popular forces organized enough to exert pressure. The survival of the system depended on the expansion of consumption by the average person. Today, post-Fordist globalism is driven by other forces, and because many of these gains are being dismantled, some nostalgia for the Fordist era is understandable.

Fordism, however, was never about equality or quality of life. It was about growth, constantly making the economic pie bigger, in whatever way possible—in ways that actually reinforced scarcity, class relationships, and personal dependence. While the exploitation of the male industrial working class was mitigated by Fordism, the system compensated by

1. the intensified exploitation of nonhuman nature, which supplied the materials,
2. the intensified exploitation of women in the home, as unpaid "domestic consumption managers" who would supposedly be covered by the male worker's "family wage," and
3. the intensified exploitation of Third World "supply regions" that would provide for the needs of both expanding production and expanding personal consumption in the First World.

To these three, we could also add the intensified exploitation of future generations of people who would pay the social and environmental costs that were deferred by waste. The monetary means of stimulating Fordist mass consumption—credit and debt—functioned explicitly to defer costs. But the super-exploitation of nature—including the creation of new forms of toxins—implicitly transferred costs to the future.

Many of the gains for socialized labor under Fordism were ambiguous and temporary. Labor union collaboration in capital-intensive development was bound to be self-defeating (Noble, 1984). It would eventually put the blue-collar working class on the streets. With the cost of natural resources radically undervalued, or discounted altogether, employers would seek to displace as much labor as possible with materials and energy. Conventional "productivity indexes" have been essentially automation indexes (Henderson, 1978). Today's "jobless growth," even during strong expansions, is a primary product of the Waste Economy.

Blue-collar workers had to make other major compromises. Their gains were achieved at the cost of management getting carte blanche to implement Taylorist job design. Technology could be implemented in ways that continued to separate mind and body, ways that would reinforce the totalitarian organization of work.

The whole Taylorist project after World War II was premised on an even more fundamental reinforcement of the chasm between socialized and nonsocialized production, between production and consumption. At the new stage of development where consumption could no longer simply be assumed, human consumption had to be planned, to some degree or another. But such planning threatened the basic values of industrialism. The consumer economy, based in suburban development, was planned nonplanning. By the same token, new forms of work had to be created to support consumption, but this work could not be recognized as real work without undermining industrial structures.

Women staffed factories and did construction work during the war effort, but many were pushed back into the home in favor of men returning from the war. The rise of the consumer society did not mean less work for women. It meant more work for less (or no) pay (Cowan, 1983; Kessler-Harris, 1982; Hayden, 1984; Matthaei, 1982; Dalla Costa and James, 1975). Galbraith (1973) called attention to the transformation of work in the home with growing consumption. Such consumption required labor to manage it efficiently. Women were turned into "domestic consumption managers," putting in more hours servicing men, children, and household. Budgeting, buying, chauffeuring, and more were added to traditional cooking, and cleaning. Because the extended family became virtually extinct, the pressures of the job had to be handled in extreme isolation. But it cannot be overemphasized how essential this work was to create the new forms of cog-labor in the factories and offices of the Waste Economy.

The rise of mass consumption, however alienated and wasteful, signified the possibility of new forms of production that would put end-use, use-value, and regenerative values first. The fact that people still had to work so hard, even as the system struggled to provide enough "effective demand" for its production, is evidence of the growing irrationality of Fordism. Chapters 4 and 5 will look more closely at the qualitative implications of the new stage of economic development for human development and social movements. Part 2 will explore the economic activities that can tap the vast potentials of postindustrial development. But first, I want to look at the problems created by the waste solution, and the subsequent industrial restructuring that is causing such upheaval today.

3

Post-Fordism: Casino Capitalism
and the Production of Illth

The waste solution provided by Fordism was inevitably temporary. It created a dynamo of growth in a number of countries, but this very growth would create problems. First, the costs of waste and constantly increasing material consumption began to come due. Secondly, the international situation that provided such stability for Fordism, with the United States as the single dominant capitalist power, changed drastically. Finally, new productive forces and new regimes of accumulation emerged that would transform both the form and content of industrial production.

The new post-Fordist stage of industrialization has not attempted to find fundamental solutions. Quite the contrary, it has functioned to perpetuate and extend the very alienated and exploitative relationships that have caused the problems in the first place. It has done this not only through a much more explicit suppression of qualitative development but also by rolling back many positive gains of mass struggle and quantitative development to date.

The main features of post-Fordism are a drastic lessening of the importance of mass consumption and higher living standards to capitalist development, and a corresponding financialization of the economy. Super-industrialism is a sick caricature of the potential for nonmaterial development. It is quantitative development that has been so abstracted that it now spins off virtually no material use-value for society as a whole. For the first time in history, money has become both the means and the ends of economic life for the species. In creating this situation, industrial growth has had to become primarily destructive and essentially cancerous. Refining waste production with financialization, capitalism is increasingly specializing in the production of *illth*. In the next few sections, I will survey some of the main features of the current system so that, in the following two chapters, we can begin to explore positive alternatives.

THE DECLINE OF MASS CONSUMPTION

Most of the positives and the negatives of the postwar Fordist system were connected to the phenomenon of mass consumption. The negatives were related to the role of waste in defining human consumption in passive and materialistic ways, chaining people to cog-labor, and destroying the environment. The positives were connected to the rising material standard of living for many, to social contracts that legitimized collective bargaining, to social safety nets and welfare measures to protect the poor, and to various other regulatory measures to protect human health, quality of life and, eventually, even the environment.

One important reason for the apparently more humane cultural consensus of this era was growing working-class power. Under capitalism, working people were theoretically free individuals. Apparently influenced by such theory, workers fought for and achieved the right to vote, forced reductions in the work day, and grew in education and knowledge. "Folk" arts like jazz became just as complex and sophisticated as the best of classical "high" art and music. Industrial unionism, like the CIO in the 1940s, helped institutionalize collective bargaining in many sectors of the economy, and grassroots power supplied massive pressure for the creation of the welfare state.

While growing working-class autonomy was a major factor in the postwar system, consolidating these gains was possible only because they were consistent with Fordist modes of accumulation. As noted in the previous chapter, very little redistribution took place in the relative shares of wealth between classes. But the new forms of mass consumption helped establish a dynamic of constant economic growth that greatly benefited corporate capital. Fordist capitalism was very much dependent on working-class consumption.

This comfy convergence of interests began to erode drastically in the 1970s. The many symptoms of this erosion included simultaneous hyperinflation and stagnation (or "stagflation") in the developed countries; state fiscal crisis; crisis in the international monetary system; new intercapitalist competition among Japan, Europe, and the United States; and the OPEC-induced energy crisis. Pressure for "belt-tightening," or austerity, began to build in the 1970s, culminating in the Thatcher and Reagan regimes in the United Kingdom and United States respectively. Thereafter, the war against mass consumption, social contracts, and the Welfare State would become the hallmark of post-Fordist accumulation.

Several key factors seem responsible for the turn against mass consumption. First, both stagnation and cost-push inflation could be at least partly attributable to the growing burden of waste and unproductive investment. Most of these costs were externalized by corporations and broadcast widely onto society and the environment. For this reason, they are difficult to quantify accurately, but this lack of quantification makes them no less real. They must be considered major contributors to state fiscal crisis and to the inflationary dynamic of the 1970s. The state was, for example, saddled with massive expenses for suburban infrastructure, which contributed to public debt and fiscal crisis. Many related costs of inefficiency, attributable to fragmented and irrational land use patterns, would be spread over the entire economy. Even more diffuse would be the pervasive health costs associated with pollution, the destruction of ecosystem services, junk food, and more.

A second important factor underlying the demise of mass consumption was the saturation of key markets. According to Charles Sabel (1987: 20):

> A fundamental cause of the slowdown of the 1970s was the saturation of domestic markets for consumer durables and hence exhaustion of new investment opportunities in the business lines that had been the mainstay of the postwar expansion. In the United States, for example, there was one car for every two residents in 1979, as against a ratio of one to four in the early 1950s. By 1970, 99 percent of American homes had refrigerators, electric irons, and radios; more than 90 percent had automatic clothes washers, vacuum cleaners, and toasters. Statistics from other advanced capitalist countries tell a similar story.

Thirdly, the declining profitability of investment in material production coincided with the growing attractiveness of purely financial investment. This was due to a number of factors: the internationalization of production and trade; the emergence of large pools of money (Eurodollars and petrodollars) outside the control of national governments; the decline of the Bretton Woods monetary system and its "gold exchange" standard; and eventually the rise of new information technologies, which enabled new forms of both speculation and money.

Burgeoning forms of financial industry would provide novel means for capitalism to create "effective demand" for its own production. Saskia Sassen (1991: 333) writes:

> Growth in the new industrial complex is less based on the expansion of final consumption by a growing middle class than on exports to the international market and on intermediate consumption by other firms and governments or, more generally, consumption by organizations rather than individuals. The key, though not necessarily the largest, markets are not the consumer markets but the global markets for capital and services. These are the markets that shape society and economy.

Consumer markets would play a role in the new economy, but the most important of these would not be mass markets; they would be niche markets for custom, luxury, or positional goods. While much of the new "flexibly specialized" manufacturing can be tailored to custom markets, so also the tastes of yuppie professionals who work in the new "producer services" are for custom production. Food, entertainment, clothing, and construction services for this market tend to be more customized and labor-intensive.

The rise of giant retailing chains selling cheap goods to the downwardly mobile has not required customers having adequate incomes. These chains are in fact cashing in on the vulnerability of growing numbers of people whose level, and quality, of consumption is declining.

THE COLLAPSE OF KEYNESIANISM: FROM INFLATION TO AUSTERITY

The decline of mass consumption is one way of describing the end of Keynesianism, which was identified with constantly rising living standards for the majority in the developed countries. As discussed earlier, it involved (1) the use of money and credit creation to stimulate demand and manage the economy, and (2) an integration of labor into the system by mildly redistributive social-contracts like the Welfare State and collective bargaining. Both of these factors entailed greater levels of state spending. They also caused inflation, or, more accurately, *employed* inflation to accomplish the goal of maintaining constant economic growth.

Inflation was a principal means of redistributing income back to capital, but this method was more preferable to the working class than the use of deflation and unemployment, because at least living standards could rise and a social service infrastructure could be created. The new social contracts both gave working people a greater stake in the system and humanized a heretofore cut-throat "survival of the fittest" capitalism.

By the 1970s, however, the inflationary strategy ran into trouble. As noted above, simultaneous runaway inflation, economic stagnation, and international monetary turmoil caused great instability.

One reason for such inflation is fairly obvious. While initially controlled inflation could be an effective stimulant and redistributive mechanism, in the long run it could not be controlled and would lose its effectiveness because, in the words of British economist Bob Rowthorn (1980: 141), "the economy adapts to take account of rising prices, so that ever larger doses of inflation are required to keep the patient healthy."

Another big reason for the collapse of the inflationary strategy was its abuse by the United States, the single dominant capitalist power, whose currency served as a means of international exchange. The stability of the Bretton Woods international monetary system, hatched in 1944, depended on the United States, which benefited greatly from the new system, to also tread a fine line of international responsibility. As expressed in the famous "Triffin dilemma," the United States had to provide its dollar as liquidity for the rest of the world, requiring a persistent balance-of-payments deficit. But to maintain international trust in the value of the dollar, the United States had to remain the top economic power, which implies a healthy trade surplus; it also needed this surplus simply to maintain effective demand for its industry. The United States needed Europe as a market, and so needed to help Europe rebuild. The temporary solution would be the combination of a trade surplus with massive foreign direct investment and loans abroad (thereby creating the overall balance-of-payments deficit and money for world trade) (Block, 1977; Guttman, 1994).

The United States' role as Free World policeman, however, proved to outweigh its international monetary responsibilities as the United States "printed money" to finance its adventures in Vietnam. Domestic unrest concerning the war and civil rights discouraged either austerity policies or tax increases, while U.S. business and government became complacent about technological improvement. Japan and Germany both began to challenge U.S. economic supremacy, undermining confidence in the dollar. Domestic inflation speeded up, as vast pools of overseas dollars (Eurodollars) began to collect in European banks, completely outside the control of national governments. This instability resulted in a run on U.S. gold reserves and forced the United States to pull off the gold-exchange standard in 1971, effectively ending the Bretton Woods system. The implementation of floating exchange rates in place of a gold standard greatly exacerbated the instability, and the oil embargo and subsequent energy crisis supplied a major inflationary hit to all the Western economies.

Planned inflation was beginning to look less and less attractive as a strategy for growth and redistribution. U.S. monetary irresponsibility, the rise in world commodity prices, the energy crisis, and more made inflation a dirty word. Although economic theory typically sees inflation and stagnation as mutually exclusive states of the business cycle, in practice—because of the built-in inflationary bias of Fordism—stagnation and inflation seemed to aggravate each other. Inflation undermined the confidence of investors, and slower growth induced producers to compensate with higher prices (Arrighi, 1994).

These inflationary factors, combined with the aforementioned saturation of markets and the burden of waste, contributed to a growing corporate consensus for new means of income redistribution. By the late 1970s, the new consensus—expressed in Thatcherism and Reaganism—was that the system could no longer afford the social contracts with labor and the poor. Cutbacks in the amount and relative proportions of state spending going to working people were coupled with a return to tight money policies that would further redistribute income back to capital via recession.

Aspects of Keynesianism were preserved—particularly the stimulative effects of deficit spending, debt, and waste production (Bonefeld, 1995). The Reagan administration, for example, while cutting back on social welfare, doubled the U.S. public debt in the period 1981–86. Its tax cuts were a windfall for the rich but did nothing for economic stimulation. Massive arms spending, however—known as "military Keynesianism"—was a substantial stimulus for the U.S. economy. The result was an economic expansion that weakened labor and effected an increasing gap between rich and poor.

The trashing of the Fordist social contracts was inspired not simply by a profitability crisis but also because new circumstances allowed capitalism to do without social contracts. As discussed above, with the financialization of production, capitalism no longer needed so much mass consumption or worker cooperation. Another reason, however, was the growing scale and scope of multinational corporate operations, which began to make these multinationals less concerned with national economic organization in any way other than short-term profit. The possibility of easily exploiting cheap labor in other parts of the world put a downward pressure on wages almost everywhere in the developed world.

Not only has organized labor not been able to extend its organization globally to counterbalance corporate flexibility, but changes in production processes have also diluted labor's organizational power at home. Subcontracting, casualized labor, de-skilling, and the like have weakened labor's power in almost all parts of the developed world. Multinational power has also weakened the state, and the postwar collective bargaining structures that integrated unions into national political structures have now weakened labor further. It was the union bureaucracies that bargained politically; the rank and file had their concerns channelled into narrow wages-and-benefits terms. The unions grew ever more cut off from their rank-and-file base, less and less able to mount vigorous fights to defend their gains.

As discussed earlier, the postwar arrangements institutionalized taxes—along with inflation—as important means of extracting capitalism's economic surplus. Collective bargaining provisions put some limits on capital's ability to exploit at the point of production and in labor markets. Taxes also became more important as state activity became a larger portion of the economy.

The neoconservative/monetarist attack on the state attempted not simply to undermine the amount of state activity in the economy but also to readjust the tax arrangements that financed this activity. Since the early 1980s, the industrialized nations have seen a substantial growth of public debt. Contrary to prevailing conventional wisdom, welfare spending has little to do with this indebtedness. Along with the massive growth of military spending in the United States in the 1980s, and interest charges on the debt caused by tight-money policies, a major cause of public indebtedness is the regressive restructuring of the tax system in Western countries.

There have been (1) a shift from taxing corporations to taxing individuals, and (2) growing taxation of the poor and the middle class, combined with lessening of tax rates for the rich and well-off classes. These tax changes have entailed increased reliance on indirect taxes, such as consumption taxes, social insurance levies, lotteries, and state-run gambling.

According to Gary Teeple (1995), the evolution of multinationals is a major factor in their lessened role in government finance. The more international capital has become, the less interested it has been in financially supporting national states. And its growing international character has also given the corporations the means to avoid taxes and play off nations against one another.

Correspondingly, cutbacks in various kinds of state services and benefits contribute to "harmonizing" social conditions on a global scale that create a "competitive" environment for corporate investment. Cutbacks are, of course, justified by state fiscal crisis, but this crisis is more an effect than a cause. Many cutbacks and forms of privatization actually increase social costs in the long term and thus aggravate the fiscal crisis. By and large, the cutback mentality of "downsizing government" has the net effect of removing larger and larger portions of the economy from political control.

Writers like John McMurtry (1999) have gone so far as to argue that the conscious creation of waste and public debt by neoconservative governments has been a deliberate domestic strategy to bankrupt the state and its life-support services—much as the Reagan administration sought to bankrupt the Soviet state by escalating the arms race.

Post-Fordist ideologies like Reaganism and Thatcherism essentially concluded that material growth sufficient to provide both capitalist profits and a general increase in living standards was no longer possible. Henceforth reverse redistribution—from poor to rich—would have to be institutionalized as a central means of economic growth. According to Brecher and Costello (1994: 29):

> In the U.S., the 1 percent with the highest incomes nearly doubled their share of national income from 8 percent in 1980 to 14.7 percent in 1989. The top 1 percent increased their share of wealth from 27 percent in the 1970s to 36 percent at the end of the 1980s. The net worth of the four hundred richest Americans trebled from $92 billion in 1982 to $270 billion in 1989. Meanwhile, one-quarter of all infants and toddlers live in poverty, including more than half of all black children under six.

A windfall for the rich would not, however, necessarily deal with systemic problems of stagnation. As with Fordism, developing productive forces would have to be channelled in ways that exploited yet contained their unique powers. But old forms of material waste would no longer provide the necessary stimulus. A new form of exploitative waste was required: this is the financialization of economic life.

BUILDING THE CASINO

The roots of the Casino Economy lay in the Keynesian Paper Economy. According to Robert Guttmann (1994: 299):

> Even though financial speculation has existed throughout the history of capitalism [see Kindleberger, 1978], fictitious capital only became an institutionalized part of our economic system with the monetary reforms of the 1930s. That form of capital is intimately tied to credit-money, a linkage which is rooted in the very process of

money creation. By loaning out (excess) reserves gained from deposits, a bank creates new money deposits, As its loan is spent, the process replicates itself with another bank. In the end the banking system as a whole has created a multiple of the original excess reserves in new money. Such money creation ex nihilo is in itself a source of fictitious capital and the reason why credit-money has no intrinsic value.

The Paper Economy began to sever the connection between real and monetary wealth by the deliberate creation of both monetary and material scarcity. The credit-money that was so central to postwar development was based on debt, and this role of debt would eventually become dominant. But Keynesianism did maintain a fragile link between real and monetary wealth through growing living standards for the working class and through its semi-gold standard. Loans were still made primarily to support profit from production. The decline of mass consumption, described above, and the displacement of gold would complete the hollowing out of global capitalism. Aided by the alienated application of new technology, money—representing nothing but pure power, or illth—would rule. Casino Capitalism is the Waste Economy's vision of nonmaterial production.

In the preceding section, we touched on the United States' abuse of its seigniorage privileges as the world's banker. U.S. opportunism basically created a monster—vast pools of money outside of any government's control—which would eventually effect a fundamental shift of financial power away from government to private finance.

After Nixon "closed the gold window," and ended the dollar's convertibility into gold (in 1971), a series of events throughout the rest of the decade prepared the way for a full-fledged Casino Economy in the 1980s. The end of Bretton Woods, with its fixed exchange rates tied to a gold value, ushered in a new era of floating exchange rates. While it was not Nixon's intention to trash fixed exchange rates for all time, experiments with fixed rates over the next two years did not work without gold, and the floating system was implemented in 1973. Joel Kurtzman (1993: 94), editor of the *Harvard Business Review,* summarizes the significance of Nixon's decision:

> By abandoning gold, Nixon enlarged the size of the finance economy by several orders of magnitude. He also moved the world onto a new standard: the interest rate standard. From that point of view all investment, finance and real, has a single benchmark: interest rates. And all investors have one single goal: to earn more than the cost of money.
>
> In high interest rate countries—the United States, Canada, and Britain—companies have been forced to abandon long-term, lower-rate-of-return investments, such as manufacturing, in favor of finance to get sufficient returns.

As noted earlier, the money generated by U.S. deficits, due primarily to its military adventures, accumulated in Europe as Eurodollars (Arrighi, 1994: 299) and eventually as petrodollars, when OPEC dollars joined the currency in international banks. They contributed to the speculation as banks awash in funds competed to lend to developing countries, many of which expected to gain by the temporary rise in commodity prices. Many of these loans went to irrational megaprojects, military buildup, and corruption.

The creation of U.S. deficits was due not only to its military expenditures but also to the multinational power of its corporations that invested abroad (Arrighi, 1994). But the increasingly speculative world economy also exaggerated the multinationalism of corporations by forcing them to protect their own dollars by having them invested around in various currencies (Strange, 1986).

These are the circumstances that explain a shift in the control of the international monetary system from government (the U.S. government) to private finance. The Bretton Woods system, designed by the United States for the post–World War II world, effectively shifted world financial control from London and New York to Washington. The floating exchange rates of the 1970s, in financial markets awash with petrodollars, gave growing power to private finance and set the scene for the "tight money" revolution and the deregulation of financial markets by the Reagan government.

The United States' decision to impose austerity on its own working class not only was a response to international pressures on the United States to "live within its means" but established a new mode of development premised on tight money for the people, and cheap money for financial capital. The national state now more or less consciously sought to support the financialization of the economy.

Many people, with some justification, see Reagan and Thatcher as throwbacks to long-discredited market and authoritarian ideologies. But it is just as important to see that the restructuring they pushed helped create the new information-based financial economy. Reagan by no means threw out the whole of Keynesianism, or the use of the state.

As noted earlier, the Reagan revolution was not monetarist in a conventional sense, but "Keynesian" in its use of military spending for economic stimulus. The Reagan Recovery was debt driven. "Sound money" policies did not mean a return to the gold standard or even to material production; they meant the use of money to control inflation by strict labor market discipline. "Sound money" was to be imposed on the people; big capital was given greater opportunities to create new forms of money and speculation. The thoroughgoing deregulation of financial markets reinforced speculation by removing many bureaucratic obstacles to the creation of new forms of financial money-making and money-trading. Deregulation of domestic financial markets was essentially a process of alignment with the new global financial markets.

The Reagan administration also spearheaded an ideology of stomp-the-weak-and-get-rich-quick that aggravated speculative behavior. The boom from 1982 to 1987 featured unprecedented levels of high-stakes maneuvering, short-term profiteering, currency speculation, stock market gambling fuelled by merger mania, and junk-bond-financed corporate raiding.

TECHNOLOGY AND MEGABYTE MONEY

The amazing scale and scope of Casino Capitalism would be unimaginable without the information revolution. In fact, the Casino Economy can be seen as the regressive diversion of the information revolution away from ecological development. Money is a form of information, and the new technology has made possible the creation of new forms of money as well as a global electronic infrastructure for moving money around. The domestic deregulation of the financial industry, as mentioned above, has been a means of aligning with this new global system.

The de facto "interest rate standard" created by cutting the dollar off from gold, along with the implementation of floating exchange rates, set the scene for a further explosion of "fictitious capital" (Guttmann, 1994) as new information and communications technology was implemented in the late 1970s and early 1980s. Information technology allowed ephemeral credit-money to be expressed as electronic impulses and to be interconnected to a global "neural network of money" or a giant electronic commons. According to Joel Kurtzman (1993: 16):

> In this new environment, millions of computers are linked in a vast 24-hour, global-trading and information exchange of unimaginable complexity. . . . Money, in its new electrical form, jumps from computer to computer. . . . Each time an electron makes its leap, units of buying-power—big and small—are exchanged. Goods, wealth, dreams and power change hands. . . . Every day [in N.Y.] more than $1.9 trillion electronically changes hands at nearly the speed of light. . . . Every three days a sum of money passes through the fiber-optic network underneath the pitted streets of New York equal to the total output for one year of all America's companies and all of its workforce. And every two weeks the annual product of the world passes through the network of New York.

Not only can money be traded more easily, but the new technology has made possible the creation of new forms of money that are ever more disconnected from material things. The most important of these forms—"derivatives"—are pure expressions of Casino Economics. They are means of managing risk—of investors both protecting themselves from and cashing in on the incredible unpredictability of the market. They are essentially contracts that can both hedge and leverage one's bets in the market. Like futures trading in commodities such as corn or oil, options or futures to buy currency or stocks at a predetermined price sometime in the future is theoretically a way of providing some stability. But the growth of such financial innovations has in fact dramatically increased the speculative nature of finance, almost completely subordinating productive to financial capital, and long-term to short-term investing. By 1995, the trading in derivatives alone in twenty-six countries was estimated at double the world economic output, and 98 percent of derivatives trading was in currency or interest rates (Strange, 1998).

Because much of this new money is cut off from gold or a material backing, it stores value poorly. It depreciates rapidly and must be traded constantly from one form to another to earn the maximum interest possible. A whole sector of producer services has been created in the financial industry to develop software and hardware that will enable investors to anticipate where returns will be greatest. Complicated combinations of currency, stock, bond, and so on are packaged together to hedge risk and maximize returns. Financial firms that once specialized in investment advice now focus on trading and devising new financial "innovations." In the United States, the financial industry is one of the most technologically advanced industries, with billions invested in sophisticated hardware, software, and technical expertise.

This technologically advanced Casino Economy has institutionalized short-term profit unlike at any time in the past. "Investing" has given way to "transacting," with little consideration given to anything but short-term paper-earnings potential. Also unsurpassed is the sheer size of the financial economy. In 1993, Kurtzman estimated that it was between thirty and fifty times larger than the material economy. Important points of connection obviously remain between the financial and material economies, but economic policy is increasingly dominated by the financial sector.

In the United States, for example, during the 1980s there was a huge expansion of financial assets relative to GNP. Earnings from interest outpaced industrial profits and aggravated the income shift from poor to rich. Because of the high cost of capital, industrial investment stagnated, aggravating unemployment. The financial economy absorbs vital resources, which would otherwise be employed in the material economy. According to Harvard's Lawrence Summers, the financial markets in 1987 absorbed 24.2 percent of U.S. corporate profits (Kurtzman, 1993).

The dominance of financial capital is the main reason even minute amounts of inflation seem to terrify governments today. This is because inflation tends to diminish the value of money as well as the profits to be made on interest. Deflation (and engineered recession), such a dirty word in the Fordist era, is today somewhat acceptable as a means of redistributing income, as long as it isn't so severe as to bring down the financial house of cards.

Stock market speculation in the 1980s also distorted the industrial restructuring that was taking place, encouraging mergers that paid off big in speculative profits for the raiders but that forced inappropriate combinations and gobbled up valuable resources.

The Casino Economy affects virtually every aspect of economic life. It is creating whole new sectors of labor. It is also reshaping the geography of the globe and defining unique patterns of development that—as will be clear in part 2—are by no means simple inevitabilities of the information economy. Writers like Saskia Sassen (1991) have emphasized the strategic role of the new "producer services"—many of which are connected to the financial sector—in the global economy. She and other writers on "world cities" have also emphasized the special importance of cities in the new regime and the establishment of hierarchies of cities in this new financial economy. While Sassen argues that the powerful global cities are not just seats of power but also sites of production, it can hardly be overlooked how wasteful and irrational most of this work is from a social point of view.

DEBT, ILLTH, AND POWER

The financialization of industrial development represents the triumph of quantitative development as an end in itself. This is something of a paradox because this victory of abstract quantity has been possible only by limiting material development—by creating scarcity through waste. Another paradox is that the triumph of money has been possible only by preventing the evolution of money into its most flexible and advanced form—money as information, money as a pure means of exchange. This is because money in this advanced form can never be a thing-in-itself; it can only be a means to qualitative development. Capitalist money, however intangible, must always remain a commodity.

Debt is the primary means by which industrialism has maintained monetary scarcity and kept information-money a commodity. Debt underlay all the credit-money created by the Keynesian Paper Economy. Although this debt chained people to cog-labor and an economic treadmill, at least it was used to create jobs, lower unemployment, and raise living standards for a good portion of the working class. In other words, debt was used to expand production and finance mass consumption.

With the collapse of the inflationary strategy of growth and redistribution, however, debt has come to play an ever more sinister and central role: to, in effect, restrict production and to actively redistribute income. Finance capital has become dominant over productive capital, and, as writers like Linda McQuaig (1995, 1998) have shown, the welfare of bondholders and other interest-earners takes precedence over manufacturing profit. The financial subsidiaries of corporations like General Motors and General Electric now contribute more profit than all of their manufacturing operations (McMurtry, 1999). Debt has become the primary means of extracting the economic surplus. As the burden of debt has become ever more enslaving, fervor concerning (state) debt has also become the key ideological tool in obtaining public acquiescence for austerity and the gutting of state life-support services.

Michael Rowbotham (1998) has shown the hypocrisy of the campaign against public debt carried out by corporate interests, which thrive on the growth of commercial and consumer debt. He describes how in the postwar world, debt has been increasingly important in supplying liquidity for the entire economy. Today this debt, primarily created by bank loans, now comprises virtually the whole of the money stock (or M4), with only 2 to 3 percent created directly by government debt-free. Because national governments have refused to create interest-free credit-money, the use of bank-credit has institutionalized chronic money-shortage. This chronic shortage is illustrated by the fact that, if all debts could be paid at once, there would be virtually no money left in the economy.

While this scarcity is disguised by continuing turnover, the reloaning of debt-money, and constant growth, its behavioral impact is hardly less significant. There can only be a situation of winners and big losers. The compulsive competition for scarce money sets in motion irrational forces based ultimately on a chronic shortage of purchasing power. It creates nonsensical export economies, forcing production and consumption loops to grow ever larger, constantly increasing the transportation component of products, and encouraging planned obsolescence of every sort.

The inefficiency involved, which was always implicit in the Fordist waste economy, has reached epidemic proportions in the current global casino in which questions of overall economic efficiency seem to be completely irrelevant. The irrationality of post-Fordist globalization will be demonstrated more graphically in part 2, where we'll look at potentials for a green economy.

The contrast between the role of debt in the Fordist and Casino Economies is illustrated in the role of mortgages. In the postwar industrialized world, mortgages were an important and successful means of increasing home ownership by the working class. In the past twenty-five years, however, mortgages have been more important as a source of issuing debt-money in the economy—now providing more than 60 percent of the money-stock in the UK and more than 70 percent in the United States—and redistributing income *away* from working people. Today, in both the United States and the UK, a smaller percentage of people own their houses outright than did thirty years ago.

The chronic scarcity of money in capitalist economies is one reason government debt has been necessary. Government debt has been a means of creating money to keep the economy going and expanding. Throughout the Fordist era, this role was implicitly recognized, particularly since government deficits helped create the social and economic infrastructures that competitive domestic economies needed.

In the Casino Economy, private capital—now based in finance—no longer believes in the necessity of this infrastructure for corporate profitability and competitiveness. Campaigns against inflation and against government deficits have, as Rowbotham (1998) argues, constituted pressure to eliminate public debt while increasing private debt, particularly individual consumer debt—for homes, transportation, and now even health care and vital social services.

Nevertheless, financial capital's campaign against public debt and Keynesianism has its limits. McQuaig (1995), McMurtry (1999), and others have documented how neoconservative governments have been much more liberal in allowing, and even encouraging, the growth of public debt due to interest charges, tax cuts, and military spending. These measures have had redistributive effects — funneling wealth to the rich — and have provided fodder for deficit panic and further cuts to social infrastructure.

SPACE OF FLOWS: THE GEOGRAPHY OF DISEMPOWERMENT

Fordism was a global system, but one with a distinct national focus. Keynesianism was a means of dealing with the contradiction between "sound money" for international trade and flexibility for national governments in managing their domestic economies. Throughout capitalism's history, the international and domestic sides of capitalism were often not a harmonious fit. As Block (1977) has shown, capitalism has always experienced tension between the capitalist ideal of the "open" economy and national economic management. Nineteenth-century capitalism, with its boom-and-bust business cycles and the rough deflationary discipline of the gold standard, was not exactly respectful of the average working person. In the twentieth century, however, structural crisis would no longer allow the business cycle to automatically impose its previously therapeutic deflation and effect a healthy recovery. Industrial elites needed the cooperation and consumption of working people to maintain growth, and so it would be politically impossible for ruling elites to allow international market forces such uncushioned impact on the national economy.

In Fordism, mass consumption and greater state control of the economy went hand in hand. This was industrialism's era of the state, the heyday of both Fordism and state socialism. It was the time of the rise of intellectual labor, white-collar work, and bureaucracy — the tools for this new management. It was the time of centralization and standardization.

In the developed countries, capitalist development needed to depend on working-class power in both production and consumption. While the power of organized labor was expressed in collective bargaining, popular power was also expressed in the Welfare State. Fordism also depended on national economic planning to provide infrastructure, education, and demand management, and even to play a role in extracting the surplus — through inflation and taxes.

One big reason domestic demand management could work was that leakage from the national economy was fairly insignificant. Government spending and monetary policies had crucial ripple or "multiplier" effects within national boundaries. The overlapping interests of state, business, and labor in domestic living standards spawned an increasingly liberal culture that acknowledged nominal equality and social responsibility.

Post-Fordism still needs the cooperation and consumption of the working class, but much less so. An increasingly globalized economy means that the purchasing power and skills of the domestic working class are much less important.

Social spending is not so necessary to prop up effective demand. National governments have much less control over levels of aggregate demand, and the "multiplier effects" of government spending tend to dissipate right across national boundaries. Increasingly transnational companies feel no allegiance to national economies and have the power to move to avoid taxes or take advantage of cheap labor, deregulated environments, and other special privileges. The role of national governments is increasingly reduced to monetary tinkering, downsizing, and competing to attract external capital.

Postindustrial productive forces bring inevitable tendencies toward both globalism and localism. New communications technologies have created a planetary nervous system, which simultaneously unifies and permits decentralization of the globe. These technologies have also redefined the relationship between hierarchy and decentralization in many areas of life.

In no way does this mean, however, that post-Fordist globalization is inevitable. In fact, the profit-driven variety of capitalist globalism we see today depends very much on suppressing key technological and organizational potentials. As we will see in part 2, the postindustrial dialectic between integration and decentralization could take a very different form in a green economy. Tapping the full potential of the new forces of cultural production requires integrating production and consumption as well as politics, economics, and culture, but industrialism depends on these separations. Post-Fordist globalization is, in fact, driven to solve the problems created by the repressive and wasteful structures of Fordism by extending these relationships further afield.

This extension involves penetrating deeper into everyday life, but it also includes a geographical extension made more possible by new technologies. One of the primary characteristics of a green economy, which is made more possible by the information revolution, is its *place-based* nature. Information-intensity allows people to make the most of natural ecosystem productivity (that is, of the ecological *context*) and to substitute information for long-distance material flows. Profit-driven post-Fordism, which is less concerned with economic efficiency, uses information in diametrically opposite ways to extend production and consumption loops globally.

One of the information economy's main intellectual advocates, Manuel Castells (1989: 169) argues that "the space of organizations in the informational economy is increasingly a space of flows," following a spatial logic derived from information production and handling that is essentially "placeless." He writes that "the more organizations depend, ultimately, upon flows and networks, the less they are influenced by the social contexts associated with the places of their location."

As discussed above, the most obvious feature of the new geography of control is the decline of the national state. It is being displaced by an increasingly powerful local/global nexus. This is a complex process. National states are still extremely important, and under industrialism, they may never be completely eclipsed. The rise and decline of various countries depend on new forms of planning and intervention, various sorts of public-private partnerships, and the provision of key infrastructure. There are some areas in which the state must play an even more important role. These areas are discussed in literature on the so-called "developmental state" on the model of Japan (Cohen, 1993). Nevertheless, national economies must sacrifice some traditional areas of sovereignty to this "space of flows" of transnational capital—as attested to by the regional trade areas of the European Union and NAFTA and the various agreements on international trade.

These trends are closely related to capital mobility. Business is increasingly able to locate wherever it finds conditions best. This flexibility has been a crucial factor in the changing balance of power between capital and labor. Since the late 1970s, capital has been in a consistently more powerful position, contributing to the current race-to-the-bottom to achieve lower labor costs.

It is interesting that, despite the importance of cheap labor, globalization is also tending to *narrow* the truly global nature of production by focusing trade and investment overwhelmingly in the richest nations (Sassen, 1994). According to Barnet and Cavanagh (1994: 284):

> The United Nations estimates that of the $196 billion in new overseas private investment made in 1989, over four-fifths flowed back and forth among twenty-four affluent countries. Only a sixth of the total flowed into the poorer nations; less than 2 percent flowed into Africa.

The Fordist era featured a role for Third World nations as sites for exploitation of natural resources and raw materials, fuelling the First World's Waste Economy. The growing informationalization and financialization of the world economy has tended to marginalize growing numbers in the former Third World. The "Three Worlds" character of the Fordist era has given way to a more complex structure, not simply because of the collapse of state socialism but also because of dynamics within the old Third World. Barnet and Cavanagh (1994) suggest seven categories:

1. the developed core countries;
2. the NICs or "newly industrialized countries" of the semi-periphery: Brazil, Mexico, Argentina, India, and the "Asian Tigers";
3. "aspiring NICs" still based in agriculture, such as China, Thailand, Malaysia, and two dozen more;
4. the former Communist states;
5. most of the OPEC countries;
6. forty or so poor countries, such as Zambia and Bolivia, still dependent on primary resource exports; and
7. the LDCs or "least developed countries": forty-seven desperately poor countries locked into dependency and virtually excluded from the thrust of the world economy.

The local aspect of the new global/local nexus for capitalism is embodied in the emergence of so-called "world cities." These cities are the dynamic production sites for the exploding producer services, especially financial services and "innovations." Researchers have charted a hierarchy of these cities, ranging from the leading global cities of Tokyo, London, and New York, to subordinate poles that play key roles in incorporating certain regions into the new "space of global accumulation" (Friedman, 1994). These world cities serve as command centers for the deployment of global capital and nodes for the "neural network of money" discussed earlier. While these cities may compete somewhat, by and large the most powerful Global Cities play a particular role in the global division of labor: generating, processing, or deploying capital.

These world cities not only are sites for global tasks and advanced services, but they embody the polarization so characteristic of the new regime of accumulation. A growing literature is documenting the rise of "Dual Cities"—sites not just for advanced producer services but also for low-paid services, flexploitation, and growing underground economies. Sassen, in particular, has made the connection between the gentrification of sections of the cores of these cities and the rise of producer services. High-paid professional workers are providing demand for labor-intensive customized services—from renovators to domestic workers to retail clerks to craft workers. Poor and immigrant communities outside the gentrified areas provide the labor for these services as well as for sweatshop manufacturing, underground community services, and even the drug trade (Sassen, 1991; Castells, 1989).

Equally significant, especially in North America, to the Dual Cities created by globalization is the emergence of suburban Edge Cities, created mainly by the decentralization of many corporate functions. Two-thirds of the United States' office facilities are now in the suburbs, 80 percent materializing in the past twenty-five years (Garreau, 1991). The prototypical commercial cities of the era, Edge Cities are designed for the automobile, for sales, for corporate efficiency. They do not possess truly public spaces—the parking lot being the closest thing, with their malls and atriums being "variations on a theme park" (Sorkin, 1992). And while they possess fairly high densities, they reinforce a pattern of megalopolitan sprawl in conjunction with their adjoining residential suburbs.

FLEXPLOITATION: MCWORK IN THE GLOBAL ECONOMY

Bill Gates and Manuel Castells notwithstanding, one of the great fallacies of "postindustrial" ideology today is that we, in the developed countries, work in a "knowledge-based economy." There can be no denying that capitalism has had to employ emerging technologies to wage the competitive struggle for profits and power. But the perpetuation of quantitative notions of wealth and development has also required suppressing, narrowing, and channelling the most radical technological potentials.

It is more correct to say that we live in a knowledge-based *society,* since the creative and multidimensional use of information permeates civil society through the vast range of subcultures, hobbies, arts, informal services, activism, and so on. Compared to these "outside" interests, the knowledge component of most people's jobs is actually quite small. Knowledge is power and is dangerous to spread around to too much of the workforce. The high-tech redirection of the information revolution has made post-Fordism much more capital intensive than information intensive. And, in certain sectors of the economy and parts of the world, post-Fordism has encouraged the most degrading and exploitative forms of labor-intensity. Industrialism has always been based on cog-labor, and as long as this is the case, real knowledge-intensity will continue to be suppressed in the formal economy. Later in this section, we'll look at the reality of jobs our vaunted "knowledge-based" economy is actually producing.

The byword of postindustrial organization is "flexibility." For capitalism, this tends to mean that the speed of change, the complexity of the economic environment, and the intensity of competition make it imperative that corporations have more flexibility in how they can use people and resources. There are many dimensions to such flexibility, very few of which benefit workers or consumers. There are certainly islands of developmental flexibility in the work world, but most forms of flexibility are euphemisms for either the elimination or the degradation of work. Unemployment and de-skilling have always been essential elements of capitalism. New technologies simply provide new means of achieving certain ends. Deregulation, downsizing, outsourcing, casualization, and reengineering are basically means of increasing the power of big capital in relation to either labor or society as a whole.

Capitalism's growing powers of displacing labor are a negative reflection of society's potential to eliminate cog-labor. Eliminating cog-labor is not necessarily a bad thing. The end of cog-labor can mean growing freedom for self-development, for leisure, for service, for management, for unalienated work. In post-Fordist capitalism, however, the obsolescence of cog-labor has meant, as implied in the title of Jeremy Rifkin's book *The End of Work,* structural unemployment, redundancy, and rejection.

In actual fact, there is no danger of industrialism completely eliminating routine labor, because the system depends on constantly reproducing cog-labor. Rather, the problem with globalization is that it is combining joblessness for millions with new forms of exploitative work, destroying communities and ecosystems on a massive scale. The joblessness is a means of disempowering those with jobs, thus exercising "labor market discipline."

The Fordist regime of mass consumption relied upon a stable and growing middle-income working class. Mass production manufacturing was the core industry that tended to spin off benefits to other sectors. Today, the new regime is eliminating that middle class as it transforms manufacturing—creating new kinds of workers and supplying new kinds of markets for itself. There is little spin-off from the new dynamic sectors, and the state has largely abandoned its redistributive role. The result is an "hourglass economy" featuring polarized workforces, income levels, and kinds of work.

The new forms of work are linked to new organizational forms that are based in flexibility. There is a growing genre of literature, most of it from a business perspective, that presents an idealized version of these new flexible forms—the end of hierarchy, flexible and lean production, reengineering, worker participation, a renaissance of craft production, and so on. In reality, the new forms of flexibility can be as destructive and exploitative as the old forms of control. Production may be decentralized, but not power.

Concentrated corporate power is not evaporating; it is changing its shape. The late Bennett Harrison (1994: 8) called this restructuring "concentration without centralization." It includes paring down corporate activities and workforces, using computer systems to coordinate far-flung operations, instituting strategic alliances between big corporations, and creating increasingly flexible arrangements with skilled labor.

The downsizing of major corporations, or their decentralization of production, does not make these corporations less dominant, but more. The smaller firms, resulting from new outsourcing and subcontracting arrangements with the large corporations, must operate within a business environment ever more defined by big capital. In many cases, skilled workers who used to work within the big corporate firms for good wages and benefits are now doing the very same work as private subcontractors to those firms for much less. These new *core-ring* production networks allow the use of cheaper and part-time labor, with much less social responsibility by the corporation (Harrison, 1994).

Robin Murray (1988) has described how this phenomenon of control-without-ownership has been a trend of capitalist development. Each major industry tends to have a "commanding height" from which control can be exercised. In the auto industry, it is assembly, but more often these commanding heights are connected with the control of technology or marketing.

The information revolution has meant a downgrading of the previously dominant position of manufacturing in the economy. The combination of automation and outsourcing has meant that, particularly in fast-growing industries like electronics, manufacturing work is no longer synonymous with secure well-paid jobs. In some industries, wages are low enough that, for example, New York City immigrant sweatshops can be cost competitive with cheap-labor imports from the Third World (Sassen, 1991).

Technological change has had a contradictory impact on production. The dominant tendency is one that has been a continuing theme throughout the life of industrialism: the de-skilling of direct production. Operations that used to be performed on the shop floor are transferred either to computers or to specialized technical staff. This allows the shop function to be either automated or downgraded to a low-paid, part-time, or outsourced status. Rifkin (1995: 5) claims that perhaps 90 million jobs in the United States, out of a total of 124 million, are vulnerable to replacement by machines.

The effect of automation and cybernation is being aggravated by the reengineering for lean production and flexibility. This reengineering is shaking up the old bureaucratic hierarchies. Whole layers of middle management are being eliminated, creating unparalleled unemployment problems for previously upper-middle-class professionals.

The evolution of work is not by any means completely negative. While the de-skilling of work continues as the dominant trend, some post-Taylorist tendencies have emerged. In many areas, upgrading worker participation and working conditions has improved productivity substantially. There is even some talk of a renaissance of "craft" production in the small, new, computerized "flexibly specialized" production of semi-custom manufacturing (Piore and Sabel, 1984). By and large, however, creative, fulfilling, and enskilled jobs are islands in a sea of work degradation. The creation of polarized job structures works against society as a whole, institutionalizing conflict and competition (Tomaney, 1994; Rifkin, 1995; Harrison and Bluestone, 1988).

The dual dynamic of de-skilling/enskilling and polarization affects sectors we might consider more privileged, such as white-collar, service, and professional work. In white-collar occupations, whole layers of middle management are being wiped out, but many front-line professional jobs are being broadened and in some cases enriched and enskilled. But these choice jobs are confined to a narrow band of the workforce, the new labor aristocracy connected with the new producer services.

There has been an explosion of specialized services, from design to communications. Traditional producer services, such as legal, accounting, and advertising services, have been joined by a plethora of other services connected to the production and transmission of information. These producer services can exist in any sector of the economy, from manufacturing to agriculture. Many of these functions were once performed in-house by corporations, but the increased complexity of the economy has caused these services to become specialized operations and separate businesses. Some of them are completely new, such as, for example, some of the "financial innovations" production arising from the Casino Economy. Other producer services result simply from the transformation of traditional manufacturing and services. As noted earlier, in contrast to the consumer services connected to Fordism, today's producer services are primarily for *organizations,* or for some of their more highly paid employees. These producer services are the driving forces of urban development in many key cities, and they are the strategic nexus of post-Fordist economic development. It is in these services that much creative work is concentrated and also where many high-income jobs are found.

The new producer services are not, however, so beneficial to all their workers. They are also a source of many low-paid jobs, because this sector is itself quite polarized, with many of the fastest-growing categories being low-paid clerical jobs (Sassen, 1991).

The explosion in producer services reshaped the urban landscape in the 1980s, creating not only office towers for the polarized services described above but also vast numbers of low-paid jobs for building attendants, sales clerks, waitresses, janitors, security guards, and so on. These services have also spun off many, largely low-paid consumer services to cater to the needs of the high-paid professionals for custom, positional, and luxury goods. For example, newly gentrified urban areas provide work for renovators, house cleaners, and retail sales clerks, among others.

Contrary to popular opinion, the largest volume of new jobs in the economy is, and will be, low-paid jobs. The U.S. Bureau of Labor Statistics projected the greatest numbers of jobs to be as cashiers, nurses, janitors, truck drivers, waiters and waitresses, and retail salespersons. Electrical engineers and computer programmers had high rates of growth projected but low absolute numbers of jobs (Harrison and Bluestone, 1988). According to Holly Sklar (1995: 26), "over half of the total job growth projected over the 1992–2005 period will be in occupations that don't require more than a high school education."

Unemployment and McJobs are the two sides of work for the majority in the post-Fordist world. Virtually everywhere in the industrialized world, average unemployment rates are creeping upward. Corporations are downsizing and reengineering to employ fewer. Between 1979 and 1992, the total worldwide employment of the Fortune 500 companies dropped from 16.2 million to 11.8 million (Sklar, 1995). Contrary to the conventional wisdom, small business cannot pick up the slack. According to studies by Bennett Harrison (1994: 13), "the proportion of Americans working for small companies and for individual establishments . . . has barely changed at all since at least the early 1960s." He claims the same is true of Japan and West Germany. Rifkin (1995: 7) writes, "By the time the first stage of re-engineering runs its course, some studies predict a loss of up to 25 million jobs" in the United States.

It is no surprise that with such polarization and degradation of work taking place, average wage rates are declining. In the United States, real wages have declined 15 percent since 1973. And, according to Brecher and Costello (1994: 22), "even for such a favored group as college-educated men in the prime earning years of 45 to 54, median real income fell by 17 percent between 1986 and 1992."

Corresponding to this trend is an explosive growth of part-time or "contingency" work. The number of involuntary part-time workers almost tripled between 1970 and 1993. Between March 1991, the official end of the last recession in the United States, and July 1993, 20 percent of new jobs created were of "people becoming self-employed" (Sklar, 1995: 32). The Milwaukee-based temporary employment service Manpower Inc. is now the largest employer in the United States (employing six hundred thousand). Statistics indicate the trend to casual and part-time work to be a global phenomenon.

The new flexibility means increasing work with much less health and safety protection, no fringe benefits, no unemployment insurance, and no pensions. It also means a growth of informal, or more accurately "underground," economic relationships outside the bounds of regulation.

Even as gender job ghettos are maintained, women's role in the paid economy is increasing because they can be paid less than men, and because they can be flexible enough for combined forms of exploitation (Barnet, 1994). According to Juliet Schor (1992), women with full-time paid jobs increased their annual hours by approximately 160 hours between 1969 and 1987. More than 50 percent of poor families are now headed by women. Even while women are engaged in more paid labor, their exploitation and poverty are increasing (Amott, 1993).

At a time when the paid work remaining is less and less directed toward socially useful production, the creation of a Dual Society of haves and have-nots is a potentially explosive development, which means purpose and community bonds tend to disappear. The system is producing vast populations of people permanently unemployed or chronically underemployed. What could and should be a stimulating cultural diversity in cities becomes an alienated fragmentation and polarization conducive to crime and violence. Police forces act as occupying armies, and the fearful privileged barricade themselves in protected shells. Already in the United States, private security guards outnumber official police. An armed camp mentality is enveloping many cities with no real community bonds besides allegiance to local spectator sports teams. Throughout the industrialized world, immigrants are coming to find work. Their labor is being exploited by the new "flexible" system. They are often scapegoated for social problems in ways that aggravate divisions in the workforce and so act to deflect attention from real causes—particularly the destructive nature of economic growth itself.

THE CANCER STAGE OF CAPITALISM

Fordism was an economic arrangement that, in the developed countries, was based on diverting growing working-class power into materialistic and bureaucratic directions. It did not try to repress this power, but in a sense to buy it off. Post-Fordism, however, cannot permit even this level of development and participation. The portions of the workforce it is prepared to buy off are much more limited, and its development processes are much more destructive. Even more, the very nature of production—focused on the abstract production of money for its own sake—is more decadent than any previous phase of economic development. It is abstract quantitative development that now depends on suppressing quantitative development. The primary spin-offs from monetary accumulation are not only scarcity but destruction and dis-ease.

It has been argued that the current dominance of finance capital is nothing special. Speculative booms have come and gone with the business cycle throughout the life of capitalism. Finance capital has enjoyed various periods of dominance, usually during times of economic restructuring when capital must be fluid (Arrighi, 1994). But the current dominance of finance cannot be simply attributed to a transition. The Casino Economy represents a new level of waste and a suppression of productive potential that is qualitatively different from boom times in previous phases of capitalism. As new productive forces are demanding a new definition of wealth and money that is essentially developmental, the "new regime of accumulation" is channelling these nonmaterial forces into the service of old material, market and class definitions of production and wealth.

The Fordist regime was certainly based on waste, but it at least recognized a level of social responsibility—as expressed in the social safety net, collective bargaining rights, public education, and so on. Controlled inflation was itself a more humane form of exploitation compared to today's austerity. Mass consumption, however alienated and opportunistic, was implicitly democratic. The bureaucratic Fordist regime harnessed century-long movement pressures for greater equality in distribution of wealth. By no means did real equality result, but there was greater official recognition of social agency and responsibility.

The Casino Economy, by contrast, represents the intensified antisocial nature of the new regime of accumulation. Based on debt and eccentric forms of credit-money, and on interest rather than manufacturing profit, the regime is ever more inflationary in a real sense. And yet its institutions carry out its austerity programs in the name of "fighting inflation," "controlling debt," and "reducing the deficit," all the while encouraging the (private) creation of new forms of money and debt. Black is white and white is black.

Our current conjuncture is completely unique. Civilizations have destroyed themselves in the past with their own exploitative tendencies, but they have never threatened our whole species or fundamental balances in the biosphere. John McMurtry (1999) is certainly justified in categorizing our present state as the "cancer stage of capitalism," a metaphor that has also been used by other writers, such as Douthwaite and Korten.

It is perhaps the most tragic fact of our current situation that paradoxically also offers the most hope for turning things around: the fact that the destructive power of this cancer has been obtained by subverting and channelling positive and growing human development potentials. This suggests that the way of fighting alienated development is by unleashing regenerative development. This is the "aikido strategy" of social change: of gently redirecting the destructive energy and transforming its quality and effects. Certainly much of the cancer will have to be cut away, but long-term survival depends on how the human organism can redirect its energy flow in a healing direction.

In the next chapter, we'll look at possibilities for qualitative development and real abundance—potentials that are ususally overlooked by the mainstream left.

4

New Productive Forces and
Emerging Human Potentials

On the flip side of the demoralizing decadence of Casino Capitalism are possibilities for unprecedented levels of human development and harmony with nature. These are possibilities for qualitative development, potentials that have been building throughout the twentieth century but that have been diverted, distorted, or suppressed by waste and financialization.

The Great Depression was a crisis not only of the overproduction of commodities but also of the overproduction of human powers. While class society is based economically on the control of scarce resources, cultural dependence is just as important in maintaining class power. When industrialization began to move into the realm of culture, possibilities for working-class autonomy increased, which posed a potential threat to the system founded on cog-labor.

Workers' skills and knowledge had always been something of a threat to capitalists, and attempts to fragment this power were often a major factor in the reorganization of production and the introduction of new technology. The appearance of new productive forces (NPFs) were an even bigger challenge because of their cultural character, that is, they provided workers the capacity to exercise power not simply in direct production or on the labor market but also over their whole lives, including the management of society.

The process of emergence of these NPFs was a gradual one, but the 1920s seems to be an important threshold, with major changes in production, consumption, and mass culture. Block and Hirschhorn (1979), following up the pioneering work of Martin Sklar (1969), cite the unprecedented decline of labor time in U.S. manufacturing even as output increased 65 percent. They argue that this marks the beginning of the era of "disaccumulation," in which both labor and capital can be released from direct production by the use of knowledge. Like Sklar, Block and Hirschhorn emphasize the qualitative dimensions of this change—the cultural ferment and the rebellion against traditional authority, work roles, sexual identities, and so on. People were increasingly moved to define themselves as something other than workers. Many of these qualitative concerns were, of course, temporarily deflected by depression and war, but they would return ever more strongly in the 1960s.

The 1920s also saw an explosion of concern with consumption, with effective demand, and even with the threat of structural unemployment (Hunnicutt, 1988). The advertising industry boomed, and the seeds of postwar suburbanization were planted in planning and architecture.

PEOPLE-PRODUCTION

The changes described above constitute a basic shift in the essence of economic development from the production of things to the production of people. Many Marxists and feminists would call people-production the "reproduction of labor-power," which was relegated to a nearly invisible status in the classical industrial economy and used as a means of subordinating women. In a postindustrial context, however, people-production must go far beyond the reproduction of cog-labor and therefore must also include the realms of art and inner spirituality, both of which are essential forms of human development.

As described in chapter 1, the industrial system was founded on growing inputs of cog-labor and physical resources. Industrialization, however, does not stop with production for primary needs. It eventually moves into the realm of culture. When this expansion happens, economic inputs and outputs both tend to become less material. More production can go toward satisfying "higher" nonprimary needs, and more creative and informational elements can be involved in actual production.

Chapter 1 also described how both domestic work and nature's materials and services were devalued even though they were absolutely essential to the system. With the appearance of the NPFs, the fastest and most efficient way to expand material production is to focus on people—on education, science, art, self-development, and quality of life. Humans should cease to be cogs in the machine; people should cease to be means to an end.

Post-Fordist capitalism, because it cannot fully embrace human development, tends to identify postindustrialism with the information revolution, which in turn is generally equated with computer technology. Authentic postindustrialism, however, cannot simply be reduced to computers, or information, or any one thing. It's a multidimensional process defined by the *new relationship of human culture to the economy* established by the industrialization of culture. Economic development spawned the process, but once started, it opened a Pandora's box, because culture or human development isn't so amenable to industrial organization.

Waste production was just as important a tool in suppressing and redirecting the overproduction of human *cultural* capacities as it was in handling the overproduction of *material* goods. Knowledge and creativity were channelled into such antisocial work as arms production and advertising, while human needs were debased through materialism, escapist mass culture, alienated sex role stereotypes, and the reinforcement of all manner of addictive behavior. Industrialism has responded to the new era of people-production by cranking out people as things, as objects or images completely out of touch with their inner potentials.

Notwithstanding their distortion by industrial capitalism, the NPFs have been evident in a wide variety of phenomena in society. These NPFs affect production, consumption, culture, regulation, and politics. The following are just a few examples of postindustrial *potentials* that may be partly, but not fully, expressed in an industrial economy:

- a new role for human creativity in production
- mass production for "higher" or nonmaterial needs
- the potential for information to displace both cog-labor and physical capital from direct production
- the new importance of quality in production
- the centrality of consumption and end-use in economic planning
- the technological extension of our minds and nervous systems through new electronic hypermedia
- the new centrality of learning to work and life
- the strategic role of organizational factors in economic life
- the emergence of more culturally defined social movements with more qualitative concerns
- growing mass pressure for an end of all forms of domination, that is, an end to all restrictions on human-potential development: class, sexism, racism, and so on
- growing potentials—and pressures—for direct democracy and popular participation
- the reemergence of aesthetic, nurturing, and intuitive/mythic sensibilities into the mainstream of human cultural development
- the birth of an unprecedented global culture and human species-consciousness, which paradoxically emphasizes the importance of cultural roots and diversity
- the emergence of new forms of individuality—particularly holistic, nondependent identities—based in equality, cooperation, and self-development
- the new importance of biological science, and of biological/ecological organization as a metaphor to model social and economic activity.

An authentic postindustrial society would, by definition, encourage all these tendencies in ways that would dramatize how pitifully they are expressed in today's industrial economy. In chapter 6, we'll see how these potentials can be embodied in organizing principles for a green economy.

The strategic focus of postindustrial productive forces is human development. But economically, this focus is inextricably connected to the need to reintegrate with nature. This is not only because environmental destruction ultimately undermines human development, but because economic efficiency requires hooking into the productivity of natural systems. Today, the concept of dematerialization (or what Sklar called "disaccumulation"), which is at the core of postindustrialism, has equally radical implications for both human development and ecological regeneration. The NPFs represent a transition from the power of matter to the power of mind, and equally from mechanics to organics.

This concept implies a fundamental long-term identity of interests between humanity and nonhuman nature. It suggests that symbiosis between human activities and natural process is both possible and necessary. As we will see, the suppression of human potential and the domination of nature have been closely linked over the past ten thousand years. The unleashing of this potential must also entail helping heal and regenerate the planet.

CIVILIZATION: PROGRESS AGAINST NATURE

The unleashing of productive forces based on human development and on integration with nature has evolutionary significance. It breaks from the main trends of the past ten thousand years and makes these postindustrial productive forces post-civilizational as well. Civilization thrived on the suppression of the very energies that are now the key factors in postindustrial development. It did facilitate the development of certain human capacities, but these capacities were the ones most closely connected with the external control of nature and of people.

Civilization—with its permanent surplus, classes, cities, irrigation agriculture, division of labor, and so on—was a major break from nature. Dane Rudhyar (1974) went so far as to call civilization the great negation of nature and the antithesis to humanity's original state, primitive or tribal society. Civilizing society meant tearing primitive humankind out of the natural rhythms it had always depended upon for its survival, largely as hunter-gatherers. The control of nature required the control of "the natural" in us—those intuitive, collective, mythic/spiritual, and mimetic (or "nature imitating") capacities most connected with tribal life. Chinese philosophy would consider these capacities *yin* or integrative, contrasted with the *yang* or separative, energies emphasized by civilization. Men projected their own *yin* qualities onto women, who were most closely associated with nature and were controlled externally (Richardson, 1971). These *yin* and mimetic capacities could not be eliminated (since they were vital regenerative forces), but they were confined within peasant culture, the world of women, and in controllable niches of the dominant patriarchal culture.

The result, as mentioned briefly at the beginning of chapter 1, was not simply a human society divided by classes but an integrated structure of domination in which the dominance of humanity over nature, of strong over weaker nations, of class over class, and of men over women worked together. This massive evolutionary control project—expressed in civilization's forms of production, technology, communication, conflict, spirituality, and and so on—seems to be premised on *creating space* between humanity and nature for a certain kind of development. This practice was common to all civilizations but evolved (for reasons too complex to cover here) to its most extreme and alienated forms in the West. It required new forms of identity, perception, social relationships, and environments that could be ever more autonomous from nature.

Increasingly powerful technologies extended the power of human senses and human muscle. The exploitation of nature could facilitate great material accumulation and the concentration of social power. Correspondingly, the control of nature required, and made possible, the increasing control of other human beings. This was the social megamachine described by Lewis Mumford (1967), which anticipated the development of industrial capitalism by millennia. In the case of the early civilized megamachines, the component parts—the cogs in the machine—were all human.

Capitalism went one step farther, putting nature and people on the market through markets for land and labor. People were now commodities as well as cogs that functioned within ever more rationalized modes of production geared to continual growth. Nature became the source of unprecedented levels of energy and material for this runaway development. The space between humanity and nature would become a chasm.

Today this chasm has begun to destabilize the biosphere in fundamental ways that threaten our survival. Relationships of domination that served to increase material accumulation and technological power are themselves becoming dysfunctional for anything but the maintenance of social power. Real development, in fact, increasingly depends on the dismantling of all forms of domination that act as restrictions on human development. The tapping of growing potentials for people-production requires unleashing the very collective, intuitive, nurturing, and mimetic capacities that civilizational development had to subordinate.

INDIVIDUATION, DEVELOPMENT, AND GENDER

Civilization was not simply devoted to suppressing human potential. Besides subordinating certain qualities, it also created space for one-sided development of other faculties—individual/universal consciousness, rationality, and historical awareness—all of which contributed to material accumulation and a particular kind of technological development. Individuation is a historical tendency of human development, a process to which civilization made major, though ambivalent or incomplete, contributions.

Three interrelated dimensions of individuation are (1) sex roles and gender equality, (2) spirituality and perception, and (3) cog-labor and working-class autonomy. I will deal with gender here, spirituality in the next section, and the political dimension of working-class autonomy in the next chapter.

In primitive societies, the possibilities for individuation were limited by the overwhelming need for band or tribal solidarity required by a hunting/gathering existence. The individual ego had to be constrained. Civilization, or class society, broke from the collective ethos of tribal societies. Initially, only kings were considered whole individuals—gods or agents of God. Through the centuries, society's philosophical notions of individuality or personhood expanded. Although individuality was generally only an attribute of elite classes, radical spiritual or cultural renaissances—such as the "axial revolutions" of the sixth century B.C. and thirteenth century A.D.—gradually democratized and universalized the notion of the individual soul or spirit. Each spiritual revolution was invariably followed by a wave of institutionalization that purged most of their egalitarian impulses. In the West, courtly romantic love, the Renaissance, the Protestant Reformation, and Cartesian rationalism helped pave the way for capitalism's competitive individualism.

When industrialization began, however, and production took on an ever more important status in society, the working masses moved onto the stage of history, as subjects and not just objects, as actors and not simply props or spoils. It would take some time before workers won the right to vote, but capitalism at least guaranteed the worker abstract equality with richer men, able to agree to a contract in the labor market. It was an equality that, as Marx noted, gave both rich and poor men equal freedom to sleep under bridges.

This new individuality, like bourgeois equality, was very abstract. It was a *dependent* individuality. It was the competitive dependent individualism of cog-labor. The male industrial worker depended on his job for survival, on bosses and politicians to run his economic and political affairs, and on his female partner for a subjective emotional life.

The true individual in classical industrial society was really the family. As discussed in chapter 1, the acclaimed ideal was the "family wage"—a wage to the male worker that would cover the sustenance of a spouse and their children in the nuclear family (Matthaei, 1982). Never mind that the average male breadwinner's wage almost never attained this lofty ideal in the whole history of industrial society, except perhaps for a twenty-year period in the richest nations. It was, however, an admirable goal from the point of view of early child labor and the super-exploitation of women.

Survival depended on the mutual dependence of man and woman. The man received material and emotional sustenance from the woman. The woman gained protection and access to cash income from the man. The male personality was conditioned by society for (cog-) work and war: the externals. The feminine personality was socialized to nurture and support: the internals. Clearly, a whole individual should encompass both sides. But the Divided Economy of industrialism—divided between paid and unpaid work, formal and informal economies—reinforced dependent personalities; one can even say that the industrial economy has been contingent on the re-creation of these dependent gender identities.

Historically, this unbalanced dependence, and women's subordination within the division of production, was possible because of the *material* focus of industrial production. Men were primarily engaged in thing-production, while women, whatever their work, were defined by people-production, which was subordinate work. With the appearance of the NPFs and culture-based production, the work of people-production had to take on much more prominence, shattering many existing relationships and personal identities.

This is the context of which Martin Sklar (1969) writes in his landmark essay on postindustrialism. Amid the social experimentation of the 1920s were new forms of sexual identity, artistic expression, and personal development, signifying possibilities to go beyond the dependent individualism of cog-labor. A harsh dose of scarcity in the Great Depression set back most experimentation with new forms of identity, and it was the 1960s before much of this experimenting would resume. But the 1940s and World War II got women out of the home and onto the assembly line, and the return of enforced domesticity in the postwar Consumer Society was a shock for many women. The privatization of consumption in the Waste Economy was a channelling of people-production into self-alienating forms. Women obviously suffered much more than men, but the apparent material gains for men were purchased at the cost of their own internal dependence.

The appearance of a new wave of feminism in the 1960s was a next step toward new levels of individual autonomy. Besides its multidimensional attack on patriarchy and its articulation of a uniquely women's way of seeing the world (Miles, 1996), it also laid a basis for the explosion of a diverse human potential movement in the 1970s. Many men, consciously or unconsciously, were forced to look deeper into themselves when their "better halves" took off on their own autonomous paths. Individuation and the self-actualization of human nature became an explicit focus of social transformation.

RATIONALISM AND ALIENATION

Much attention is usually given to Cartesian dualism in the West as the philosophical source of industrialism's massive materialistic upheaval. But Western rationalism was itself the culmination of a civilizational process already under way for many centuries. More important may be the contrast between primitive society and civilization. Civilization ripped humanity from within natural cycles, and today, humanity's survival depends on reintegrating with natural process. Some of the most important qualities cultivated by primitive humanity are therefore crucial to develop today, albeit in a very different context of human development.

While it is important not to romanticize or idealize primitive societies, it is equally important to understand the fundamental differences between these diverse societies and civilization. *All* primitive societies were not necessarily sustainable, but tribal societies had, over millennia of evolution, by and large adapted to their diverse environments in ingenious ways. Top priority had to be collective, not individual, survival. Survival needs made them much more egalitarian than later class societies, and the need for flexibility precluded much division of labor, save by age and sex.

Primitive society's connection to nature was through its collective/tribal character. Material survival encouraged this, but so did the largely collective character of oral culture. Hunting/gathering subsistence made integrated sense perception essential, and being so dependent on natural cycles, context was all-important. Space was not neutral and objective but, rather, pregnant with meaning and a crucial aspect of relationship. All places were unique and living.

Time, on the other hand, was something to overcome, to be periodically abolished. Social, spiritual, and environmental cohesion was rooted in tradition, not in innovation. One's acts became real only insofar as they repeated an act—building a structure, eating a meal, consummating a marriage, going on a hunt—originally done in "that time" by a god, hero, or ancestor. Actually, the intention of this "eternal recurrence" was not to *repeat* the archetypal act but to mystically *participate* in it, in an eternal present moment. Profane historical acts and events which couldn't be experienced on this plane had to be periodically abolished, through rite, ritual, and symbol. Mythic consciousness was therefore oriented to the "vertical" plane of timelessness and permanence, not the "horizontal" dimension of time, relativity, and materiality. This focus on the eternal present moment and the qualitative character of space are aspects of the multisensual *field consciousness* of the primitive.

This mode of consciousness was increasingly suppressed by civilizational development—not completely and all at once, but persistently over the course of civilization. Civilization's dominant materialistic forms moved in an ever more westward direction, influenced by the very ecology of the globe (Rudhyar, 1974; Ribiero, 1968). Civilization unleashed *yang*—or separative—forces, which freed humanity from some limits of collective and naturalistic living, governed by the *yin*—or integrative—qualities of collectivity, intuition, orality, spirituality, integration, and space. Individualism, materialism, rational/analytical thought and literacy, historical/temporal consciousness, division of labor—all served to increase human external control over nature and society.

One of the great tools developed by civilization was rational analytical consciousness. Rationality involves breaking things down and putting them back together again. It decontextualizes, abstracts, and then recontextualizes. This cognitive process takes time, and the civilized literate human is ever time conscious (Watts, 1967). (By contrast, intuitive knowledge is grasped all at once, in an instant). The increasing valuation of rational knowledge in the West roughly parallels the development of historical consciousness: from Judaism, to Christianity, Protestantism, Darwinian/Newtonian science, and ultimately secular Marxism.

Language was our first and most important technology, affecting our very way of thinking and perceiving. Writing, however, was an application of language that took giant steps in contributing to our powers of decontextualizing, rational abstraction, and external control. Various writers have also commented on the likely connection between the use of writing and the use of money (DeKerckhove, 1995). (As discussed elsewhere in this book, commodity-money is the abstracted impersonal expression of human value, quantitative value.) The phonetic alphabet in particular provided a tool for segmenting, abstracting, and impersonalizing reality. Alphabetic literacy was the ultimate expression of the "left brain" analytical capacities, which dissect and reassemble experience.

Literacy was an important element of mass individuation. Protestantism's call for a direct individual relationship to God coincided with an explosion of literacy among common people, which was spawned by the printing press. As DeKerckhove (1995: 197) emphasizes, "Reading and writing are the fundamental conditions for the privatization of the mind." Literacy fosters conceptual, rather than experiential, notions of identity, encouraging introspection as well as a more visual orientation to the world.

This tendency of rational (or left-brain) development to create vision dominance among the senses is a crucial aspect of modern modes of perception, since vision is a sense that is much more separative than hearing or touch. Particularly in Western civilization, personal identity has become increasingly detached from the body and trapped in the head (Berman, 1984). Besides alienating us from our physical and biological being, it serves to isolate our minds and spirits from the rest of world. This detachment, of course, tends to be more extreme in men.

There are many different kinds of technology and modes of employing them, as Ursula Franklin (1990) has written. Many hunting/gathering peoples had quite sophisticated technologies. Neolithic cultures and Eastern civilizations utilized technologies like geomancy and feng shui which situated humans within natural process and which complemented rational knowledge with other forms of knowing. The dominant technologies of civilization, however, have worked by *segmenting and extending our senses and bodily functions.* (Simple examples of technological extensions might be a hammer or knife as an extension of the human arm, and the wheel as an extension of the foot). This dynamic, emphasized by Marshall McLuhan and the media theorists, suggests how the very process of technological extension has been, until recently, intrinsically a form of alienation. The sequential segmentation involved has had a destabilizing effect on the existing human sensual structure and the psyche. Influenced by Hans Selye, McLuhan (1964: 53) wrote, "Any invention or technology is an extension or self-amputation of our physical bodies, and such extension also demands new ratios or equilibriums among the other organs and extensions of the body." That is, every technological extension is a fairly traumatic experience that creates a new balance among the senses. The new ratio, in fact, usually tends to be precarious and unbalanced. Overall, technological development has served to fragment human consciousness and experience. In industrial society, this tendency has made it much easier for the elites to employ technological innovation to disempower people as both workers and consumers. It has contributed to the dependent individualism created by coglabor, the class nature of social power, and the gender dependence structured by the Divided Economy.

POSTINDUSTRIAL PERCEPTION

The industrialization of culture coincided with a new dynamic to our technological extension. As McLuhan argued, through electronic media and information systems we began to extend our minds and nervous systems, a process that has radically different implications than the extension of our muscles. It integrates rather than fragments our sensual balance. In the words of McLuhan (1964: 64),

> By putting our physical bodies inside our extended nervous systems, by means of electric media, we set up a dynamic by which all previous technologies that are mere extensions of hands and feet and teeth and bodily heat-controls—all such extensions of our bodies, including cities—will be translated into information systems. Electromagnetic technology requires utter human docility and quiescence of meditation such as befits an organism that now wears its brain outside its skull and its nerves outside its hide.

McLuhan suggested that the very speed of electronic change forces us to forsake processing reality in an analytic, sequential way and to take it in "mythically," all at once, using all our senses, like a hunter-gatherer, a Zen monk, or an aikido master. Such a state of mind emphasizes *field-consciousness*. It encourages identity to be derived more from the mind than from the contents of the mind—from the *screen* rather than from the *images* projected on it. With such a basis for identity, a healthy balanced relationship to the information explosion would encourage us to go beyond processing innumerable bits of information, to see (and feel) the *patterns* of flow of knowledge and reality. The focus would again, as in primitive society, be on *context*.

Whereas the industrial era is distinguished by the domination of the visual sense, a postindustrial society would feature a much greater balance of the senses, with a particular emphasis on hearing and touch, which are more integrating and inclusive forms of perception. Being more anchored in sensing than simply thinking, consciousness and identity would reside in a better balance between mind and body. Or rather, the mind would be centered in the whole organism, not simply our heads.

This balanced perception would be conducive to a more holistic individuality that combined real autonomy with cooperation. Paradoxically, identity that is more anchored internally, rather than in external social roles or cog-labor identities, is much more flexible externally, exhibiting what Leonard (1972) called "psychic mobility." It provides an identity that can be less self-preoccupied, more sensitive to social context and environment, and more amenable to service. By contrast, the competitive individual of industrial capitalism is only a part-person — isolated but incomplete — necessarily dependent on a spouse or higher authority.

Technological change, as an extension of our own being, can encourage and facilitate human individuation. By recapturing some of the multisensual perception of primitive humanity, but employing it as a mode of individuation, postindustrial human development constitutes an evolutionary synthesis of key aspects of primitive society and civilization. Technology cannot do this, however, as an impersonal megatrend; it must be *conscious*. Today, technology, like most other elements of the NPFs, is being employed to amplify the objectifying and commodifying inclinations of capitalism. For this reason, tapping technology's potential for human development requires a prior commitment to spiritual and social transformation.

Holistic forms of individuality need not be created in a vacuum. Even while the dominant civilizational processes have encouraged dependent and separative individualism, there have been minority elements within civilization that have been devoted to the cultivation of holistic individuality. Among the most important are the inner spiritual, or mystical, traditions that have existed both on the fringes of civilization and at the cores of all the major religions. Not primarily concerned with belief systems, their concern has been more perceptual and psychological. Their focus has been not simply preserving the intuitive or field consciousness of primitive consciousness but sharpening and deepening this consciousness in the individual.

These traditions have recognized that the five primary senses provide us with useful information in part because they act as filters, screening out other aspects of reality. They understood that in daily life we use only a small portion of our brain/mind's capacity. For this reason, they developed sophisticated disciplines and techniques to "cleanse the doors of perception," to plunge more deeply into individual identity, and to directly experience the "worlds within worlds" existing in the present moment. Developing this kind of awareness typically combined disciplines to limit the addictive power of habit and superficial ego gratification, with disciplines to integrate mind/body perception.

Traditions like Sufism, Zen, Taoism, Kabballah, and mystical Christianity have typically existed in an ambivalent relationship to the dominant religions. On one hand, they have served as the "inner cores" of these religions, providing real experiential substance to religious symbol and belief. They have often been progressive revolutionary forces, establishing greater social equality, deeper levels of individuality, and wider notions of universality. They have also been creative impulses in the development of science and art. On the other hand, their more revolutionary contributions have typically been diluted or reversed by institutionalization, as civilization, particularly in the West, tended to transmute these developments into more individualistic, rationalistic, and materialistic forms. Often these disciplines of direct spiritual experience and self-actualization have also been persecuted as threatening external authority and dogma.

Despite their universalistic philosophies, the inner mystical traditions of civilization had to communicate in the terms and patterns of their originating cultures, most of which were patriarchal. To be relevant to an emerging postindustrial spirituality, therefore, most of these traditions will have to leave behind a lot of oppressive cultural baggage. This will not be an easy task, since the richness of postindustrial society will also depend upon the preservation of a diversity of traditional culture in both social and spiritual life. Combining a critical egalitarian approach with spiritual insight will be an incredibly difficult challenge. Nevertheless, the disciplines and insights provided us by older spiritual traditions can be invaluable in helping us ground social change in authentic personal transformation.

MASS CONSUMPTION AS PEOPLE-PRODUCTION

One of the strongest indications of the potential for people-production in the economy is the rise of mass consumption. In the classical industrial economy, human consumption—and the unpaid domestic work involved—originally could be left to take care of itself. But with the Great Depression and the crisis of overproduction, something basic changed: consumption could no longer be left to itself; in fact, it would have to be encouraged.

In 1968, just as Russian tanks were about to roll into Czechoslovakia, a new book was released in the cultural ferment of the "Prague Spring." Put together by an interdisciplinary team of the Czech National Academy of Sciences headed by Radovan Richta (1969), *Civilization at the Crossroads* was a breathtakingly radical look at the implications of the "scientific and technological revolution."

One of the many insights of the Richta book was that the rise of mass consumption in the industrialized world—however wasteful and alienated a form it took—nevertheless signalled a historic threshold in humanity's development. It upset the long-standing investment/consumption relationship upon which the accumulation of wealth in civilization had always depended. Previously, the majority of people—the proverbial "masses"—had always to "defer consumption" as much as possible to make social investment possible. Now, with the crisis of effective demand, such mass consumption became a *prerequisite* for investment. It signalled a new importance of human self-development in the economy.

What is, after all, human consumption? It is the self-production of human beings. Through the reign of industrialism, and indeed from the dawn of the civilized megamachine, people have taken a back seat to things. But for modern industrialism, domestic markets were required for dramatically increasing production, and a more cultured and sophisticated workforce was required to maintain technological progress. A new importance for the reproduction of labor-power coincided with a need for new markets. We had entered the era of people-production.

Industrialism was faced with the aforementioned dilemma of how to encourage this consumption without undermining scarcity or unduly facilitating working-class autonomy. Waste production was, of course, the ingenious solution. Industrialism could have its sufficiently (but not too) skilled working class, and its markets, and its patriarchal privileges—even as people reproduced themselves as alienated, dependent, addicted, and escapist individuals.

To co-opt people-production, industrialism had to overcome some important inclinations of the NPFs. On one hand, human self-development defies productivism, a mindless focus on production for production's sake. Like a conserver-economy, human development means putting end-use in command. It means consumption planning, and ultimately it means a subordination of exchange-value to use-value. This, of course, undermines the very basis of capitalism.

People-production also implies a special new importance of spatial organization and new efficiencies derived from organizational factors. The waste economy utilized this new importance of spatial organization in reverse, by deliberately creating a wasteful and inefficient built environment.

As discussed in chapter 2, the wasteful suburban infrastructure that was implemented after World War II in North America had the effect of reinforcing the Divided Economy—the artificial division of "production" and "consumption." The Waste Economy pent up passive consumption in isolated residences, creating more unpaid work there without acknowledging its value to the economy. Vast numbers of women were booted out of the postwar formal economy into isolated unpaid work as "domestic consumption managers." Women's actual work hours, always greater than men's, increased as men's declined (Cowan, 1983). Gender stereotypes became ever more important in Fordist people-production as women's roles were made over to suit the new culture of privatized consumption. Women were to be either consumers (homemakers) or objects of consumption (playmates) in a new economy based on addiction, alienation, and the waste of human potential.

PROSUMPTION AND THE RESURGENCE OF THE INFORMAL ECONOMY

Even in distorted development, the NPFs tend to work against the economic straitjacket of industrialism's Divided Economy. People-production has continually threatened the boundaries between production and consumption. A big reason for this, of course, is the resistance of industrialism to making the economy truly "knowledge-based" by putting human development in command. The result is that much of the really developmental work takes place in civil society and the informal economy.

As discussed in chapter 1, industrialization happened by pulling production out of, and away from, the home and concentrating it in central "workplaces," be they factories, shops, or offices. The intensification of industrialization meant more and more productive labor was pulled from the home in what's been called the "socialization of labor" process. Education, health care, and even home repair have been pulled into the formal economy.

This shift was always considered to be an inevitable irreversible trend of economic progress, but in recent decades, that process has begun to reverse itself. While many home-based functions continue to be formalized—child care, fast foods, and so on—the home and community is the scene of an almost invisible but explosive countertrend (Burns, 1975; Brandt, 1995). More and more work is taking place in and around the home and community. Much of this work is what Toffler (1980) called "prosumption"—the food growing, self-help building, preventive health care, small appliance repair, and so on that conventional economics would simply characterize as forms of consumption. But this prosumption is far from passive, and it is an important part of an exploding informal economy that is producing increasing portions of society's real wealth, with some estimates going over 40 percent (Pietila, 1993; Henderson, 1978; Quarter, 1992).

The Divided Economy is not a rigid duality but rather a spectrum of activities from unpaid household work, on one extreme, to the transnational corporation, on the other. In between, we find other informal and formal enterprises and those that combine elements of both worlds. There are neighborhood and mutual aid organizations, barter and skills exchanges, voluntary associations, community development enterprises, co-operatives, small businesses, and state enterprises. Among all these, there are some that are more private and others that are more social (Ross and Usher, 1986). Embedded amorphously along this spectrum, there is what has been called the "social economy"—a diverse third sector whose common identity is its commitment to put profit second to social purpose (Quarter, 1992).

Definitions can be only so hard and fast, but the informal economy is characterized primarily by familiarity and by production for use, use not necessarily within the household but within a shared community. Not all of the production is nonmonetary, but the portion that uses money employs it primarily as a simple means of exchange. The informal economy allows other social, environmental, and personal values to come into its operation. The social economy, for its part, tends to overlap the formal and informal economies and, to some degree, the private and public sector of the formal economy.

As mentioned earlier, the new productive forces of people-production resist easy commodification. Their quantification into the cash nexus of the paper economy suppressed much of them, made invisible other portions, and distorted much of their other formal manifestations. But a combination of the new demands for economic "flexibility" and the inherent tendency of the super-industrial economy toward stagnation, has spawned a new dynamism of informal and formal/informal hybrid activities.

One not-so-benign example is the underground economy that has boomed with growing corporate competition and the emergence of economies increasingly polarized between rich and poor (Castells, 1989; Mattera, 1985; Ed Ayres, 1996). Many left academics tend to refer to these negative developments as "informalization," but there is a more positive element to many growing informal activities that have taken off over the past two decades. These activities embody alternative values, focused on community economic development, on environmental regeneration, and on human physical and spiritual health. James Robertson (1985) has written of the phenomenon of "own-work": of self- and community work outside the bounds of conventional cash "employment." There is a growing recognition of centrality of community to real human development. New processes and institutions of grassroots participation, with local control, and democratically targeted development are being improvised.

The paper-cum-megabyte economy in the 1980s almost completely disconnected itself from real production in an orgy of speculation and the creation of gigantic financial infrastructures in our cities. But the existing informal economy is in itself no satisfactory alternative to this destructiveness. It is still the place of women's isolated exploitation, although now it typically ranks as a second job, along with the low-paid work she must endure in the formal sector to make ends meet. The physical structure of the built-environment and the lack of proper remuneration for informal work have made the home a locale of increasing exploitation. Exploitative "homeworking" is booming, as is all sorts of underground economic activity (Sassen, 1991).

Glorification of the informal economy, and its expansion in its current form, is therefore not desirable. The new social movements are recognizing that what is necessary are new kinds of links between formal and informal economic activities, transformative links that deflate purely paper economics and focus *all* economic activities on community development. A key example of this transformative linkage is the community currency, which will be described in more detail later in this book. It helps to eliminate poverty, links formal and informal activities, and fuels local development, all while undercutting capital-accumulation as an end in itself.

A recognition is growing that an economics that facilitates human self-development cannot penalize or devalue work that takes place in the home or community. Such work has to be encouraged, enriched, expanded, and de-isolated. This can happen not by monetarizing the household, but only by bringing the values of the household and community to the formal sector and beginning to spatially reintegrate sectors of production and consumption.

Human self- and community development demand a new integration of the old sectors of socialized and unsocialized labor. In a sense, what is required is an expansion of the "social economy" to encompass more of the mainstream economy. But the existing social economy has to a great degree been dependent on the mainstream (private and public sector) economy. Except on the margins, it has lacked a self-regulating dynamic.

The possibility of society's prioritizing human development to the extent that it would move to create community-based economies would seem to be far-fetched. But our biological survival may depend on it, and ecology provides another powerful force pressing for integrating production and consumption. It also provides the model for self-regulation needed by complex economies.

ECOLOGY AS A PRODUCTIVE FORCE

A central dimension of people-production is the substitution of human intelligence for materials, energy, and cog-labor in direct production. This substitution is what industrial ecologists speak of as "dematerialization," and what Martin Sklar (1969), and Fred Block and Larry Hirschhorn (1979) referred to as disaccumulation. It means doing more with less, particularly less energy and fewer material resources. And it means doing this on the level of the whole economy, not just on the level of the individual firm or production process. Dematerialization is one of the most important characteristics of qualitative development, one which industrial capitalism is incapable of expressing in any truly fundamental way.

As we will see in more detail in part 2, the two key ways a postindustrial economy can dematerialize is (1) to focus on end-use, and (2) to integrate human economic activities within natural processes. In many respects, the very process of economic development is forcing this reintegration with nature upon us, for better or worse. An example is the role of scientific knowledge. Rational knowledge, which has long been a means of separating ourselves from nature for the purpose of control, is, in effect, now forcing us to reintegrate, simply because of how deeply our investigations have penetrated into nature. We must make a choice, however, about *how* we want to do this. Will it be another form of domination of nature or a harmonious relationship of co-evolution?

On the negative side, powerful interests are engaging in dangerous genetic and biological engineering simply for the sake of power and short-term profit. Humans are now making machines out of living organisms. Scientists, states, and corporations are playing a dangerous game of imitating God by eliminating ecodiversity and subtle balances established over many years. This kind of imperialistic intrusion into nature will surely result in our own destruction.

On the positive side, a more respectful form of integration with nature is possible. Ecological innovators are exploring new possibilities for benign and regenerative use of natural systems, which both respect their integrity and offer many legitimate benefits to human communities. For example, John Todd (1994) and his fellow eco-technologists are devising "living machines" that purify water naturally without destroying diversity and ecosystem integrity. Permacultural systems of food production and settlement design are also employing sophisticated scientific knowledge of nature, coupled with traditional local knowledge, to benignly harness the natural productivity of ecosystems without harming them.

What distinguishes this form of scientific knowledge from the conventional science behind high-tech bioengineering is that all other scientific considerations are subsumed to ecology. As with primitive peoples, context is all-important. The relationship and interaction of all living systems are considered and valued as sacred in their own right. And yet, because this perspective is deeply aware of the working of natural productivity everywhere, it can tap possibilities for human benefit over the entire landscape. The emphasis is on nature doing the work, as much as possible on its own terms. The economy is seen a sailboat in the winds of natural process, and ecology is employed as a key productive force.

This knowledge is important not only in integrating human activities within natural processes, as in urban rooftop agriculture or wind power, but it is also crucial in designing human systems that mimic the elegance and efficiency of ecosystems. Industrial ecology—which will be examined more closely in chapter 9—applies just such design principles to manufacturing.

Even in our destructive industrial economy, potentials for reintegrating with nature are reflected in organizational change. Today, as our economies and societies are increasing in complexity, they are beginning to exhibit an organic character similar to natural systems. This is a real contrast to mechanical systems. As Geddes (1915) and Lyle (1994) have pointed out, the "machine model" upon which industrial organization, science, and philosophy have been based is incredibly crude and simplistic, making industrialism the "paleotechnic era."

The speed and complexity of change today, however, fostered by perpetual technological revolution, have gotten to the point where they defy traditional forms of external control. "Fast, cheap and out of control" is a theme of advanced technological design today (Kelly, 1994), with rank-hierarchies having to give ground to network-hierarchies. The details of a process cannot be managed from above, deterministically, but rather only the general directions and parameters can be established, managed stochastically, or statistically, with much operational autonomy given to the base. Complex systems, be they production systems or whole economies, literally must be allowed to evolve, like ecosystems.

The organic character of postindustrial organization suggests a trend toward growing democracy. It implies that political consciousness and control must be more integrated into everyday work life. Of course, capitalist globalization must block or defuse such potentials, but ecological production depends on them. In part 2, we will see how, in most cases, the appropriate scale for ecological production is much smaller than that of industrial production. Besides the fact that the speed of change means that planning must be closer to execution and impact, the complexity of needs, circumstances, and technologies makes local observation and management essential. Ecological forms of development must be specific to microclimates and eco-regions, and efficiency depends on tight production/consumption loops.

These trends are enhanced by the impact of electronic communications technology, which makes possible the coordination of widely decentralized units. Authentic postindustrialism therefore facilitates direct democracy—not via electronic polling, but by making community-based participation a practical means of global regulation and cooperation. Network organization allows the creation of "communities of communities." The extension of our minds and nervous systems through new communications technologies—which today is most often used to reinforce centralized control—is actually more appropriately used to empower communities and regions, allowing them to be integrated with nature's bioregions.

DEMATERIALIZATION AND LABOR

The reorganization of production along ecosystems lines has major implications for labor. In the same way that feminists have attacked the Divided Economy as inimical to human development, in recent decades, environmentalists have attacked it as repressive of ecological productivity. Greens have argued that the creation of ecological economies depends on making homes and residences places of production for food, energy, water, and so on and not simply places of passive consumption. Rooftops, back alleys, and public gardens and squares can and should be productive places. This, of course, has major implications for labor, since our current system penalizes home- and community-based work.

Years ago, Sklar, Block and Hirschhorn, Gorz, and others pointed out some of the positive implications of the elimination of cog-labor from direct production. In contrast to the structural unemployment that is the actual course capitalism has taken, they highlighted the possibility of releasing humans from drudge-labor for more creative work and for more leisure time.

As Hirschhorn wrote in *Beyond Mechanization* (1984), the myth of the Perfect Machine—an automated process that totally displaces human labor—has long captured the imagination of both establishment and radical visionaries. For establishment thinkers, it poses the possibility of production and profit without rebellious and unpredictable workers. For radicals, like French Marxist Andre Gorz (1980, 1983), it has suggested new forms of human "autonomous activity"—creative leisure, re-creation and art, freedom from drudgery.

Both versions of this myth, however, are premised on a Divided Economy, and the presumed eternal separation of work and leisure, or production and consumption. Today the radical view of the end of cog-labor is being transformed by an ecological vision. The liberation of the human being from the industrial production machine does not mean an escape to an "autonomous" zone, but a total reorganization of society to reintegrate production and consumption in a way that would make both work and leisure *regenerative*. The information-intensive ecological economy does not abolish cog-labor by completely eliminating routine labor but by transforming (what remains of) it into developmental forms. By decommodifying it, by instilling it with social relevance, and by reintegrating it with design and decision, even routine work can be developmental. As with eco-agriculture and eco-building, it may involve a greater balance of mental and physical work. In many instances, it represents a recapturing of traditional values of craft.

The point is that industrial development has caused incredible damage to both communities and ecosystems. To increase real wealth, this damage must be repaired. There is no shortage of work to be done, just a shortage of work in the formal sector of the industrialism's Divided Economy. This has tremendous implications for our economic strategies. While "work-sharing" may play an important role in our development strategy, our primary focus must be *to design systems to ensure socially and ecologically necessary work gets done and somehow remunerated*. Part of this might involve the sharing out of existing paid work, but it will also entail designing processes that tap community (and ecosystem) energies outside regular market forms. We must look seriously at ways of *directly* remunerating regenerative labor, that is, encouraging work which *in itself* creates wealth for the worker and the worker's community. Some of these means will be considered in part 2.

This kind of integration of the formal and informal economies is a way of making visible previously invisible forms of essential labor. But this can only be completely successful if nature's equally invisible inputs into the economy are acknowledged. Despite recent assaults on workers' wages, resources are still relatively much cheaper than labor, and this hurts labor tremendously. As Hawken (1993) emphasizes, we live in a society that insanely continues to displace labor from production as population grows. We are using information to replace labor rather than materials and energy—even as we suffer increasing environmental degradation resulting from our linear resource flows. The key to creating jobs in the formal sector is not work-sharing, but reversing the labor/materials relationship by incorporating the full costs of the use of nature's materials and services into market prices. Then there is incentive to employ people rather than resources.

While Block and Hirschhorn (1979) claimed that the ratio of capital to output had declined since the 1920s, in retrospect the displacement of *labor* has far exceeded *materials* displacement. From the point of view of the firm or even a product, a certain degree of capital savings seems undeniable. But from the point of view of the economy as a whole, even considering gains in living standards in the postwar industrialized economies, overall efficiency gains are questionable. Per capita materials consumption in North America, for instance, has generally been increasing since World War II, and at a much greater rate than the standard of living. What has declined has been the market price of materials. Industrialization, therefore, has been marked by a dual tendency through most of the twentieth century: the displacement of labor from direct production by information, materials, and energy, and the increasing devaluation of what many environmentalists call "natural capital"—the earth's materials, air, water, systems, and creatures.

By definition, the green economy is capital-, materials- and energy-saving, and people-intensive. For this reason, ecological development is the only way to maintain a place for humanity in the economy. It is not, of course, simply a matter of changing the relative prices of labor and materials. Real qualitative wealth must be increased, and new forms of remuneration must also be created. If this is done, however, it promises a fulfilling future for human work in every sector of the economy.

5

The New Ecology of Politics

The industrialization of culture transforms not only the economy but also the basic nature of politics. Politics is not simply about the balance of social power between groups, but about how we move collectively into the future—the rules, goals, and activities that set the tone for our entire society. Politics in the industrial era is largely about control and distribution of quantitative wealth—money and material—and about the relative power between groups in social structures based on domination. At its most basic level, it is about "control of the means of production"—all that hardware in the formal sector that produces so much *stuff*.

The appearance of new productive forces has changed fundamentally what we should think of as the "means of production." It is not information or computer hardware that is the key productive force, but human creativity. Economically, the full utilization of these productive forces requires that human development become both the prime means and ends of economic development. Politically, "seizing the means of production" entails *seizing ourselves*. Politics can no longer be a separate sphere; it must be integrated into daily life—everywhere people-production takes place. For this reason, real green politics, or postindustrial politics, is not primarily a politics of ecology. It is about realizing a new *ecology of politics*, in which the fundamental strategies of social movements and the goals and means of social regulation have changed substantially.

Chapter 11 will look more specifically at forms of community-based regulation. In this chapter, I want to review more generally two key dimensions of postindustrial politics:

- the new relationship between opposition and alternatives in social change strategy, which reflects a very different role for the state in society; and
- the necessity of new rules of the game that institutionalize service as the main output of economic activity and return matter and money to being strictly means to the end of satisfying social and environmental need.

WORKING-CLASS AUTONOMY AND CULTURAL PRODUCTION

Authentic postindustrialism can only mean the complete integration of politics, economics, and culture, with human development at the core of this new complex. A new relationship between politics and economics in the post-Depression era was somewhat evident in the new interventionist powers of the Fordist state and in the social contracts for workers and the poor. But these arrangements also disguised even greater potentials for the politicization of daily life and actually increased people's dependence in many ways.

As discussed earlier, capitalism's crisis of overproduction was just as much a crisis of the overproduction of human powers as it was of the overproduction of commodities. The industrialization of culture accelerated the scientific and technological revolution that resulted in market failure, but it also began to provide working people with educational and cultural powers that could ultimately undermine the cultural basis of class power. Class societies have always been based both in elite control of scarce resources and in the cultural dependence of the masses.

While workers in the industrial era gained the right to formal equality and political participation, cultural, political, and economic dependence circumscribed worker power. This dependence was defined by cog-labor. The worker, immersed in cog-labor within the production machine, depended on the managers to run the factory, the owners to run industry, and the politicians to run society.

Class dependence has always been mutual, of course. Rulers throughout history have depended on working people for hard labor, to generate the economic surplus, to man the armies. But working masses have been culturally dependent—even the newly equal industrial working class. All civilizations have had dual cultures—the "high" culture of sophisticated art and science and the "folk" culture of peasants and workers. Perhaps even more than political/military control of the surplus, this cultural monopoly of the ruling classes has been their real source of power.

The industrial ruling classes—be they capitalist or socialist—have nevertheless had to be more apprehensive about their cultural hegemony than did earlier aristocratic elites. Representative democracy was one great concession that industrial elites had to make early on, expressing their own economic dependence on workers. Political concessions could be made, however, as long as they didn't affect economic control, which rested in turn on cultural monopoly. Any threat to this cultural monopoly would open a whole new Pandora's box.

It's in the nature of industrialization to open this box. One early sign of growing cultural possibilities for the average person was the rise of white-collar work. The complexity of management, combined with the inadequacy of markets in distributing resources, made for a growing importance of bureaucracy. Whether public or private, bureaucracies are mechanisms of planning. They are hierarchies of white-collar cog-labor (Bennis, 1966; Toffler, 1980). Regardless of its routine nature, this work requires more education and more cultural sophistication. At the same time that management began to require more knowledge, so also production involved more scientific and technological knowledge. Science was becoming less an aspect of upper-class culture and more a crucial sector of industry. Thus, there was a need for more cultured and knowing workers and for educational workers to train them.

Ultimately, technological development begins to eliminate cog-labor itself through automation, which "completes the internal linkages" in the production process and puts humans outside direct production altogether to manage, coordinate, and maintain (Block and Hirschhorn, 1979; Hirschhorn, 1984). Again—at least potentially—it generates more cultured and autonomous workers.

Nowhere perhaps is the potential for working-class autonomy so clear as in the arts. In a substantial and growing portion of the world, there can be no distinction between "high" culture and "folk" culture. Is the best jazz or ethno-fusion music any less sophisticated than Western classical music? The twentieth century witnessed a historically unparalleled fusion of high and folk culture. Certainly there are levels of sophistication, ranging from commercial pop music to experimental computer music and onward. But these are not primarily class-based differences.

The concept of working-class autonomy is simply another way of expressing the potential for the elimination of class altogether. The same can be said for the potential of autonomous individuation to eliminate class, gender dependence, and patriarchy.

For industrial society to survive, it has had to find a way of reproducing unhealthy dependencies. The strongest expression of possibilities for working-class autonomy in the Depression era came not from cultural workers but from the vanguard sector of industrial production at that time—the mass production industries. The very scope and scale of those industries gave workers the opportunity to achieve unprecedented forms of solidarity by organizing themselves in the new industrial unions of the CIO (Brody, 1980). As discussed earlier, this was the peak of power for the "worker as cog" within socialized production. Further possibilities for real autonomy—beyond cog-labor—were circumvented by the institutionalization of collective bargaining and the turning of unions into organizations of labor management. In effect, workers at a certain level of bureaucracy began to fulfil the functions of management, keeping workers as dependent as ever on existing structures.

The same can be said for virtually all organizations in industrial society. As touched on in chapter 2, class power tends to become depersonalized, and the Rockefellers and Carnegies are replaced by faceless bureaucracies, staffed by workers whose job it is to manipulate or exploit other workers. There are certainly extreme differences in income levels among the different levels of workers. But the fact remains that class power doesn't disappear but is objectified into giant organizations and internally structured into the working class. Class relationships are not only structured into bureaucracy, but today—as many forms of bureaucracy are being undermined by technological change and flexible organization—are being structured into the network organization of the Global Casino.

The institutionalization of class power parallels the growing importance throughout the twentieth century of internalized forms of cultural control. These are forms of people-production channelled in alienated ways. The economy of privatized mass consumption is one example of the way the industrialization of culture has made oppression and exploitation into an internal complex—internal not simply to the class, but to the individual. In the era of cultural production, brainwashing has become an essential function of the economy, expressed in advertising, media, fashion, sport, education, diet, and so on. Along with brainwashing goes addiction, or identification with and dependence on the externals we've been conditioned to desire: sex, success, food, control, attention, and so on.

POLITICS AND THE WITHERING AWAY OF THE LEFT

The dependence of the early industrial working class was reflected in its forms of political involvement and in its main strategies for radical (that is, fundamental) social change. Early industrial workers were too preoccupied with cog-labor to represent themselves in politics. And the very nature of classical industrial society divided politics from economics (Polanyi, 1957). Workers needed politicians to represent them. Socially conscious workers were, of course, not fooled by the demagoguery of assorted bourgeois politicians; rather, they had their own politicians: the organized left. The left was typically a collection of advanced workers, small farmers, and sympathetic intellectuals. The intellectuals had the tools to fight the bosses' hacks on their own turf, and even win elections—for the Labor Party, or Socialist Party, or Populist Party, or Social Democratic Party or whichever party. The left acted as the workers' "shadow-state" at a time when the workers could not represent themselves directly. The left had a very important historical role to play, both intellectually/culturally and organizationally.

Needless to say, that role changed substantially as industrialization moved into culture. The boundaries between politics and economics were becoming blurred because of the need for greater planning, and thus these boundaries had to be artificially reinforced. Maintaining politics as a separate sphere has become a crucial means of reproducing the industrial system and preempting potentials for direct democracy.

We touched on these potentials for direct democracy in the previous chapter, and they will be discussed more in part 2 of this book. What should be emphasized here is that, notwithstanding global trends toward deregulation, the need for planning is not lessening; rather, it is growing. There are two forces at work, one potentially positive and one quite reactionary. On one hand, there is a crisis of bureaucracy. This is because the speed and complexity of the modern economy is forcing planning to take place closer to production—further down the corporate hierarchy. Deterministic planning from above is now often not flexible enough. New forms of organic management, incorporating greater levels of departmental autonomy, internal self-regulation, and feedback, are increasingly being employed in large organizations. While corporations are generally not using this trend to facilitate democracy, there is some potential to do so.

On the other hand, current trends toward corporate rule are minimizing or eliminating many forms of planning. But this has little to do with efficiency and much to do with brute power. Corporations are seeking greater freedom from accountability. It is not a question of markets versus planning, but one of state planning versus corporate planning.

Growing potentials for direct democracy result from a combination of the growing cultural power of people, new electronic communications technology, and the intrinsically decentralizing tendency of much technological development—particularly in eco-production. While the technological possibilities for democracy are by no means obvious to most people, many people do sense an incredible waste of human potential. They sense that the system denies their participation. For this reason, representative democracy since World War II, particularly in North America, has felt like a superficial sham. If in fact the suppressed democratic potential of emerging productive forces could be tapped, this would not only make conventional party politics obsolete but also render superfluous the left's traditional role of representing the working class. People today should be able to represent themselves.

Marx saw the working class coming to power well before the classical industrial period gave way to the Fordist era of integrated power. He saw it happening through its representatives, the organized left, whom he apparently believed could be made accountable enough to eventually allow the "withering away of the state" as postindustrial productive forces facilitated the blossoming of direct democracy. Marx, clearly, was an optimist.

The actual situation is, of course, that the new production forces (NPFs) have emerged, making possible both working-class autonomy and direct democracy, but prior to the revolution. Put another way, originally the revolution was to be made in order to attain such autonomy and democracy. But the reality is that *building autonomy and democracy is what's necessary in order to make the revolution.* What we find today, therefore, is the "withering away of the organized left," as the new social movements, which have emerged in response to the new conditions, employ a different strategy. In contrast to the left's "organizing" of other people, the new movements emphasize the self-activity and networking of coequals. And instead of the left's state-focused oppositional activism, they work on the creation of grassroots alternatives.

This new strategic focus reflects a different role for the state in a postindustrial economy, where the state functions more as a coordinator than a policeman, and where the emphasis is on establishing new rules of the game and new driving forces of economic development. Again, this particular role is possible because the most advanced forms of production/consumption can (and must) be initiated on a small scale, usually on a community level. These forms of production are not simply those providing food, energy, equipment, and so on, but—as described in the previous chapter—those of people-production, or human development. From this standpoint, it is worthwhile to look at the relationship of new social movements to the positive focus on alternatives.

NEW SOCIAL MOVEMENTS AND THE REDEFINITION OF WEALTH

It has been typical of much of the orthodox left to characterize the new social movements that emerged in the Fordist era as "particularistic" and distracting from more fundamental "class" issues. They raise, it is said, peripheral quality-of-life issues that divert our attention from the down-to-earth bread-and-butter issues of control of the economic surplus and means of production.

Yet, from the point of view of the new forces of people-production, these movements can, in themselves, be considered important productive forces. Once production moves from production for primary needs to cultural production, questions of quality take on a special importance. The old left and the old labor movement had little quibble with the content of industrial production last century; it was its *distribution* that they contested (Paelhke, 1989), along with the conditions of work. Once, however, that waste production began disconnecting the accumulation of paper from real development, questions of content became extremely important.

The new social movements—feminism, peace, ecology, human potential, aboriginal rights, anti-racism—have raised fundamental questions about the nature and content of production, the very "why" and "how" of our work, in addition to traditional questions of equality of distribution. (My concern here is only with *progressive* social movements. As with fascism earlier this century, emerging potentials also produce retrograde movements, composed essentially of people who fear their own freedom and who take refuge in ever more alienated images when traditional social roles are threatened. While dealing with these inevitable developments in civil society is important, it is not my focus here.) In this sense, these new movements are the successors of the early labor movement, the "new working class" movements of our day. Not only do they anticipate the end of class itself by their more cultural identities, but they anticipate the end of civilization, which since its emergence from hunting/gathering societies has been based not simply in class domination but in multiple layers of domination: environmental, sexual, national, racial, and so on. Today, there is a movement against every level of domination, with increasingly explicit visions of how human beings should interact on this planet.

The central importance of eliminating domination per se is one reason the new social movements are implicitly postindustrial. The full realization of human potential is impossible with the perpetuation of existing forms of racism, sexism, ageism, and the like. While each movement has come from some particular concern, there has been a growing recognition over the past couple of decades that most forms of oppression, domination, and exploitation are related in some way. In most situations, curbing or dissolving other forms of domination can help tremendously in overcoming the kind of oppression one is most concerned with.

Each social movement tends to have different insights about the origins of domination. Feminists have pointed to male supremacy and insecurity. Deep ecologists have pointed to human desires to control nature. All of these insights can be enlightening. Strategically, however, our top priority is not necessarily to agree on which form of domination or oppression is most important or fundamental but to see how they are all interconnected in practice, so that domination can be attacked and ultimately eliminated on all levels of human experience. This attitude has been spreading consistently in the main social movements.

As the social movements have worked to cooperate more and see oppression on various levels, they have also tended to move toward creating positive alternatives. It is probably true that the more enlightened elements in each movement are always in a minority, but they have nevertheless played the biggest role in defining horizons for the movements and having the most impact on mainstream culture.

The green movement that emerged in the late 1970s in various parts of the world was the product of a convergence of social movement perspectives. In some places, the peace or feminist movements played bigger roles than did environmentalists in establishing the new green parties and organizations. The green movement has not been a simple coalition movement, but a *synthetic* one—an autonomous movement that has synthesized various social movement concerns. At its best, it has combined this quality of synthesis with a distinct focus on creating positive alternatives.

Over the last decade or so, institutionalization has set in on most of the green parties, and, in contrast to their original intention to be "anti-party parties," they have become conventional industrial parties. Most radical greens have left the parties, and the green movement has continued to evolve outside the confines of narrow electoral politics. It should be emphasized, though, that many of the important initiatives I characterize as "green" do not always explicitly define themselves this way. Many of the more progressive elements of the labor movement and the left have also been part of these developments, and this heterogenous trend has been a big part of the emergence of more distinct qualitative alternatives to globalization around the world.

Much of the left, as well as large sections of each social movement, however, still hasn't made the jump from preoccupation with distribution to the redefinition of wealth itself. The left still tends to see the social movements as bases of opposition to capitalism but fails to see them as contributing to alternative forms of seeing and living. For this reason, it hasn't made the jump from oppositionalism, focused on the state, to an emphasis on the grassroots creation of alternatives. "Seizing the means of production" today means moving as directly as possible to establish regenerative production and new forms of community. Oppositional activity is still very important, but today its success depends very much on the power we can establish by creating practical alternatives.

THREE MOVEMENTS

Three movements in particular must be mentioned in connection with this redefinition of wealth: the feminist, human potential, and environmental movements.

Feminism not only represents an attack on oppressive forces of patriarchy but also expresses a different way of seeing and being in the world. It expresses holistic alternatives based in long-suppressed *yin*-integrative energies. Because the oppression of women has been equally social and psychological, women's struggle has had to combine the "personal and political" in ways unparalleled for Western movements. It has had to be equally oppositional and alternative, critical and visionary. Women's situations have given them insights into politics, economics, technology, art, psychology, and much more that are crucial for a postindustrial transformation. The diversity of women's situations—across class, racial, and cultural boundaries—has not simply enriched these insights but also contributed to an understanding of patriarchy as a whole and the common situation of women everywhere (Miles, 1996). Women's traditional life/work—concerned with people-production (or the reproduction of labor-power) and which made them peripheral to the megamachine—now makes them central to postindustrial development.

While mainstream discussions of gender and the economy today tend to focus on equality of opportunity and income, for over a century, feminists also have been critical of the industrial division of production and its corresponding values. Tendencies of integrative or transformative feminists have thus called for the *domestication of political and economic life* by reintegrating the Divided Economy and by putting social and ecological values in command of the economy.

Today, enlightened environmentalists are calling for an end to the Divided Economy by integrating home and "workplaces" for slightly different reasons: closing loops and harnessing the natural productivity of every place. But the necessity of integrating production and consumption for efficiency was recognized by many feminists long ago (Hayden, 1981). Feminists are emphasizing the human development side of NPFs more; environmentalists are stressing the ecological regeneration side. Structurally, they both are raising the need to eliminate the Divided Economy. Despite the importance of establishing new forms of ecological production in the home and community—food and energy production, water purification, even goods production—the starting point for this transformation must be the recognition, and remuneration, of the important work that has always been done in the home.

The modern renaissance of feminism, beginning in the 1960s, has also played a crucial role in highlighting the necessity of disciplined personal transformation to social change. The women's movement has pioneered exciting new forms of individual/collective development and purged some older forms of authoritarian and patriarchal cultural baggage. The range of services, art, and recreation spawned by the women's movement is mind-boggling. And, as mentioned earlier, women's quest for full individuation both preceded men's and catalyzed men's (to the minimal degree that men have indeed begun to work on themselves).

The *human-potential movement* is, of course, less a traditional social movement than many others, simply because it is so focused on individual change. It is often criticized as escapist—sometimes justifiably. Social transformation, however, is impossible today without personal transformation. This task, moreover, is much more difficult than is usually acknowledged. It is not simply a matter of living ethically, of substituting a new self-image for an old one, or employing a new interpretation of reality. Having new stories, myths, and interpretations that are more regenerative is, of course, desirable—something emphasized by writers like Thomas Berry (1988). But ultimately these must be based on deeper levels of *perception,* and the direct experience of more subtle realities. These realities tend to be obscured by superficial concerns, ingrained habits, and a reactive consciousness that is usually the prisoner of its most recent thought or emotion.

Sophisticated disciplines of personal transformation, of real individuation, evolved throughout the civilized period. These disciplines typically stood in an ambivalent relationship to orthodox religion and patriarchy. In all cases, however, they were a minority phenomena. Such self-development could not be permitted for the majority of people.

Today, our survival depends on the generalization of self-development to everyone. This means freeing many of the traditional spiritual disciplines of counterproductive (patriarchal, racist, or elitist) cultural baggage without throwing out the baby with the bathwater. This danger is real, as are the dangers of new forms of escapism, narcissism, and individualism. The industrialization of culture has also been accompanied by a wealth of new psychological disciplines, techniques, and philosophies. They serve a diversity of purposes, from short-term mental health to long-term individual self-actualization. Many simply reinforce industrial forms of ego-consciousness. Others are legitimate postindustrial spiritual paths.

Because of the centrality of human self-development, individual transformation is essential to social change. Some people may be more inclined to focus on one form of change, but our social movements will have to acknowledge that individual and social transformation are interconnected. This acknowledgment indeed seems to be happening, as spiritual concerns are growing more explicit in most of the social movements.

The *ecology movement* is somewhat of a grounding force. On one hand, ecology must become the basis for our relationship to the material world. Economics would be a subdiscipline of ecology that describes how we can sustain ourselves within the ecosystems around us while helping us to play a role in sustaining life. On the other hand, there are inescapably social and spiritual sides to ecology. Ecological alternatives require not just a transformation of personal values and behavior but also community action and solidarity. Ecology not only provides the understanding to prevent environmental destruction but also the model and ethos for creating harmonious and regenerative human economic activities. The design perspective that is emerging from cutting-edge environmentalism is providing the development model that can serve as an alternative to both the capitalist free market model and the (socialist or welfare) state model of economics. The ideal is self-regulation, which is driven by use-value, not exchange-value. But the ideal also includes a strong collective consciousness—one that is expressed mainly in the rules of the game and positive incentives rather than in bureaucratic intervention.

Ecology can also provide many of the symbols that can unify humankind in this era of cultural cross-fertilization, an aspect that is stressed by geologian Thomas Berry. Whether one is a secular materialist or a Sufi mystic, one can acknowledge the sacred aspect of the Earth, which gives us life on many levels. The use of symbols is one of the most important elements of political life, which is now deeply integrated with economic, cultural, and spiritual life. In contrast to the dominant political images today, our symbols must wake us up, not put us to sleep. They must help broaden and deepen our sense of identity, not narrow it. The new movements can help us create symbols and celebrations for a new political culture of historical transformation, which is simultaneously grounded in an experience of the present moment.

THE ECOLOGICAL SERVICE ECONOMY

Closely related to the importance of alternatives, human development, and the grassroots politics of everyday life is a new role for the state in a postindustrial society. On one hand, this new role is essential because of the growing potentials for, and the necessity of, decentralized production and management. Power can and must be concentrated at the base of society, particularly at the community and bioregional levels. Rather than being a policeman or a megamachine, the state must be a facilitator and coordinator.

On the other hand, a new role for the state is necessary to transform the very goals and driving forces of economic development. The traditional goals of industrial development—accumulation and expansion of material output—must actually be discouraged. And yet this must be done in a way that provides *more and better service* to people and the environment. Our main economic outputs must be defined primarily in terms of service—nutrition, transportation/access, housing, entertainment—rather than in terms of the commodities currently used to satisfy these needs. This end-use approach, which specifically targets human need, allows us to work backward to meet these needs with the least use of material resources and energy.

A key role for the state is the implementation of new rules and regulations that encourage service outputs and continual dematerialization. These New Rules must be embodied in new incentives and disincentives to support qualitative development. This is a complex matter because the state wants mainly to support people's regenerative inclinations, not to impose burdensome pressures on them. The New Rules can work only in tandem with economic redesign that facilitates regenerative activity. A principal example would be product stewardship systems that enforce comprehensive forms of producer liability (these systems will be discussed in more detail in chapter 9). Coupled with activity to create closed-loop production systems, such stewardship legislation could provide great benefits to all participants.

The New Rules themselves not only must apply to different levels of the economy but also must ultimately be expressions of the community in question, be it local, regional, national, or international. Sustainable Community Indicators, which will be discussed in chapter 10, can act as the sources of qualitative value to displace the values of accumulation.

It is crucial to understand how the organic relationship between the New Rules and driving forces, on one hand, and the ecological design of each sector of the economy, on the other hand, actually works. Today, the "guardian" values embodied in the state and the "commercial" value of private enterprise are largely at odds with each other. Part 2 will show more clearly how the scale, methods, and goals of different forms of eco-production can work in radical ways for regeneration. The role of the state is to support and generalize this activity.

One of the major tasks for the state is to help build social and environmental costs into market prices, through methods like tax shifting, where pollution and extraction is taxed rather than work and income. This helps reverse the relationship between labor and materials and make visible long invisible subsidies to the economy. In the long run, however, this is not enough to support regenerative production, since monetary accumulation will still create unhealthy relationships. Ultimately, institutional action to support qualitative development and dematerialization must include measures to undercut the power of money and monetary accumulation.

Besides the rules, devices like community currencies, particularly account-money systems, are essential in undercutting the power of monetary accumulation and focusing the economy on use-value and social need.   The process of creating what David Korten (1999) calls "mindful markets" is essentially one of creating markets driven by use-value rather than exchange-value, where money is strictly a means of exchange. As I will argue later, monetary reform alone is insufficient in creating regenerative economic activity. What is essential is comprehensive redesign where new monetary forms can be supports for regenerative activity in various sectors of the economy. This involves the state because of its central position in the community network.

II

Designing the Green Economy

The time has come to lower our voices, to cease imposing our mechanistic patterns on the biological processes of the earth, to resist the impulse to control, to command, to force, to oppress, and to begin quite humbly to follow the guidance of the larger community on which all life depends.

—Thomas Berry, *The Dream of the Earth*

6

Eco-Design: Principles of the Green Economy

Ecological design is a crucial means of redefining wealth and implementing qualitative development. It is a process of making human and ecosystem regeneration both the *means* and the *ends* of economic development. Authentic ecological design is truly revolutionary because it cannot achieve its goals as a spin-off or trickle-down of capital accumulation. It expresses intrinsic value, not exchange-value. This means that the green economy cannot, by definition, be capitalist, even though it may employ markets and be self-regulating in many ways. Social and environmental need must come first and be the starting and finishing point of economic activity.

A growing literature on green economics describes this situation by defining the output of the entire economy as "service." It is this status of the green economy as basically a service economy that allows it to be "disaccumulationist." This service concept is, however, completely different from the current prevailing notion of a so-called "postindustrial service economy." The latter refers to a shift away from manufacturing to services in the industrialized countries, with manufacturing jobs shipped to the Third World. This kind of service economy is a symptom of social decadence, exploitation, global inequity, and waste.

The *green* service economy is an appropriate expression of people-production, productive forces centered around human development. It means that the economy is designed to maintain and increase human quality of life first and foremost. This is the "end-use" perspective that has gained widest use in the energy sector, where Amory Lovins (1977) has popularized the idea that we want "hot showers and cold beer," not necessarily power plants and fossil fuels. By the same token, we want nutrition, access, entertainment, and health, not necessarily McBurgers, sport utility vehicles, and innumerable consumer "durables." That is, we start with the needs we want to satisfy and then work backward to design the most elegant and efficient means of accomplishing the task. We may extract resources, we may manufacture things, we may use energy—but all of those things are *means* to an end, not the primary outputs of the economy. Because they are means, we can creatively minimize the matter and energy embodied in them and, in doing so, increase the quality of life for all.

While there is a growing recognition that material things can no longer be conceived of as the goals and primary outputs of the economy, it is not yet so widely appreciated that money must be dethroned as the goal of the economy. Just like matter, it is a means and not an end, and just like matter, its open-ended accumulation is a force destructive to both society and nature. This is not to say that green economic redesign can't redirect the profit motive. Doing precisely this is one significant, if not sufficient, means of a postindustrial transition. In our current economies, eco-design can save lots of money as well as resources and can provide good jobs for growing numbers of people—a theme emphasized by Roberts and Brandum, Bill Mollison (1990), Amory Lovins, and many others. But full-blown eco-design must ultimately overturn capitalism's means/ends separation, involving a transformation of markets as much as the state. In a green economic transition, the role of money as a conveyer of value must be increasingly displaced by social and environmental indicators developed by our communities.

As mentioned earlier, because we have gone beyond the era of socialist and welfare states, this does not mean planning is dead. The speed and complexity of change demands a new kind of planning, intentionality, and consciousness that is much more sophisticated than old top-down deterministic planning. A design perspective is much more subtle than a management perspective and does not need to *impose* its intentions. It does not need to control the details of development; rather, it aims at redefining the rules of the game and the basic incentives and disincentives that shape the economic environment—not simply by discouraging selfish activity but by reinforcing individuals' regenerative inclinations. This might involve the use of markets or money for certain purposes. It might include direct expenditure by the state. But it would also include a whole range of other means, such as product stewardship, product or material bans, performance standards, local currencies, and green taxes.

Design is an expression of the fairly new and growing role of culture in economic life. It reflects the special role of organization in economic efficiency today and the possibility of displacing vast amounts of capital, resources, and energy with human intelligence. Thus design is closely connected to establishing new relationships—and ultimately eliminating the distinctions—between production and consumption, between the formal and informal economies, and among politics, economics, and culture.

The imperative of a design perspective springs partly from the qualitative nature of the changes that are required simply for our species to survive. Given demographic projections indicating a human population of 14 billion before 2050, many analysts say resource throughputs must be reduced by at least 90 percent in the industrialized world, an impossible task for technological fixes alone (Hawken, 1996).

As mentioned above, the most effective means of increasing efficiency today are organizational. There are two main elements to this restructuring for greater efficiency: (1) organizing to let nature do the work by benignly situating activities within natural processes, and (2) modeling human economic organization on the ecosystem. These two dimensions are, in practice, closely linked, and both imply the possibility of a symbiosis between human culture and nonhuman nature.

The ecological model comes from the need not simply for greater efficiency but also for more organic forms of organizing and regulating complexity. The increasing complexity of economic activity both requires and makes possible ecological design principles in the economy. Old forms of deterministic control are failing; this failure has been a major factor in the breakdown of state socialism and in the rise of decentralized forms of corporate organization. The post-Fordist super-industrial economy is applying more organic regulatory processes in its advanced technology and through its information and control networks. But only an ecologically based economy can apply organic principles comprehensively. In the next few sections I want to show that the green economy is not a return to the Stone Age but a major step forward in terms of both efficiency and regulation.

The green economy is a holistic paradigm. The following ten principles convey the basic elements of a green economy, although, by definition, they have a unique application in every specific situation. Although expressed as separate principles, they require one another and in some cases are just different ways of expressing the same thing.

1. **The primacy of use-value, intrinsic value and quality.** This is the fundamental principle of the green economy as a *service economy,* focused on end-use or human and environment needs. Matter is a means to the end of satisfying real need and can be radically conserved. Money similarly must be returned to a status as a means to facilitate regenerative exchanges rather than an end in itself. When this is done in even a significant portion of the economy, it can undercut the totalitarian power of money in the entire economy.

2. **Following natural flows.** The economy moves like a proverbial sailboat in the wind of natural processes by flowing not only with solar, renewable, and "negawatt" energy but also with natural hydrological cycles, with regional vegetation and food webs, and with local materials. As society becomes more ecological, political and economic boundaries tend to coincide with ecosystem boundaries, that is, society becomes bioregional.

3. **Waste equals food.** In nature there is no waste, because every process output is an input for some other process. This principle implies not only a high degree of organizational complementarity but also that outputs and by-products are nutritious and nontoxic enough to be food for something.

4. **Elegance and multifunctionality.** Complex food webs are implied by the previous principle: integrated relationships that are antithetical to in-

dustrial society's segmentation and fragmentation. What Roberts and Brandum (1995: 93) call "economics with peripheral vision," this elegance features "problem-solving strategies that develop multiple wins and positive side-effects from any one set of actions."

5. **Appropriate scale/linked scale.** This does not simply mean "small is beautiful," but that every regenerative activity has its most appropriate scale of operation. Even the smallest activities have larger impacts, however, and truly ecological activity "integrates design across multiple scales," reflecting influence of larger on smaller and smaller on larger (Van der Ryn and Cowan, 1996).

6. **Diversity.** In a world of constant flux, health and stability seem to depend on diversity. This applies to all levels (diversity of species, of ecosystems, of regions) and to social as well as ecological organization.

7. **Self-reliance, self-organization, self-design.** Complex systems necessarily rely on "nested hierarchies" of intelligence (Kelly, 1994), which coordinate among themselves in a kind of resonant dance. These hierarchies are built from the bottom up, and—in contrast to civilization's social hierarchies—the base levels are the most important. In an economy that moves with ecosystem processes, tremendous scope for local response, design, and adaptation must be provided (although these local and regional domains must be attuned to larger processes). Self-reliance is not self-sufficiency, but it facilitates a more flexible and holistic interdependence.

8. **Participation and direct democracy.** To enable flexibility and resilience, ecological economic design features a high "eyes to acres" ratio (Van der Ryn and Cowan, 1996), that is, lots of local observation and participation. Conversely, ecological organization and new information/communications technologies can provide the means for deeper levels of participation in the decisions that count in society.

9. **Human creativity and development.** The need for grassroots participation and innovation puts a premium on all-around human development. While the high-tech waste economy concentrates human development in narrow bands of the population, ecological economics depends on both generalizing human development to everyone and widening and deepening this development. Social, aesthetic, and spiritual capacities become as important as analytic ones.

10. **The strategic role of the built-environment, the landscape, and spatial design.** As permaculturalist Bill Mollison (1983) has emphasized, the greatest efficiency gains can often be achieved by a simple spatial rearrangement of system components. Elegant, mixed-use integrated design that moves with nature is place based. In addition, our buildings, in one way or another, absorb around 40 percent of materials and energy throughput in North America (Roodman and Lenssen, 1995). Thus, conservation and efficiency improvements in this sector have a tremendous impact on the entire economy.

These principles can and must be applied differently in every situation. In the following chapters, I will explore what this might mean in different sectors of the economy. By no means is this very schematic treatment intended to be encyclopaedic, but simply demonstrative of the basic principles and relationships, with just enough examples to indicate that these possibilities are in fact already being actualized in the interstices of globalization.

Having a positive vision of what our economies can be is essential for basic change in specific communities. This would not be a detailed blueprint, since ecological change must include a large measure of flexibility and spontaneity. But this vision would convey the large qualitative changes, and approximate targets, for the locale in question. Today, in many places, there is an exciting diversity of alternative economic projects and enterprises. What is more rare are local and regional economic development plans or guidelines that articulate how all these activities can combine into a cohesive economic development strategy. Until we can articulate how our alternative projects constitute a comprehensive alternative to corporate globalization, we will have big problems trying to level the playing field for regenerative enterprise.

One of the most pressing needs of the alternative movements today is the development of Green City and Bioregional Development Plans, which can be the basis for both local development policy and grassroots activity. The following sections suggest, in the barest and most schematic way, possible directions for these participatory plans.

7

The Ecological Space of Flows: The Built-Environment

Postindustrial productive forces inevitably diminish the role of the nation-state with a local/global nexus. But in full-blown postindustrialism, geared to qualitative wealth-creation, this nexus would look very different from its distorted expression in the current super-industrial corporate-global order. While the "space of flows" of profit-driven information is increasingly placeless, the economic flows of the ecological economy move with, or extend, natural flows. Qualitative wealth, almost by definition, cannot be placeless. The green economy is preeminently place based, and even its planetary character derives from this specificity and rootedness—expressed from the bottom up through an organic linking of scales. Reestablishing the sense of place—and learning to live there fully—is what bioregionalists call "reinhabitation." This chapter will highlight some strategic elements of reinhabiting and redesigning our cities.

From a *social* point of view, to put human development in command the green economy has to bring together the Divided Economy, integrating the formal and informal economies, paid and unpaid labor, "workplace" and "home," production and consumption. This is the physical and economic division that has drawn the criticism of feminist writers and activists for well over a hundred years. It corresponds to what Marxists would call the division of labor between production and reproduction, or between the production of things and the reproduction of labor-power. New productive forces put special emphasis on the reproduction of labor-power—on people-production or human development—and so healing this division is a crucial priority for achieving authentic postindustrialism.

This split also roughly corresponds in cities to the distinction that landscape architect Michael Hough (1995) makes between the "official" landscape of commercial developments, public places, and so on and the "vernacular" residential landscape of vegetable gardens, religious ornaments, gingerbread, brightly painted houses, and fancy fences. A crucial task of green urban design is to un-

leash the riotous diversity and creativity of the vernacular on official society by
enriching the vernacular with social and ecological knowledge and vision.

The role of economic reintegration is crucial. But this physical integration also
has a crucial psychological dimension, so it must bring together the prevailing
mentalities of the two realms. This synthesis cannot weight the two mind-sets
equally but has to put a relatively greater emphasis on the nurturing/organic ethos
of the domestic sphere. It requires, in Delores Hayden's (1984) words, a "domestication of public space" in the very process of de-isolating domestic life. For
this to happen, it will not be enough for conventional planning and architecture
to augment their rational/visual focus with new ecological insights. They must ultimately give way to a more holistic design process, which, while making better
use of science, would involve *all* of the senses and a greater *depth* of feeling.

From an *environmental* point of view, there exists in industrial cities another
pair of landscapes that must also be integrated to tap the spontaneous productivity of nature. Michael Hough contrasts the formal "pedigreed" landscape of
lawns, trees, flower beds, fountains, and other planned elements, which we find
in highly visible areas like streets, squares, malls, parks, and front yards, with the
informal landscape of industrial lands, railways, vacant lots, and back alleys. The
latter tend to be dominated by "weed" plants, shrubs, and groundcovers. They are
nonplaces "in between" that, while often considered degraded, usually contain a
much greater biological diversity than the formal landscape. The pedigree landscape, considered attractive and acceptable, tends to be monotonous and mono-
cultural, requiring great inputs of energy to maintain.

Green urban design works to tap the natural productivity of the indigenous (if
no longer native) landscape in the same way it tries to unleash the vernacular
power of community. As we will see in this and later chapters, growing cultural
and technological potentials make this more necessary and possible. These potentials, however, can only be realized through spatial design.

PATTERNS OF HUMAN DEVELOPMENT

If we simply consider its various elements, the green or postindustrial built-
environment doesn't involve anything new. What makes a city ecological or regenerative can be found in many cities of the past, but generally not all together
in one city or as fully developed as we need today. Whatever their precise origins (Jacobs, 1970), cities are essentially expressions of civilization, or class societies, which, not incidentally, have also been patriarchal societies. Notwithstanding their achievements, cities have always been involved, to some degree
or another, with the exploitation of nature and people. No fully regenerative
city—one that tapped the full human potential of its inhabitants and the ecological productivity of its landscape—has ever existed.

In industrial society, cities and buildings have both been seen as "machines for living." The creative, liberatory, and regenerative aspects of the city were not lost, but the machine mentality did erode much of the holistic quality of older urban design and architecture. Patriarchy, like class power, would now be enforced less by political and religious means and more by economics. Industrialization dictated a chasm between public and private life, which was reflected in the built environment.

Two competing but alienated visions of domestic life contended through most of the nineteenth and twentieth centuries: the nuclear family "sacred hut," which isolated women in the home; and the "machine aesthetic" of collectivized consumption and industrial efficiency. The sacred hut triumphed in North American postwar suburbanization; it stimulated mass consumption to drive industrial production. The machine aesthetic had many proponents in the West, beginning with Bentham, but triumphed (ideologically at least) in the state-socialist bloc; it tried to minimize consumption to devote resources to industry. In the West, the less physical, but increasingly complex, unpaid work involved in consumption-management super-exploited women. In the East, sheer lack of resources put different kinds of burdens on women.

A third stream, which Delores Hayden describes as the "neighborhood strategy" of design, included feminist designers like Melusina Peirce and Alice Constance Austin. It was inspired by the aesthetic models of the village and the cloister, and it influenced some of the designs of the Garden Cities movement earlier this century. One of this strategy's crucial concerns was providing some alternative to the polarized industrial landscape where there has been no middle ground between isolated private life in the home and impersonal (increasingly mass) public life. It sought to link private to public space with a range of semiprivate, semipublic spaces that corresponded to various levels of community.

The wonderful writings of Delores Hayden (1981, 1984) survey the range of feminist and "neighborhood strategy" design that constitutes a great resource for alternative design today. As the sacred hut model in North America is increasingly undermined by cultural, economic, and demographic changes, there is a growing need to reshape urban and suburban spaces to serve human need and restore community. Community kitchens and eating areas, common green space, semiprivate outdoor rooms, shared child-care facilities and laundry services, community and rooftop gardens—all these are elements that feminists have advocated designing into residential developments. A much greater diversity of living arrangements is necessary to accommodate people's needs and life-choices.

Later in this and following chapters, I will touch on topics, such as ecological infill and cooperative consumption, that are directly connected to women's initiatives for more regenerative environments. Because of women's particular relationship to built-form, their perspectives on design can be especially strategic in creating holistic alternatives.

Many of the most crucial aspects of Green City design are revealed in long-standing regenerative functions of cities, which must be distilled and generalized. Victor Papanek (1995) writes about five positive functions of cities, which I have taken some liberties to rephrase:

1. **Economic/functional:** to facilitate trade and exchange through markets, workshops, and so on, but could also include industry, infrastructure, and housing.
2. **Political/regulatory:** administration and self-governance, expressed town halls, meeting halls and centers.
3. **Developmental:** the aesthetic/ intellectual capacities expressed in galleries, theatres, forums, schools, and so on.
4. **Convivial:** the vitality conveyed by overall design of public space.
5. **Spiritual:** expressed conventionally in structures like cathedrals or temples but also as a deeper quality that underlies and supports the conviviality of all urban design, and particularly public space.

Such writers on cities as William Whyte (1988), Jan Gehl (1987), Jane Jacobs (1961), Terry Fowler (1992), and others have highlighted crucial relationships that help make a city alive, interesting, and safe, relationships that can be built right into the physical structure of a city. Many have to do with appropriate human scale. Jane Jacobs, in particular, has been influential in changing the thinking of planners and academics as well as citizens about the patterns that create healthy urban environments. In taking on the conventional planning wisdom of the 1960s, she called attention to the importance of a diversity of land uses and building types, of positive effects of urban density, of small parks that really suit neighborhoods, of short city blocks that optimize crossing paths and so chance encounters, of "eyes on the street" in discouraging crime, and much more.

Writer/architect Witold Rybczynski (1986) makes clear, in tracing the concept of "comfort" through building design history, that many of our criteria for design have changed substantially over time, paralleling human development, individuation, class and gender awareness, and technological development. Nevertheless, there does seem to be a nearly universal quality to holistic design, which a green society can employ. As Rybczynski (1986: 231) notes, "what is striking is that the idea of comfort, even as it has changed, has preserved most of its earlier meanings."

University of California architect Christopher Alexander (1977, 1979) has focused his work on both identifying universal qualities or patterns and discovering the organic design *process* that will produce the unity and diversity that echo the beauty, order, and spontaneity of nature.

In *The Timeless Way of Building* (1979), Alexander writes that underlying all good design is what he calls the "quality without a name," which can be approximated only with adjectives like "whole," "comfortable," "alive," and "ego-less." In *A Pattern Language* (1977), Alexander and his colleagues offer hundreds of design patterns based on this quality, as well as a participatory process whereby holistic design can be incorporated in any building or planning project. These patterns, comprising a virtual physiology of building and design, have had a major impact on the way design professionals and laypeople alike view the built-environment. Ranging from large patterns for whole cities to carpentry finishing details, the patterns have titles that speak for themselves: Scattered Work, Community of 7000, Neighborhood Boundary, Mini-Buses, House Cluster, University as Marketplace, Public Outdoor Room, Shopfront Schools, Wings of Light, Sheltering Roof, Intimacy Gradient, Light on Two Sides of Every Room, Alcoves, Interior Windows, and so on. Many of these patterns strike most people as common sense, and yet they are systematically ignored, or violated, by mainstream design professionals.

It is Alexander's view of the *process* of design, however, that may have the most significance for the creation of green cities. In *A New Theory of Urban Design* (1987), he and his collaborators lay out an organic planning process premised on these key principles:

- The primary purpose of any act of construction is to heal the city.
- This construction must contribute to the creation of a continuous structure of wholes around itself.
- This structure of wholes is always specific to its circumstances.
- The structure is generated by creating a field of centers, with a center being a physical thing (like a building) and not simply a point.
- This field is always created incrementally and gradually, and cannot be implemented as an abstract blueprint.

Because of this incremental quality, organic design is quite different from conventional planning. It is always somewhat unpredictable, and it depends on deeply felt experience, which is not just visual. It is also quite different than conventional architecture in that it does not see a building floating individually in space but requires that the building create "positive outdoor space"—well-shaped public space next to the building, which helps to complete a larger pattern of wholeness among surrounding buildings.

Whereas conventional design builds up from component parts, organic design differentiates like an embryo growing slowly in the womb. The designer tries to feel for the larger pattern and then to make the project fit within and complete this pattern. All building is, in this sense, a process of *repair*, because it is always healing and complementing preexisting patterns. These principles apply to a project whether it is an entire university, a civic center, a rooming house, a garden, or a window alcove.

In a community, the mix of commercial buildings, residential buildings, public buildings, and parks will depend not only on the desires of the community but also on rules of thumb that guide a healthy diversity and balance of activities in a community. With regard to transportation, Alexander's organic design goes further than current environmentally oriented planning, which prioritizes land-use planning before considering transportation (for example, by locating workplaces and homes nearby). Alexander argues that holistic design must completely reverse the sequence of conventional planning today, which usually begins with transportation routes (for example, roads), then provides buildings, and lastly fills in pedestrian space. Organic community design *begins with the creation of convivial pedestrian space,* then provides buildings, and lastly provides transportation to the buildings. This process generates spaces that resonate with a very different quality.

The establishment and development of green cities depends on implementing community design processes that encourage broad citizen participation. These processes would utilize "design pattern languages," which would be developed by the communities themselves. Alexander argues that, although many holistic patterns express virtually universal relationships, living pattern languages can only be developed by the people using them. Design professionals must reorient themselves to roles as facilitators, resource-people, and educators, providing citizens with the tools to make the most fundamental design decisions.

Storefront design centers in every community can provide places for people to educate and express themselves on design issues. Centers, workshops, and other strategies have been employed by Alexander and other advocates of participatory design like Stanley King and Sim Van der Ryn. Alexander's system was the basis for a new planning process for the University of Oregon in Eugene and is described in his book *The Oregon Experiment* (Alexander et al., 1975). Vancouver's Brittania Community Centre was developed by a participatory pattern language process in the 1970s. Pattern language processes have also been employed in the building of the Eishin Gakuen school outside Tokyo and a housing project in Mexicali Mexico (Alexander et al, 1985).

The development and implementation of community design pattern languages would complement the development of community indicators and green city plans, to be discussed in chapters below. They would function as crucial means of green community self-regulation.

THE CENTRALITY OF THE LANDSCAPE

A green economy involves "doing more with less" not only by going with natural flows but also by helping to *regenerate* those natural systems. For this reason, the landscape must play an especially strategic role in the economy. The landscape is so important that people like John Tillman Lyle use it to differentiate the industrial from the postindustrial economy. According to Lyle (1994: 29), "The industrial age replaced the natural processes of the landscape with the global machine . . . while regenerative design seeks now to replace the machine with land-scape." These are not just idealistic yearnings, but practical possibilities made viable by growing ecological knowledge, "economies of *appropriate* scale," and advances toward decentralized technology.

For this reason, the term "infrastructure" takes on a new meaning and plays a strategic role. Green infrastructure forms the lifeblood of economic life. It is one reason ecological restoration is one of the most important economic activities in a green economy. Soil, vegetation, and natural drainage, wind, and precipitation patterns become extremely important in determining the kind and quality of human economic activity. Ecological engineering of this infrastructure consists in augmenting the self-design of natural flows, or perhaps mimicking these flows with engineered designs that nevertheless allow natural flows much scope for taking their own course.

Peter Warshall (1998) has outlined the relationship between infrastructure and what he calls "ecostructure"—the web structures found in nature: the patterns of bird migration, salmon runs, floodplains, watersheds, and so on. He describes how human infrastructures—such as for energy, transportation, and water—have tended to clash with ecostructures because the infrastructures are designed for overly narrow goals. Vast potentials exist to design infrastructures to not undermine ecostructures and to even support and complement them.

All infrastructures are control systems, but the difference between conventional infrastructures and eco-infrastructures is like the difference between a World Wrestling Federation "rassler" and an aikido master who employs no offensive actions. Not only do eco-infrastructures avoid damage to the environment, but they can also be designed to include ecostructures in their functioning, letting nature do the work. The incredible potential for green infrastructure is one reason why the radical green emphasis is not to "protect the environment" by sealing off cities from wilderness, but to bring nature into the city in various ways. While industrial infrastructures are designed to be as invisible as possible, eco-infrastructures are meant to be visible to everyone. This visibility gives people a sense of place, showing them how their sustenance comes to them and where it goes after they use it. Eco-infrastructures make nature's services and cycles visible, dramatizing how, in Barry Commoner's (1971) words, "everything is connected to everything else."

Eco-infrastructure includes much more than our conventional notion of infrastructure. It includes not only energy, transportation, and water but also food, raw materials, and even provision for wildlife. Clearly then, its form would have to correspond to a great extent with ecosystem boundaries, and eco-infrastructure would thus be one of the major factors making green economies bioregional.

Industrial technologies tend to concentrate resources in a small area and add major infusions of energy to process them. According to Lyle (1994: 29), "In contrast, regenerative systems tend to follow a strategy of dispersal, or spreading out over the landscape, combined with some degree of augmentation. The effort is to make full use of basic landscape processes—even more complete use than nature herself makes."

In the case of *water,* instead of speeding up its flow, and removing it to treatment plants for processing or to large bodies of water to pollute, the ecological strategy is to slow and disperse. Storm water can be purified through natural filtration by the soil on which it lands, recharging groundwater, and can also be taken up by plants for food, climate control, and so on—on rooftops, in parks, in playgrounds, and in wetlands. It can be stored in ponds, marshlands, and rain barrels. "Graywater" waste from homes can be cascaded for productive use watering lawns and washing vehicles. Sewage can be treated using "living machine" or solar aquatic systems, in which toxins are removed by plants and sunlight. These systems can also serve as highly visible aesthetic features, in public lobbies—as in the Boyne River Conservation School in Ontario—or on the street—as in the "sidewalk solar sewage walls" designed by biologist John Todd. Todd, in his many projects, and the engineering team of the Healthy House in Toronto have also made clear that the use of rainwater for drinking and washing is practical and economic even now in our polluted cities. A green economy that drastically reduces car use while gradually phasing out most toxic chemicals would make both rainwater use and natural water treatment even more effective and inexpensive.

Restoring watersheds can even (and especially) in cities be a tremendous source of economic, environmental, and social vitality. In Toronto, the city is helping restore the wetlands at the foot of the long-abused Don River, purifying the water while creating places for wildlife, cycling, and hiking amid the beauty of the river valley. Across town, the Garrison Creek Linkage Project is working to restore much of a buried creek, partly as a means to avoid pollution problems in Lake Ontario resulting from the disruption of natural water purification processes. Besides saving millions of dollars for water treatment, the project hopes to create new parks, bike lanes, and food-growing and neighborhood-gathering places all along the ravine.

In the case of *food,* a Green City would reverse trends in industrial agriculture and make the city once again a center for food growing. For millennia, the city has, for its own survival, had to maintain a close relationship with the countryside. Rural occupations and livestock also thrived within the city, until the industrial energy economy began to drastically reshape all spatial relationships. Even today, in the less industrialized countries, food production in cities is still important. Cities in China, for example, produce 20 percent of their own food, and Havana is responsible for 5 percent of Cuba's total agricultural production.

Jane Jacobs (1970) has argued, counter to the long-standing belief that cities emerged from the agricultural revolution, that agriculture originated in cities. We don't need to agree or disagree with this position to appreciate the importance of agriculture to urban life prior to the industrial revolution. Wendell Berry has pointed out that preindustrial civilization's "governing metaphor" for humanity's relationship to nature was pastoral agriculture, whereas today it is the machine. John Lyle suggests that postindustrialism's governing metaphor should be the garden.

There can be no doubt that a postindustrial transformation of agriculture would stem from cities, that it would represent a major decentralization of food production, and that it would take the primary form of a *gardening revolution*. Perhaps most importantly, it would see the entire city as a kind of garden, attempting to tap the latent permacultural productivity of back alleys, rooftops, walls, sidewalks, parks, industrial lands, plazas, and more. Edible landscaping would be a big part of multifunctional use of plants, which could also help purify air, soil, and water; shape outdoor space; and provide air conditioning, shade, windbreaks, food and habitat for wildlife, a productive sink for organic wastes, and even industrial feedstocks. As we'll see in chapter 9, eco-manufacturing must increasingly move away from petrochemical-based production toward plant-based materials, the so-called Carbohydrate Economy. This shift could have a tremendous revitalizing impact on rural communities, but even Green Cities could provide a certain amount of feedstocks for local industry, with manufacturing increasingly linked to horticulture.

Because a green economy is, as much as possible, a closed-loop system, food production is an obvious way of dealing with the volumes of organic waste that a city produces. This would mean not only composting food scraps and yard waste but also putting human waste to better use than polluting water. Like renewable energy, modern composting toilet technology is safe and cost-effective but suffers from cultural and institutional barriers. An explosion of urban food production would likely be the biggest factor spurring more ecological handling of organic waste. Support for more conventional organic farms is also, of course, essential in creating regenerative food systems. Besides providing healthy food for city people, they can help redefine city/country boundaries and roll back suburban sprawl.

Because a green economy would put stress on self-reliance—especially in food, shelter, and energy—creating a regenerative food system is one of the most strategic areas of concern for community development (Roberts, MacRae and Stahlbrand, 1999). It must both ecologically decentralize over the landscape and create new kinds of relationships between producers and consumers. It does the latter both by encouraging more self-production (or prosumption) of food and by encouraging Community Supported Agriculture (or CSA). CSAs—which originated in Japan in the 1960s (Kneen, 1995) and Germany and Switzerland in the 1970s (Douthwaite, 1996) but, since the mid-1980s, have been spreading like wildfire throughout North America (Van En, 1995)—are usually small business, nonprofit, or cooperative enterprises in which member-consumers receive seasonal organic food in return for reliable support for the local farm or farmers involved. They are basically a form of direct selling by farmers in which CSA consumer-members "share the costs to share the harvest." Members thus share the

risk with the farmer and usually have an option of visiting the farm and helping
with the work if they wish.

Urban ecological food networks in many cities are already combining activities on various levels of the food system:

- education about food, nutrition, and ecology,
- training in organic gardening, farming, and permaculture,
- support for CSA,
- support for rooftop gardening and community gardens, and
- special organic food programs for the poor and unemployed.

The creation of economic processes based on natural cycles in the landscape
also includes the use of *materials.* In chapter 9, I will look more closely at the role
of resources in green industry. It should be emphasized here, however, that the
need to run the green economy on current solar income, to minimize the embodied transport energy in materials, and to reuse and recycle materials means that
localities and regions must learn to develop their own sources of supply.

Of course, a tremendous source of supply for cities is their own waste streams.
As with organic matter, cities are potential sources of vast quantities of materials,
which today are simply disposed. For this process to work properly, wastes must
be kept separate to make recycling possible, and products and buildings must be
designed to be easily disassembled.

Communities must know their resources well, both renewable and nonrenewable, and they must cultivate their strengths. Buildings can be designed to make
use of indigenous resources. An ecological building materials industry is growing that is creating more durable products, products made from waste, and products made from benign renewable materials. An example is the boom in straw
bale construction and building materials made from straw, hemp, and so on.
Rammed earth is feasible in most areas, and almost all regions have a history of
vernacular design based on indigenous materials.

Not only building but also the production of clothing and consumer durables
can be carried out in ways that make the best use of local resources and materials. As noted above, a shift to the Carbohydrate Economy and industry based in
plant materials can increase the bioregional potentials of green manufacturing
and resource use.

Because it must be so integrated into natural process—and because this involves
a radical social agenda of unleashing domestic and vernacular creativity—green infrastructure comprises the "deepest green" of green industry in the economy. It can
provide tremendous amounts of productive work for people, because it is so labor-
intensive, and this work also tends to be high skilled and learning based.

The above survey represents only a small selection of all the landscape features
central to Green City development—and to the efficiencies of a green economy.
Linkages for wildlife movement, the relationship of "edge" to interior landscapes,

life in the forest canopy, questions of plant succession, and much more are vital elements of not only urban ecology but also urban economics.

ECOLOGICAL INFILL AND PATTERNS OF ECO-DEVELOPMENT

The process of repair with which Christopher Alexander has been concerned applies just as much to environmental as to social design. The energy-intensive sprawl of the Fordist Waste Economy created lots of largely dead space between buildings and places. A priority for eco-development is to fill that space in ways that both create community and support the natural productivity of the landscape.

The Waste Economy had it own patterns that must be transformed if ecological development is to take place. According to Van der Ryn and Cowan (1996: 9):

> The poverty of the industrial imagination is manifested in the limited number of templates used to meet every imaginable need. There are strip malls, mini-malls, regional malls, industrial parks, edge cities, detached single-family homes, townhouses, and sealed high rises, all hooked up with an environmentally devastating infrastructure of roads, highways, storm and sanitary sewers, power lines, and the rest.

While the built-form should depend on the specific circumstances of the place in question, ecological design of settlements usually calls for more compact development. Greater densities make walking, cycling, and public transit more efficient. Conventional urban intensification, or simply increasing density in existing cities, is not in itself ecological. *Eco-infill* also attempts to create stimulating mixed-use environments, which include food and energy production, help provide for local water and materials recycling, and provide a range of local jobs to serve community needs. The pattern of infill is crucial, and context is all-important. Solar access, for example, might require lower densities than places where district heating is more sensible. Wind conditions, existing building heights, vegetation, drainage, access to water, wildlife, and more must be considered.

It is essential that environmental criteria are not applied narrowly, as in the case of some supposedly energy-efficient buildings, which are ugly, create negative outdoor space, and feel like tombs inside. The use of pattern languages developed by community people themselves, as described above, can help designers save space and material by generating places that create wholeness and psychological space in small areas. Designers like Peter Calthorpe (1993), who first put single-minded emphasis on environmental considerations, have come increasingly to recognize the ecological importance of building community through design.

High and medium densities do not necessarily cause the feelings of crowdedness and alienation associated with high-rise development. But if we want to attain such densities while maintaining a feeling of psychic space in low-rise or medium-rise buildings, land must be reclaimed from the automobile. The car today dominates as much as 50 percent of space in many North American cities.

Much of that asphalt can be turned over to vegetation. The emphasis of ecological design is on *access,* which can be provided with much more elegance, equity, and convenience than expensive modes of transport.

Progressive planners and designers have made considerable strides in outlining different green conversion strategies for existing cities, suburbs, and rural areas. What might be done with the suburbs has been a particularly tricky subject. Many environmentalists, who ordinarily have a great aversion to heavy equipment, would just as soon send in the bulldozers and let natural regeneration take its course. But levelling the suburbs, of course, is no solution to sprawl.

Designers like California's Sim Van der Ryn and Ontario's Martin Liefhebber have suggested transitional alterations to the basic suburban patterns of strip arterials, shopping malls, and blocks of detached housing. Measures include closing streets, clustering parking, infilling with new and more diversified housing types, clustering housing near the stores on the arterial, and (as densities increase) opening corner stores in the residential blocks. Peter Calthorpe and other advocates of the New Urbanism have articulated horizons for new suburban development (like Calthorpe's "pedestrian pockets") that represent something of a compromise between conventional commuter suburbs and more self-reliant Green Cities.

Perhaps the biggest barrier to more radical urban development strategies is the reticence of most planners, developers, and politicians to recognize that green local self-reliance is a practical economic development alternative. It will take a combination of more grassroots development initiatives and a growing dissatisfaction with corporate globalization to affect public policy. Fortunately this seems to be just a matter of time at the local level, as evidenced by the growth of a movement for sustainable communities and, to a lesser degree, of national "green plans."

Eco-infill provides conditions for optimal levels of both human and biological efficiency. There is a growing recognition even in conventional planning circles of the waste intrinsic to a separation of paid workplaces and residences. An ecological perspective multiplies the efficiencies of mixed-use development several times over. On one hand, eco-infrastructure lets "nature do the work," saving vast amounts of capital and resources. On the other hand, the design and maintenance of multilayered eco-infrastructure—which provides water, food, energy, and more—requires lots of skilled work, and much of this work dissolves boundaries between home and workplace. Residences can cease to be places of strictly passive consumption (in the eyes of official society) and become fully supported places of food, energy, and (recycled) resource production. Making this switch involves more direct support for vernacular creativity and the home's traditional role of people-production.

GREEN BUILDING

The built-environment is responsible for about 40 percent of materials and energy use in industrialized economies. The building industry is therefore in a position not only to achieve great efficiencies but also to strongly influence the manufacturing and extraction sectors.

Cheap energy made possible a building style that extracted buildings from their environmental context. The international style presaged globalization in creating structures that looked the same in Edmonton, London, or Bangkok. Skyscrapers and tract bungalows alike depended on massive energy input for heating and cooling.

The energy crisis of the 1970s spawned a movement of environmentally oriented building. Initial preoccupations with active solar technology gave way to simpler systems of passive solar heating and cooling, and eventually to super-conserver construction. In the past decade, advances like super-windows, which can be considered forms of "transparent insulation," have made possible super-efficient buildings that require very little energy to heat and cool. At the same time, eco-building has become increasingly concerned with materials, from both a health and an environmental point of view.

Most governmental green building programs in the developed world have refrained from questioning the patterns of built-form. Canada's well-known R-2000 program, for example, has always been geared to enlisting the tract builder in energy-efficient or healthy home building. As discussed above, the industry has worked to reinforce a nuclear family form that is now in decline. More recently, the development industry has seized on condominium construction as a means to cater to new markets while avoiding more authentic social and ecological building.

Nevertheless, a grassroots green building movement is growing throughout the world and is looking comprehensively at energy use, development patterns, transport, materials, human health, building preservation, and the role of building in economic development. It is concerned at least as much with renovation and retrofit as it is with new construction, because so much of the building stock that will exist in fifty years exists right now.

In the coming period, we can look forward to some interesting developments in construction. First is the appearance of more and more eco-materials—building products that do not outgas harmful vapors, that are produced with recycled resources, that are incredibly durable, and so on. Second is the widespread use of regional benign materials and indigenous building techniques enriched with eco-efficiency. Third, buildings will increasingly be designed to accommodate community-based eco-production of energy, food, handicraft, health care, and other kinds of services. Fourth, many materials will be designed to be dismantled and reused.

The latter will likely be part of a major reorientation in building to "plan for change." That is, since buildings are always changed over their lifetime, they would be designed to accommodate change. The basic structure of a building should last for anywhere from thirty to three hundred years, according to Stewart Brand (1994) in *How Buildings Learn*. Exterior surfaces change about every twenty years. Wiring, plumbing, and other surfaces tend to wear out or go obsolete every seven to fifteen years. Interior walls and other elements of the floor plan tend to change every few years in some buildings, especially commercial ones, so they would be designed for easy dismantling.

POWER, MONEY, AND BUILT-FORM

The existing built-environment of the industrial world is not simply the product of economic development or happenstance. It also embodies power relationships that reflect power imbalances in industrial society. Many tendencies of ecological design and planning at least give lip service to the idea of participatory planning. It should be understood that, notwithstanding the exciting variety of win/win scenarios provided by eco-development, the standpoint of more powerful members of society may conflict in significant ways with that of the less powerful. Authentic participatory design puts particular emphasis on empowering the disempowered. Even the most apparently ecological notions of efficiency are subject to narrow interpretation and abuse by those (for example, white men) who have traditionally monopolized social, ideological, and design power. This is a special concern at a time when the new definitions of wealth revolve around human development.

Earlier in this chapter, we mentioned some of the contributions of the feminist tradition of design to the neighborhood perspective on development (Hayden, 1981; Wekerle, Peterson, and Morley, 1980; Sprague, 1991; Eichler, 1995). Also touched on was the dynamism of the vernacular in residential renovation and landscaping. Many aboriginal peoples have managed to keep up traditions of self-governance, education, craft, design, stewardship, appropriate technology, horticulture, and more—most of which can have great relevance to the creation of regenerative communities. Because the Green City model depends on social as well as ecological diversity, it is crucial that progressive community identities find expression in the built-environment. Participatory forms of community political self-regulation—as discussed in chapter 11—make this more possible. Citizen assemblies and participatory planning also allow diverse communities to find common ground to deal with common (and sometimes divergent) concerns.

It is unfortunate that much discussion of urban eco-design focuses almost exclusively on land use. Because real ecological design is somewhat antithetical to capitalist property relationships, many problems of land use will be impossible to solve without dealing with questions of land tenure and ownership. Current forms of both rental and ownership often discourage the kind of *stewardship* that should characterize healthy relationships between people, land, and shelter. Speculation in land is a particular barrier to regenerative land use almost everywhere.

Perhaps the most important means of undermining the power of money in land are community currencies that can undercut the power of exchange-value altogether. Pure credit-money (or account-money) systems like Local Employment Trading System (LETS) provide a means of exchange that is not a means of private accumulation. As will be discussed more thoroughly in the section on money, they focus economic activity on *use,* completely eliminating speculation.

Until community currencies are sufficiently developed to affect markets in land, other avenues are available to help undercut speculation. Daly and Cobb (1989) and others have suggested the use of Georgist "ground rent" or a land tax that is levied only on the market value of land and not on improvements to the land or on wealth-creating activities taking place on the land. This also has the net effect of putting the emphasis on the *use* of land, since any speculation value is taxed away. Such redefinition of property taxes is one possibility that should be considered as part of a more general overhaul of the tax system, and it will be discussed in chapter 11.

New forms of ownership are ultimately necessary to institutionalize ecological relationships. Community land trusts are means by which people can enjoy the independence of home ownership even as the ownership of the land is held in trust for the community and future generations (Institute for Community Economics, 1982). In urban areas, municipalities can engage in land banking, which takes land off the market and allows it to be used in any number of regenerative ways.

Collaborative housing, or cohousing, combines elements of cooperative ownership and stewardship with participatory design. Members of a cohousing group participate in the design of their community (McCamant, 1988). Cohousing, land trusts, and enlightened housing co-ops are important means of providing the security and responsibility of individual ownership while at the same time fostering stewardship and providing the flexibility for regenerative evolution of the land.

A crucial struggle for community control over the built-environment is the one against *shelter poverty,* which is an especially important form of social control in capitalist society (Stone, 1993) and one that helps enforce scarcity relationships. Housing is a major cost of living for the average person, and the threat of losing one's home is a Sword of Damocles hanging precariously over many people's heads, particularly in North America. Homelessness is not exclusively the plight of a small under class but is the temporary condition of large numbers of people, and an imminent threat for many more. The reality or threat of homelessness is absolutely central to most capitalist societies in maintaining relationships of exploitation and mentalities of fear and competition. Couple with this the psychological importance of one's own home, and we can see why a great priority must be placed on providing everyone adequate housing.

"Housing is a right" is an important principle promoted by social struggles going on around the world. Green community economic development, however, calls attention to the fact that this struggle can go far beyond demands on the Welfare State. Poor and unemployed people have the right not only to housing but also to skills for self-reliant living, including skills in solar energy, building renovation, and city farming and gardening. Some squatter movements in Europe have incorporated some of these concerns into their activism, but most other housing groups would also do well to incorporate regenerative skills-building into their strategies. A person's involvement in the physical transformation of his or her environment can be a liberating and empowering experience.

STRATEGIC OPPORTUNITIES IN THE BUILT-ENVIRONMENT

As noted above, the built-environment is a strategic area of change. One additional reason for this is that, because it is relatively decentralized compared to, for example, manufacturing, alternative projects are easier to get going and changes made in this sector can ripple widely into the rest of economy.

Energy retrofit and "home greenup" programs have played a major role in various community economic development initiatives. Many communities have found that "plugging the leaks" in the local economy can begin with plugging the energy leaks in local buildings. In Ontario, the Green Communities Initiative (GCI) in the early 1990s embarked on an ambitious program to support green businesses and create new demand for green industry. Not only did the "greenup" building inspectors make recommendations to homeowners for retrofit options and provide lists of certified contractors, but they also provided a directory of local manufacturers and retailers of green products. This directory had tremendous potential to expand demand for eco-products, even while substantially reducing resource and energy throughput. Such a program of collective green consumerism, therefore, goes far beyond the limitations of individual consumerism and could be a crucial means of creating green manufacturing. In Ontario, unfortunately, the program was quashed by a right-wing provincial government that came to power in the 1995 elections, shortly after the completion of the first directory. Elements of the program, however, are slowly being reconstructed by various community groups.

The situation of *organized labor* also offers an example of opportunities in the built environment. Consider briefly the role of the building trades compared to labor in the manufacturing sector. Historically, the construction trades have been a conservative element in the labor movement. Their original status as itinerant craftspeople made them much more individualistic and vulnerable to narrow business-unionism than many other workers. Their source of power was their craft skills, in contrast to the unskilled and semiskilled industrial workers, whose power base was not their skill but their solidarity across whole industries (such as auto, steel, and mining). The carpenters union in North America, for example, opposed the rise of the industrial unions and became a stronghold of racist and sexist "hard hat" machismo in the 1950s and 1960s.

In a postindustrial context, what was once a weakness may now be a strength. Progressive unionism today must create more decentralized forms, raise qualitative concerns about the purpose of work, and recapture labor's heritage of workers' control and cooperation. The building trades workers' base in craft, and their decentralized industry, may allow them to take initiative to fully restore craft skills. They could move to have a say in urban development and could form small eco-companies and worker co-ops that are deeply connected to community life. It takes much less capital and organization for carpenters to redirect the content of their work than it does production-line workers.

In the era of quality, work must recover its craft dimension. Building trades work has been segmented, de-skilled, and purged of many of its craft elements, but to a far less extent than has industrial manufacturing. In North America, building trades work is largely divided between residential and commercial, the commercial area being the area of highest wages and the greatest subordination of craft autonomy. Except for large apartments, condominiums, and some subdivisions, the residential and renovation sector features workers working for other workers (that is, homeowners), and so wages are much less. Regulation and standards are also less, and although this sector of construction has lots of fly-by-night activity, it is also a preserve of craft independence. Great efficiency gains are possible in both the commercial and residential sectors, but it is the residential sector that may be more strategic in the long run, since more and more of society's production should be done in, or closer to, home.

Besides gaining greater levels of self-management by forming co-ops and small businesses, building tradespeople can cooperate with ecological designers and landscapers and work as consultants for do-it-yourselfers in their communities. They can also provide substantial markets for ecological materials, thereby creating a powerful force for the transformation of manufacturing and extraction industry. And they can provide raw materials themselves by "mining the waste stream" and transforming demolition into dismantling.

Existing building trades unions that have the courage to plunge into unfamiliar waters can form worker co-ops and energy service companies (ESCOs), which can work with their communities to create prosperous and efficient local economies. They can lobby against construction megaprojects (which provide many fewer jobs than do eco-development and retrofit). They can gear training to energy-efficient building and knowledge of ecological building materials, and they can use their pension funds and other labor investment funds to finance regenerative development that creates good work and a greater quality of life. This implies no small reform of construction unionism, however, because it undermines the sectoral split between residential and commercial work as well as the unions' role of labor-brokering for the big construction companies. Some aspects of this transformation may be forced on unions anyway, however, since megaproject development and heavy construction is ever more capital-intensive and open to exploitative nounion companies.

8

Transformative Energy: The Soft-Energy Path

Understanding energy is important in understanding any system, but it has particular relevance for a postindustrial transformation because of the central role energy has played in the industrial economy. Industrialization took place because of the application of new energy sources to production. Manufacture and a fairly rigorous division of labor existed prior to the industrial revolution, but the application of hydro and especially steam power to production unleashed a leviathan.

The role of energy is particularly illustrative of the qualitative changes required by an authentic postindustrial society. The evolution of forms of energy indicate growing potentials for participatory democracy as well as the need to move from quantity to quality. Amory Lovins's articulation in the 1970s of the central importance of end-use was one of the first economic expressions, coming from the environmental movement, of the necessity of overturning industrialism's fundamental relationship of means and ends. This is despite the fact that Lovins, an advocate of eco-capitalism, has never acknowledged the subversive implications for capitalism of a comprehensive end-use economics.

Before going any farther, it might be best to offer a succinct description of the soft-energy path, roughly based on Lovins's original description, in order to highlight the fact that this path is a paradigm in itself. The path involves the following elements:

- **A flexible diverse mix of energy supply.** In this mix specific to local conditions, solar, wind, biomass, hydro, and even limited fossil fuel use have their place. Contrary to popular misconception, an ecological energy system is not simply a matter of substituting solar energy for oil, or wind power for nuclear energy. Defenders of the status quo have usually made their case by arguing that such a substitution is unrealistic. But the green economy is created by gradually dissolving energy monocultures—in favor of flexible, diverse mixes of energy—and also by turning attention away from energy *sup-*

ply toward energy *use.* The fact that a soft-energy path does not provide single substitutions is not a weakness of this strategy but a strength. Single sources imply vulnerability, inflexibility, centralization, and pollution. Conventional energy-supply projects are typically associated with environmental destruction, capital-intensity, and boom-and-bust cycles.

- **Primacy of renewable energy sources.** The green economy runs primarily on "current solar income" from various sources, not by using up stored "natural capital" embodied by fossil fuels.
- **Focus on end-use, on conservation, and on efficiency of use.** The renewable mix can work only if we use much less energy and use it much more efficiently. It makes no sense to pour water into a leaky sieve.
- **Energy matched to the task at hand in both quality and scale.** It's irrational, for example, to use temperatures of thousands of degrees hundreds of miles away to heat and cool buildings, when sensible building design can provide these things, and we can save a high-quality energy like electricity for more appropriate uses, such as running electric motors and public transit.
- **Participation-oriented structure in both production and consumption.** A flexible, diverse mix involves decentralized production and people's active involvement in conserving and flowing with natural processes. The efficiencies of the soft path are possible very much because of everyone's participation in getting the most out of the least. Questions of end-use and use-value are usually very specific to the people and situations involved.
- **People-intensive development and job-creation.** While the energy sector is industrial society's most capital-intensive sector, a soft-energy infrastructure of renewables and conservation is labor-intensive. Even in today's industrial economy, the ratio of tradespeople to professional, scientific, and technical people in nuclear energy is two to one. In solar energy, it is nine to one (Grossman, 1978). These trades jobs are precisely the kinds of work—good-paying, skilled, midrange blue- and white-collar jobs—that are fast evaporating in the polarized "Dual Economies" being created by corporate globalization.

HISTORICAL TRENDS: FROM QUANTITY TO QUALITY

Industrialism's use of energy has been powerful but far from efficient. From a thermodynamic point of view, the industrial economy has been fantastically inefficient. Geddes (1915) and more recently Lyle (1994) have described industrialization as the "Paleotechnic Era" because industrial technology is so crude. Its power has been in the sheer volume of energy and resources it has mined and processed. This incredible throughput has disguised the fact that the real costs of these resources have been drastically undervalued.

While questions of efficiency are certainly important, a green perspective has to begin with understanding *qualitative* potentials. Decades ago, Ivan Illich (1974) in his classic work *Energy and Equity* highlighted the negative impacts of massive energy throughput. He argued that, up to a certain point, or "below a threshold of per capita wattage, motors improve conditions for social progress." Above this threshold, energy grows at the expense of social equity, community, and control over technology. Illich emphasized the role of excess transportation energy and speed in degrading human relationships, but a parallel argument can also be made with regard to energy use in manufacture, communications, and other activities. "Participatory democracy," he wrote, "demands low energy technology, and free people must travel the road to productive social relations at the speed of a bicycle."

Illich was essentially demonstrating how an excess of quantity can create a scarcity of quality. Historically, the threshold he refers to is actually the point where economic development had to move from quantity to quality (approximately the time of the Great Depression). Industrialism's "hard-energy path" has always been an energy monoculture, focused on single sources of supply for fairly indiscriminate uses. Most of this energy has come from destruction of some sort, be it combustion of fossil fuels or wood, or the splitting of the atom in nuclear fission. But the notion of a "hard path" has had practical relevance only in the postwar nuclear era, when possibilities for a "soft path" have emerged from the very logic of cultural/scientific/technological development.

In the realm of energy, qualitative potentials have been expressed since the beginning of the twentieth century in three main ways: as long-term trends toward dematerialization, decarbonization, and decentralization. For our English-speaking friends, this means the creation of energy systems that are more efficient, cleaner, and more democratic. The polysyllabic terms, however, express some subtleties that are fairly important. And, although these tendencies have not necessarily developed in lockstep with one another, they are all the result of technological development and the growing importance of information.

Dematerialization, a concept used by industrial ecologists, refers to the potential of technology to do "more with less" by substituting information for capital, energy, and resources. Notwithstanding the incredible and needless waste created by both postwar and current industrial development, an efficiency revolution is taking place. While today the full costs of energy are still not being paid, somewhat higher prices (especially for new supply) and competitive pressures are making energy-productivity more important to the mainstream economy. Analysts like Skip Laitner (1995) and Amory Lovins (1989) both point to Germany and Japan's leadership in energy-productivity as major factors in their economic leadership. By and large, it has become less expensive to save, rather than to produce, a unit of energy. The full potential for saving, however, is unrealized not simply because of what Lovins calls "institutional inefficiencies" but because of social power relationships and the subversive implications of radical dematerialization for the industrial economy.

Nevertheless, even the most wasteful industrial economy—the United States—has benefited from energy-efficiency. Lovins (1989; 1986) writes that, from 1979 to 1989, the United States got seven times as much new energy from savings as it did from all net increases in supply, and, of that new supply, more came from renewables than from nonrenewables. Laitner (1995) cites a report by the U.S. Office of Technology Assessment (OTA) that explicitly connects productivity gains in the U.S. economy with substantial gains in energy-efficiency from 1973 to 1987.

Advances in technology for both production and end-use efficiency are taking place; some have been implemented, some are awaiting application, and other radical gains are on the immediate horizon.

Among renewables, solar electric and wind power are becoming increasingly viable. Combined-cycle natural gas–fuelled power plants coming on line in the early 1990s were in many cases 50 percent more efficient than plants of only a decade before. Efficiencies in lighting have more than tripled since the introduction of the compact fluorescent bulb in the early 1980s. Similar gains have been made in a host of household appliances, including refrigerators (electricity use cut in half in less than twenty years), furnaces, water heaters, and ranges. In industry, the United States and Japan raised their energy productivity by more than 37 percent between 1973 and 1988. It has been estimated that users of electric motors could slash their electricity use by as much as 60 percent by using more efficient motors and better matching motor size to drivetrain components (Flavin and Lenssen, 1994).

Decarbonization refers to an overall trend toward cleaner, less polluting sources of energy. The Worldwatch Institute's Flavin and Lenssen (1994: 288) write:

> Humanity first relied on solid fuels—moving from wood to coal—and then began to shift to liquid oil early in this century. In recent decades, a new trend has developed, as natural gas has begun to displace both liquid and solid fuels in many applications. This shift to gas is in effect a continuation of a long-term trend to ever more efficient, less carbon-intensive fuels—part of the gradual "decarbonization" of the world energy system.

The maturation of renewable energy technologies, and a soft-energy path, is the ultimate development of decarbonization.

Decentralization is typical of almost all forms of postindustrial production, although, as I have argued throughout, the character of this decentralization has been severely circumscribed by industrial institutions. The most positive examples of decentralized energy production are renewable energy technologies, which can often be applied on the community or household level. Such examples include solar photovoltaics, wind turbines, and small hydro. Coupled with conservation technologies and other innovations like fuel cells and flywheel batteries, renewables are the most advanced expressions of "distributed generation" and can provide the energy infrastructure for economic democracy.

At the moment, renewables are still marginal phenomena. But decentralization has also affected the mainstream. The current restructuring of the electrical industry is an example of a decentralization driven by technological development. As Lyle (1994) has written, industrialism centralized great concentrations of energy. In North America, early market competition gave way to the rise of large vertically integrated energy companies and electrical utilities. There came a time (certainly by the 1970s) when big power plants became much more expensive than new smaller and more efficient energy sources—be they fossil fuel or renewable. In subsequent decades, the costs of the old monopoly systems have risen, and it has suddenly looked much less sensible to consider power generation a natural monopoly. With lots of smaller independent generators being able to supply power more inexpensively, it makes sense for the distribution network to become a kind of common carrier, but generation then would become an arena of competition among many providers.

Decentralization in the mainstream is, of course, a mixed blessing at best, because most of the powerful players in today's economy are not particularly interested in the democratic potential of decentralization. They are interested in either protecting their own economic power or cashing in on a new market, or both. As with the evaporation of state socialism, electrical restructuring has opened a Pandora's box of greed, chicanery, and power struggle. The utilities, big corporate energy consumers, and independent generators (most of whom aren't in renewables) are all pushing their agendas for restructuring, and most of these agendas have little to do with society's overall interest. Deregulation has too often meant freedom from environmental regulation and consumer protection. In the case of troubled public sector monopolies like Ontario Hydro, plans for privatization have been justifiably characterized as "piratization."

DECENTRALIZATION, INTEGRATION, AND THE LANDSCAPE

It is convenient to discuss energy in industrial society as a separate sector, a supply sector. But because of the postindustrial possibility of distributing energy production throughout society and over the landscape, it is difficult to separate energy production from its use in manufacturing, transportation, agriculture, and other areas. Implementing a green energy system does not mean performing a simple substitution of solar energy for fossil fuels; it means transforming all aspects of economic life.

Industrial society has not only centralized energy production but has also fragmented its use. The green economy "closes loops." That is, it not only decentralizes energy production, but it would also integrate various uses, and integrate production and use, so that energy can be used more fully and can be reused. In the next section, we will see how industrial ecology and closed-loop manufacturing work to locate firms and processes together in complementary ways to allow waste heat (and production by-products) to be of productive use, and thus save resources.

But here special mention can be made of cogeneration, the simultaneous production of electricity and heat. "Cogen" is a growing source of energy and an example of possibilities for creative integration of production. One function of industrial redesign is to *cascade* energy into various useful purposes as it degrades from each higher-level use.

In the previous section on the built-environment, we considered briefly the role of elegant urban redesign in achieving new levels of efficiency through eco-infrastructure and other methods. Here it might be useful to call attention to possibilities for energy savings and clean energy production.

The obvious starting point is the connection between urban design and transportation energy. Perhaps 30 percent of energy use in the advanced countries is related to transportation, and that figure may actually be higher if one includes the manufacturing energy devoted to supporting long-distance transport, either in packaging or in transportation infrastructure (Douthwaite, 1996). Douthwaite convincingly demonstrates how transportation expenses are, for almost all communities, a major drain of money from local economies. As mentioned earlier, planning and design tendencies have emerged to articulate many different ways to decrease cities' dependence on the automobile (for example, the New Urbanism and Eco-Cities movement). Imaginative transportation alternatives are being implemented (such as car-sharing co-ops, bike-based municipal recycling systems, traffic calming, street closings, road pricing, bus "tube stations," and discounted public transit). The focus of the most progressive initiatives is on easy *access* (to all of society's services by everyone) rather than on *mobility* (Zielinski, 1995).

In comparing energy use in various cities around the world, the International Congress for Local Environmental Initiatives (ICLEI) found that density may be the single most important factor affecting a city's energy-efficiency (Jessup, 1992). Buildings with common or party walls, of course, use less energy than isolated buildings. Urban density provides the appropriate scale to make public transit and cycling economical and lessens the relative cost of infrastructure.

Urban intensification, or "densification," is therefore an essential dimension of a soft-energy path. Conventional intensification strategies involve encouraging multiple-unit residential development; integrating work, residences, and shopping in the same area; and implementing higher density zoning along main transit routes. *Eco*-intensification and infill can multiply efficiencies many times over by overlapping functions of food growing, climate control, and natural water treatment. Eco-infrastructure is geared to save energy in many forms: to reduce the need for supply, to provide renewable sources, and to minimize the use of materials and thus their "embodied energy."

There are many possible examples. Infrastructure design for water can at the same time eliminate much energy use by eliminating the need for water pumps (a major energy sink in most cities today). Restoration of watersheds and other ecological landscape features can save or provide vast amounts of energy for water treatment, cooling, and other functions. Such simple landscaping measures as tree planting can reduce the heating and cooling load on a building by as much as 50 percent. A major part of the Sacramento Municipal Utility District's conservation initiatives to displace nuclear power from a closed reactor was tree planting. The SMUD program had as many as 140 trees a day being planted in 1995, with mature trees estimated to reduce air conditioning costs by 30 percent. Village Homes in Davis, California, have designed their tree cultivation to also produce substantial quantities of fruit and nuts.

Rooftop gardens are a vast untapped potential for saving heating and cooling energy while at the same time tapping photosynthetic energy for food and natural waste treatment. According to Mark Roseland (1998), the German cities of Mannheim and Frankfurt grant permits for flat roofs only if they are the "living" variety, a policy that, if duplicated by other cities, could in itself have major implications for reducing global energy consumption, reducing urban heat islands, improving urban air quality, and saving billions of dollars on stormwater treatment.

RENEWABLE ENERGY AND DISTRIBUTED GENERATION

Organizational decentralization is complemented by technological development, which makes possible smaller and cleaner forms of energy production. Today, various forms of renewable energy are becoming more economic, in some cases even competing against highly subsidized forms of dirty energy. But the combination of the industrial economy and renewable energy is generally a very poor fit. The industrial economy tends toward centralization, mass production, and monoculture. A comprehensive development of renewable energy, which demands diversity, flexibility, and participation, can come into its own only in a postindustrial green economy.

A green economy can emerge, however, only from the interstices of the old order, so it is imperative to find ways of making space for renewable energy production and use wherever possible. It is unlikely that renewable energy can be fully developed without much greater levels of democracy, but it is equally true that more renewable energy helps lay a basis for more participation and democracy. Whatever institutional mechanisms they employ, communities should try to incorporate as much renewable energy as possible into their energy restructuring.

In recent years, a number of studies have demonstrated the potential of renewables. A Union of Concerned Scientists report in 1991 concluded that, coupled with strong conservation measures, renewable energy could provide more than half of U.S. energy supply by 2030, at a net savings to consumers of about $2.3 trillion (Cole and Skerrett, 1995). A Cambridge University report, cited by Richard Douthwaite, suggested that renewables could contribute up to 50 percent of the net energy contribution in the United Kingdom by 2040. Finally, a Stockholm Institute study for Greenpeace indicated that renewables could provide 62 percent of Western Europe's energy by 2030, rising to 100 percent by 2100 (Douthwaite, 1996). These projections do not, of course, presume most of the radical/qualitative changes described by this book, so the possibilities can be considered much greater.

Any discussion of solar energy must begin with *passive solar,* the simplest and most decentralized form of solar energy. This form involves simply capturing the natural warmth of the sun with the intelligent design and siting of buildings. It has to be combined with conservation and energy-saving measures to be effective, as well as be intelligently matched to the task at hand. Therefore, it is deeply embedded into, and widely distributed over, the built-environment. Passive solar can provide not only heating but also cooling capacity and power for natural ventilation. The possibilities of good building design are magnified by passive technology breakthroughs like phase-change thermal storage materials and super-windows. Super-window technology has now advanced to the point where advanced windows are actually "transparent insulation." They allow the capture of ever greater amounts of solar energy and will eventually permit north-facing solar greenhouses.

Solar thermal technologies, such as hot-water heating, suffered economic setbacks in the 1980s when many industrial governments cut back financial support, but, technologically, progress was still being made. The cost of a flat-plate collector dropped 30 percent between 1980 and 1990 (Flavin and Lenssen, 1994). The pioneering Sacramento Municipal Utility District made the replacement of electric hot-water heating with solar one of its priorities in its energy system overhaul, with more than 3,500 solar systems installed from 1992 to 1996. According to Smeloff and Asmus (1997), the program saved on average 2465 kilowatts per year, or approximately 67 percent of the total household consumption of water. Another solar thermal technology is the parabolic dish with a Stirling or heat engine mounted at the focal point. The engine converts heat into electricity.

The cost of solar electricity, or photovoltaics, has been declining substantially over the past two decades. While it is still generally too expensive for most grid-connected uses, it has become much less expensive than extending the grid where that would previously have been required. In 1989, Lovins wrote that the breakeven point for the extension of the electrical grid was down to a mere 400 meters, due to the decreasing cost of photovoltaic technology. He feels this already makes obsolete the extension of the grid into rural areas.

The situation is even more optimistic if one considers the real or full costs of electricity generated by nuclear or fossil fuels. From this perspective, photovoltaics is competitive in almost all areas. Lovins's Rocky Mountain Institute insists that household electricity usage could be lowered from 11 kilowatts per day to 3 by using efficient lighting and motors, passive solar, better fridges, and so on. For these needs, a small array of solar collectors could supply all of a home's needs (Berman and O'Connor, 1996).

Collectors are now being produced as roof shingles, allowing them to be incorporated into the building structure, thus saving roofing costs as well. More and more elegant and inexpensive mounting systems are being developed to meet the needs of all kinds of buildings.

Wind power is a renewable energy that has become a competitive energy source during the past decade, even on today's sloped playing field. Mid-1990s estimates were that the average cost of wind power would fall to four cents per kilowatt hour by 2000. Although almost 90 percent of wind generation is in California, Denmark provides the model for grassroots wind power development. In barely twenty years, activists have, in Douthwaite's words, "started a movement and created an industry." By 1994, Denmark had about 3,600 wind turbines in operation, with a capacity of 500 megawatts. This provided 3 percent of the country's electricity, and Danish planners have targeted a 10-percent share by 2005 (Flavin and Lenssen, 1994).

The dynamic forces in Denmark have been the rural wind guilds, which have helped people buy and operate turbines cooperatively. These grassroots operators have even helped shape the technological development of the turbines, which are known for their reliability. Danish farm equipment manufacturers got into the production end quickly and actively sought the input of the farmer-operators (Berman & O'Connor, 1996). Wind is a renewable power source that has vast immediate potential for community development. The Danish wind guilds are providing the inspiration for a new generation of community wind power developments all over the world. In Canada, the Toronto Renewable Energy Co-op is financing the construction of a large windmill downtown on the shores of Lake Ontario, which will supply energy to the grid.

In addition to solar thermal, photovoltaics, and wind, renewables like *small hydro, biomass* (and biogas), and even *geothermal energy* have tremendous untapped potential for community self-reliance. Coupled with technologies like the *fuel cell* (which today is used as a power source for large buildings) and combined with conservation, they offer almost unlimited opportunities for place-based energy production.

There are a number of other developments that reinforce this trend toward distributed generation. While megaproject-minded engineers seem to have frighteningly big plans for *hydrogen,* the greatest potentials for hydrogen—as a fuel or a means of storage—are really decentralized on a small scale, since the equipment to produce it is just about as economical on a small scale as on a large one. Hydrogen can be produced from water, using rooftop solar collectors as a power source, and stored for use on the community, or even household, level.

Flywheel batteries, which store energy mechanically rather than chemically, also promise much greater autonomy for home- and community-based electrical storage. Richard Douthwaite (1996) describes a small combined electrical generation system developed in Ireland, which consists of a wind generator and a bank of PV cells coupled to an engine running on biogas. The system can run anytime, powered by whatever fuel is appropriate for the moment.

The restructuring of the electrical industry has invited comparisons with the telecommunications industry, which has also recently undergone substantial change. Although there are some fundamental differences between these industries, there are some parallels, particularly the desirability of establishing a "common carrier" distribution arrangement.

A closer relationship between the information/communications industry and the energy sector is also suggested by a progressive energy system's basis in distributed generation and energy/conservation services. In the new decentralized energy economy, new kinds of load management will be required. This is because so many consumers are also producers of energy; because the grid serves the function of a battery (that is, storage) for the small producers; and because adaptation to daily weather and seasonal climate conditions will be ever more important. The same cable that provides buildings with computer and telecommunications services may also provide energy management information and services while providing the municipal utility a means of coordinating supply and demand. This assumes, of course, that the telecommunications system would be as community oriented and community controlled as the energy system, and that the telecommunications system would augment rather than undermine face-to-face communication.

END-USE AND DEMATERIALIZATION

Perhaps the most radical concept of the soft energy path is the primacy of end-use. Soft energy guru Amory Lovins has long stressed the importance of an *end-use* and *energy-services* approach to energy. He insists that what we want are "*hot* showers and *cold* beer," not oil or power plants. We don't necessary want *things,* but we want our needs satisfied, and we should be looking for the most elegant, inexpensive and efficient ways to satisfy these needs.

A focus on end-use, however, raises questions about the *quality* of human need. All needs are not equal, and end-use decision making should lead to a careful examination of the needs we want to satisfy. Are these needs healthy and regenerative, or alienated and antisocial? Such questions are not only political but spiritual. Individually and collectively, we should be constantly distinguishing wants from needs and exploring the total implications of our choices. This reflection is essential in reducing unnecessary energy and materials use, since the industrial waste economy has made such an effort to channel so many of our social and psychological needs in crass materialistic directions. But a dialogue on needs is also essential to our development as human beings—the people-production that is really the nexus of postindustrial development.

Despite trends toward niche markets (for those who can afford them) and multistakeholder collaboration (for those who accept the rules of the game), it seems more than unlikely that the industrial economy can implement needs-based development or sufficient participatory democracy to create authentic end-use economic or energy systems. Something more community based is necessary, something that doesn't simply engineer better spin-offs from capital accumulation but actually displaces accumulation with more qualitative incentives. We'll look at this more closely in the section on money, finance, and alternative indicators.

The whole point of an end-use approach is to increase our quality of life while reducing materials and energy throughput. As mentioned earlier, even simple sustainability for the planet requires a materials and energy use reduction of 90 percent in the "rich" countries. Dematerialization does not therefore simply mean increasing the efficiency of particular firms or operations. It means reducing the total mass of materials and energy use in the economy. It means the end of (quantitative) "economic growth." Clearly, this is just a potential, because until now, efficiency gains have invariably meant that we just *do more* so that the economy continues to balloon.

Because we live in such a wasteful society, the opportunities to create wealth by saving are enormous, and there is potential to create indefinite numbers of jobs that reduce material growth. "Ecopreneurialism" evangelist Wayne Roberts goes so far as to hold up the ESCO as the model for the entire green economy. An ESCO typically will contract to save a company, household, or government a certain amount of energy and money, and the ESCO is paid over time directly from the savings it has achieved. This strategy can be applied just as easily to saving water and other resources. It is real wealth production that does not require more resource-throughput, but less.

Analysts at the U.S. Department of Energy write that a $100 billion investment in energy efficiency upgrading could reduce annual energy bills by $25 billion, while providing many jobs, reducing pollution, and allowing capital to be more productively redeployed (Kats, Rosenfeld, and McGaraghan, 1998). Municipal governments can work with ESCOs to create jobs and major savings. In Toronto, the Better Buildings Partnership is a pilot project worth $38 million, which in only two years has cut the city's carbon dioxide emissions by 65,000 tons and created around two thousand jobs. Not only has the project made good money for energy management companies, but the returns on the project have created a revolving loan fund that continues to provide new financing for further upgrades and more savings.

Despite government and utility cutbacks in energy-efficiency programs due to electrical industry restructuring, continual progress is being made in achieving efficiency gains as real-time monitoring and electronic controls are being employed.

The potential for business and worker co-op development based on the ESCO model is virtually unlimited. In recent years, some ESCOs have extended their scope of operation from efficiency retrofit work to encompass small-scale generation and cogeneration. This is a sensible fit, since the greatest levels of efficiency can often be achieved by considering production and consumption simultaneously.

ESCOs and ESCO-like organizations can also be more consciously designed for the purpose of community economic development. The Green Communities Initiative (GCI) in Ontario, a combination of separate but associated programs in ten Ontario cities, has employed building "greenup" inspections to spin off substantial retrofit work in homes and small businesses. An outgrowth of the Toronto GCI has been Green$avers, which does building audits, air leakage testing, and air sealing and insulation work.

The ESCO model is also a great opportunity for unions hard-pressed by globalization. A number of unions have invested their pension fund money in Toronto's Retrocom, a fairly large ESCO that does work in the commercial sector. The greatest opportunities, however, are for building trades unions, which can create union ESCOs staffed by union workers. Because the job creation potential of building retrofit is so great, unions can have much more control over the creation of their own work. They can use their own pension funds to create this work and bring them benefits during their own worklives. In many areas, legislation will have to be changed to allow the unions to use their pension funds in such a progressive manner, but given the many allies such a plan might win, creating the political clout to revise the legislation does not seem an impossible task.

DEREGULATION: COMPETITION FOR WHAT?

Even though it is certainly a strategic factor in establishing regenerative activity, green entrepreneurialism can never be a complete strategy for postindustrial transformation. Something else is needed, on a social or community level, that not only provides context and support for green enterprise but also changes the driving forces of the economy as a whole. This means fundamental changes in the economic rules of the game, gearing the game to reduce the *total amount* of material growth.

One theme of this book is that of qualitative change, which is change that can only emerge gradually and organically. But all gradual change is not necessarily qualitative. The utilities' embracing of end-use concerns is a case in point. Concern with end-use is ostensibly the reason behind the Demand-Side Management

(DSM) programs implemented by large electrical utilities. Certainly, there is some reason to celebrate the fact that utilities have embraced some of the early recommendations of conservation activists. In the past couple of decades, DSM programs moved from the environmental fringe to the mainstream as utilities realized that the cost of new generation capacity was far more expensive than conservation and energy-efficiency programs. But as Berman and O'Connor (1996) have demonstrated, DSM has been employed not really to reduce overall energy use but as a means of load management that could, in the long run, allow the utilities to sell more electricity. These programs have also been major forms of public relations. As Berman, O'Connor, and other writers have shown, most utilities have also been more than willing to trash their energy-efficiency programs during the current restructuring as part of a cost-cutting mania.

By the same token, this whole restructuring has not really been driven by efficiency but by the hypnotic appeal of lower energy prices. Politically, the process has been powered not by the utilities' longtime nemeses—grassroots environmental groups—but by large energy-intensive manufacturers, who want cheaper energy and want "direct access" to cheaper independent generators. Most of these independents aren't providing renewable energy.

It seems unlikely that energy consumers' "direct access" to energy producers will provide lower prices to anyone but the largest industrial consumers. And, in the absence of proper information and regulation, small consumers will be increasingly vulnerable to marketing scams, especially "green [that is, high] pricing" for supposedly clean power.

As long as energy prices do not "tell the ecological truth" and reflect full environmental costs, a "least cost" energy strategy is more than bogus. Even more to the point is the question of whether we *want* low energy prices. Ideally, energy prices should not only reflect full costs but encourage the reduction of energy use as well as more people-intensive forms of development. That is, energy and material prices should be relatively greater than the price of labor.

Certainly we do not want overall remuneration for workers to fall, and we want to protect and support low-income people as prices change. But these are challenges that can and should be overcome by proper economic design; they do not constitute an valid argument for low energy prices.

This said, it seems unwise for pricing to be the major means of redirecting the economy. Pricing has an appropriate role but only within a complex of economic redesign, including product stewardship, community currencies, and performance standards. The main point I want to stress in this section is that we must question energy industry restructuring based primarily on the mania for low energy prices.

The current restructuring of the electrical industry amounts to a kind of semi- (or quasi-) decentralization that is intended (consciously or unconsciously) to avoid a real democratization of energy. As the status of utilities as legally sanctioned "natural monopolies" is being changed, many private utilities are actually merging to become bigger and so maintain their market power by becoming "unnatural" monopolies. In other cases, the breakup of the utilities and the institution of market competition has unleashed a plethora of exploitative forces. The "direct access" or "retail wheeling" arrangement mentioned above has pitted the big industrial consumers somewhat against the utilities. Direct access threatens to leave the old monopolies stuck with the "stranded costs" of their past nuclear follies, and it leaves the average retail consumer without protection or power in the market. But the utilities have seemed more than willing to protect their markets by offering industrial consumers special deals to stave off the new competition from independent generators. This means that residential and small business consumers get stuck with paying for the utilities' stranded assets (Shuman, 1998; Berman and O'Connor, 1996; Smeloff & Asmus, 1997).

THE GREEN MUNICIPAL UTILITY

The municipality is a vitally strategic arena of energy action, and the establishment of a municipal conservation economy is an essential part of the creation of a green energy system. I have chosen to focus on the concept of a green municipal utility, but the role of such an organization could actually be carried out by a network of collaborating community-based organizations or by a democratic municipal government. The precise organizational form green energy development takes is very much contingent on local circumstances, but some kind of conscious direction at the community level does seem necessary.

Most progressive writing on energy seems to concur that divorcing distribution (and the grid) from generation and allowing competition among generators is a good idea, as long as measures are taken to make sure energy prices reflect real energy costs. But the most appropriate buyers of energy external to a community are the community itself, not individual consumers. Among other reasons, this is because the community level is a place where so many efficiency measures are taken. Some energy analysts have suggested forms of "wholesale wheeling" where the municipal utility or purchasing co-op would purchase the energy the community required, carry out conservation programs, and coordinate small generator distribution within the community.

Strong municipal coordination is necessary both because of the number of independent generators in the system (potentially every household and business), and because qualitative choices about energy development depend on specific community values and ecological circumstances, which are different everywhere.

One of the great assets of a municipal utility is that it can play such a major role in dealing with financing of efficiency measures. It can provide the up-front money to pay for building retrofit or renewable energy equipment and recoup its investments like an ESCO—from returns on the monthly savings. A utility can make this process even simpler than a private ESCO by using a check-off scheme on its monthly billing. (For example, a homeowner who once paid $100 a month for energy might now use only $50 worth after retrofit and pay $75 a month—the $25 difference going to pay for the initial work and profit on that work to the utility and retrofit firms. Without having to pay out anything for up-front costs, the homeowner notices only that he or she is paying $25 less per month).

The clear prototype for green municipal utilities in North America is the Sacramento Municipal Utility District, or SMUD. Although created several decades before, SMUD began to realize its potential for self-reliance and clean energy when recurrent problems with its nuclear power plant triggered a movement to close the plant. The plant was closed in 1988, and SMUD improvised a number of strategies to provide alternative energy sources and services. It bargained for power from outside sources while it devised comprehensive conservation programs, including tree planting, home audits, rebates and financing for efficient appliances and equipment, weatherization for the homes of low-income people, and commercial/industrial retrofit. It also initiated or expanded investments in cogeneration and renewable energy. The latter has included programs in solar hot water heating, photovoltaics, fuel cells, and biomass.

In the context of today's electrical industry restructuring, SMUD's achievements are notable. Just as significant, though, is the kind of potential it suggests for municipalities that go one step further: toward fully green regional economies. A municipality consciously committed to creating much greater levels of economic self-reliance could multiply opportunities for conservation and renewables simply because every sector would prioritize this move. This kind of ambitious vision would, of course, create many new obstacles, but possibilities for support, inside and outside the community, would be great.

Not only are there ways other than municipal utilities to create green municipal economies, but there are different ways a green municipal utility might be created. One way might be a community takeover of an existing municipal utility. Many existing municipal electrical systems, such as Toronto Hydro, have little or no responsibility for generation. They may engage in conservation programs, but their main interest is in selling energy, which they receive from the big generation utility (such as Ontario Hydro). Such municipal utilities will have to be transformed if green energy systems are to be created, and it may be possible for grassroots energy activists to be elected to the utilities' governing boards and hire progressive staff, much like SMUD hired David Freeman, the maverick energy administrator.

In some cases, the municipal utility may have to be created from scratch. This might require a lot of preliminary activism and education, but it provides a clear slate on which a community can draw up its energy future. In some cases, existing local government entities may be the appropriate coordinators of the energy system. In any case, communities will want to democratically decide what forms of energy they want to prioritize, what kinds of conservation activities they prefer, and how to coordinate supply and demand in a way that encourages optimal self-reliance.

ELEMENTS OF GREEN ENERGY STRATEGY

We can summarize a green energy strategy here while adding a few relevant considerations:

1. **Ecological urban and industrial redesign.** Because a green economy moves from a linear to a cyclical model of resource use, thereby integrating production and consumption, and because it distributes energy production throughout society, design is the key to energy efficiency. Goods production and food production are also more decentralized, and energy efficiency is to a great extent contingent on the success of industrial ecology and eco-agriculture.

2. **The grid: A common-carrier transmission system.** One of the most significant characteristics of a green electrical infrastructure is the de-coupling of energy production and supply from distribution. This separation should also mean a de-coupling of energy sales and profits in the energy industry, but this is certainly not the case in today's capitalist electrical restructuring. As we have discussed, in a green system, the electrical grid would be a means of distribution for many suppliers, including independent power producers, large and small, and lots of NUGs, or "nonutility generators." With such dispersed generation and so many consumers also being producers, the common-carrier grid becomes in effect a kind of battery—storing the excess production of local producers and allowing them to take back energy when they need it.

   An important means of creating this flexibility is "net metering," which allows a household or company's electrical meter to run backward when they are feeding electricity into the grid and forward when they are taking energy out. To date, small producers have usually not been allowed to receive the full market price of their energy. A variation on this theme is Germany's "electricity feed law," which requires that electric utilities purchase all power generated from solar, wind, and biomass energy and mandates the price at which it is purchased (Dunn, 1997).

3. **The green municipal utility (GMU).** The GMU would make available all of the relevant information and research necessary for the community to develop its soft-energy vision.Then it would work to coordinate and actualize this vision, facilitating more energy self-reliance, with less energy use and cleaner sources. It would play a central role in helping to actualize the area's Community Economic Development Plan. The GMU would embody the community's control of the grid, and it would implement the community's choices of sources and saving.

   While SMUD is the most discussed model of progressive energy development in North America, there are many other places that provide examples of green energy strategies, emphasizing one dimension or another.

These locations include Austin, Texas's "conservation power plant"; Portland, Oregon's solar access laws; Springfield, Illinois' "comprehensive energy plan" (Cole and Skerrett, 1995); and Osage (Iowa) Municipal Utilities (Berman and O'Connor, 1996).

4. **Regenerative financing.** Although the GMU can be a major source of financing, it is important to acknowledge the special role of financing per se in creating green energy alternatives. Compared to hard-energy technologies, soft-energy systems are inexpensive. But because they are so decentralized and not simply the preserve of big corporations and governments, the "first costs" they involve can present major problems for people and small firms. It has been widely noted that the spread of soft-energy technologies and systems is not a technological or even an economic problem; it's a problem of financing.

There are many off-the-shelf eco-technologies that would be more than competitive but simply haven't been commercialized, very often because of insufficient financing. In many cases, scaling up production—such as for photovoltaics, wind turbines, and compact florescent bulbs—can bring down prices substantially (Flavin and Lenssen, 1994).

Other progressive financial institutions, such as credit unions, can play an important role in a region's energy transformation. Because they create real qualitative wealth, these investments promise reliable returns. Energy-efficient mortgages, low-interest financing, rebates for solar equipment, and various kinds of first-cost financing must all play an important role.

"Green pricing" is a popular but controversial means of supporting green energy development. Many utilities and power providers are taking advantage of people's environmental concerns to charge premium prices for dirty energy. Even in cases of the sources being legitimately renewable and ecological, we must be careful about reinforcing the notion that it is appropriate for dirty energy to cost less than clean energy. Green pricing can be an important means for the initial financing of soft-energy projects, but growing pressure must be exerted politically to force environmental costs to be incorporated into market prices.

5. **Incentives for green energy/disincentives for hard energy.** Market mechanisms may be insufficient in themselves to create a green economy, but levelling the playing field for green energy is certainly a crucial arena of struggle. There are many areas in which the rules of the game must be changed.

To begin with, *subsidies, direct and indirect, to hard energy supply must cease.* This is one way that prices can "tell the ecological truth" (von Weizsacker, 1994). According to Flavin and Lenssen (1994: 299):

In 1991, direct fossil fuel subsidies totalled some $220 billion a year worldwide, according to World Bank estimates, equivalent to 20 to 25 percent of the value of all fossil fuels sold. . . . In the United States, energy industries received federal subsidies worth more than $36 billion in 1989, with the fossil fuel and nuclear industries reaping nearly 60 percent and 30 percent, respectively, of the total.

Of course, there is nothing wrong with directly subsidizing clean energy because its paybacks are so positive. The rate-based incentives that are widespread in Germany as a means of stimulating photovoltaic development are a good example. A 1-percent surcharge on all electric bills finances especially favorable buyback rates for electricity from home-installed photovoltaic systems.

Carbon taxes, as an element of *ecological tax reform,* are another way real costs can be built into energy prices. The degree of taxation for any particular energy source would reflect its contribution to carbon dioxide buildup (von Weizsacker and Jesinghaus, 1992). Levels of taxation could be introduced gradually and be coupled with measures to ensure that lower-income people would benefit, not suffer, from the restructuring.

Until such time as GMUs, or their equivalents, are prevalent, it seems desirable that governments, where possible, actually require that utilities include externalities in their energy pricing. According to Flavin and Lenssen (1994: 69):

> Massachusetts, for instance, has assessed environmental costs of $7,934 per ton of nitrogen oxides, $1,873 per ton of sulfur dioxide, and $26.45 per ton of carbon dioxide emitted at power plants. Including these costs would increase the delivered price of coal at a typical East Coast power plant by a factor of four.

Governments have more traditional regulatory options available, for example, building codes and appliance and equipment standards. Performance standards are means whereby levels of quality are prescribed, but the means to meet those standards are left up to the manufacturers or builders.

Information is another tool for change. Consumers, be they communities or individuals, need to know how ecological is the power they purchase. Energy can be certified and labelled in the same way products can be. This is especially important when price does not yet reflect environmental costs. Programs in Sweden and Australia suggest how a labelling and logo program might work (Dunn, 1997). Certification criteria could also be worked out by GMUs or community power-buying co-ops and applied to their bulk purchases. GMUs and green community economic development programs (like Ontario's Green Communities Initiative) can apply their own criteria and standards and even provide guidebooks for consumer and co-op purchases of energy.

9

Living in De-Material World: Manufacturing, Resource Use, and Media

In a green economy, manufacturing, resource extraction, and waste management must be considered together. In nature, there is virtually no waste; every output is an input for some other process. Waste equals food. This is completely different than the industrial economy, which is marked by linear resource flows, from extraction to disposal. Our current economic cycles, limited largely to dollars, do not correspond to nature's biocycles and materials cycles. For this reason, goods production would look quite different in a green economy.

Establishing green manufacturing is perhaps the most difficult nut to crack in creating an ecological economy. While it is true that food, shelter, and energy play primary roles in creating economic self-reliance, ultimately any real transformation must take on industry. Implementing alternatives in manufacturing, however, is more difficult than in the other sectors because manufacturing requires much greater capital, and power is more centralized. It is dominated by big business, the most conservative element of society.

Manufacturing is the sector that has been the heart of industrial capitalism. Producing *things* is the core of industrialism, and, appropriately, Marx's analysis of capitalism began, in volume 1 of *Capital,* with an analysis of the commodity and how things derive their exchange-value. Once the means of production became forms of capital, the accumulation of money became synonymous with the accumulation of material things. Despite the optimism of proponents of eco-capitalism, that relationship will not change easily. By contrast, a green or postindustrial economy, as discussed earlier, is about the production of *services* and use-value.

It must be reemphasized that this has nothing to do with the pop version of the term "service economy" in countries of the North, which describes capitalism's tendency to push manufacturing into cheap labor areas of the world. In a green economy, manufacturing remains local, while *itself* becoming service-oriented, that is, it becomes fully integrated into economic processes geared to serve

human and environmental needs with the least possible consumption of resources.

Until fairly recently, substantial thinking on the question of green manufacturing was sparse, particularly in North America. What little there was came mainly
from outside mainstream industry, from critics like ecologist Barry Commoner
(1990) and designer Victor Papanek (1973). The environmental movement was
overwhelmed with largely defensive struggles, but these struggles over toxic pollution and other issues generated tremendous self-education and "citizen science"
within the movements. This helped create growing regulatory pressure that would
eventually encourage individuals within industry itself to think more seriously
about the environment.

In the past decade or so, the perspective of "industrial ecology" has emerged
from the business world and associated academics in management, engineering,
and science. Industrial ecology (or IE) basically looks at production systems as
kinds of ecosystems, as subsystems of the biosphere. Although a fairly narrow
business mentality permeates much of IE writing, the literature also exhibits a
down-to-earth understanding about industrial processes and the practical measures required to close loops. A fairly young perspective, in recent years it has become increasingly diverse, holistic and, in some cases, quite visionary. Hardin
Tibbs, for example, writing in the summer 1998 issue of *Whole Earth Review,*
put IE in the context of Lovelock's *Gaia* hypothesis of the Earth as a living
superorganism:

> Industrial ecology is the need to place the whole global-industrial system in the
> context of planetary physiology. . . . This means the emergence of a technological
> infrastructure that can harmonize with the Earth's unique biogeochemical
> processes and cycles.

Until now, IE's most practical impacts have been in company pollution-
prevention and in the design of industrial parks, but, as we will see, its basic principles have radical implications for larger social reorganization. In this section, I
will survey some of the most basic aspects of green production. To begin with,
here are a few basic principles:

1. **Production contributes to qualitative wealth.** This is the ultimate meaning
   of service- and end-use–oriented production. Wealth in a legitimately postindustrial economy can be defined only in terms of human self-development,
   community, and ecosystem regeneration. And, as Gunter Pauli (1998) argues, most forms of ecological production will be designed to target multiple purposes—such as providing gainful employment and eliminating
   poverty—in addition to their functional goals of providing for specific service needs: food, shelter, heat and light, and so on.
2. **Waste equals food.** As mentioned earlier, this principle means that all outputs and by-products should be useful. It also implies that all of these re-

source flows should be benign and nontoxic enough to be healthy food for something. Alternatively, any necessary toxic substance that serves as a "technical nutrient" must be in a tightly sealed closed loop that cannot possibly contaminate anything outside this loop. *Substitution* is an important tendency of industrial progress that is geared to replace dangerous substances with benign ones.

3. **Dematerialization of production and higher resource efficiency.** A long-term trend of economic development is the displacement of materials by information and human creativity, that is, greater resource-productivity. While this trend is partially visible in the advanced economies (in terms of per-unit inputs), it has been offset by the absolute volume of waste production and materials throughput due to economic growth. In short, the potential for resource productivity has barely been tapped. In order to really unleash this potential, the cost relationship between materials and labor must be reversed. In the "developed" capitalist economies, materials are extremely undervalued in comparison to labor. A green economy reverses this relationship, while at the same time increasing the human quality of life and quality of work.

4. **Reduction of the speed of resource flow through the economy.** This reduction is a matter not simply of cycling and recycling but of minimizing the number of transformations (which all require energy) and shortening the length of the loops. This is a big reason why reuse is more ecological than recycling.

5. **Appropriate scale.** There will likely always be "world-scale" industries and markets, simply because some technologies can be utilized, and products can be produced, more efficiently on that scale. But, in most cases, the green imperative to close loops and move with natural processes will amplify already visible postindustrial trends toward regionalization and customized production.

6. **Regenerative work is created.** Eco-industry must consider the amount and quality of work it provides. It should, whenever possible, express a bias toward *people-intensity,* given our problems of unemployment, population growth, and resource-intensity. But the *nature* of the work is also important. Not only should health and safety be a major consideration in job design, but also the need to tap and enhance human creativity should be considered. Work can be designed to be fulfilling and enjoyable. In the appropriate context, however, even routine labor can be intentionally developmental, as we see in the tedious chores of monks in a Zen monastery. Other necessary routine work can take on a regenerative quality from its social importance. For many, if not most, situations, creating meaningful work means greater levels of worker self-management and ownership. In any case, a green economy has to provide a diversity of work activities that allow a fit with the dispositions and life-situations of different people and communities.

SCALE, CRAFT, AND COMMUNITY

A common reproach to green recommendations for self-reliance and decentralization is, "Are you suggesting a return to craft production?" The simple answer is "partly."

Most of the current advocates of industrial ecology are fixated on large-scale production, very much because this is how we currently do things in the industrialized world. Concerns with mass production are certainly necessary, and I will review some key elements below. If, however, we are really serious about end-use and quality, there is a much bigger role for craft than many people imagine.

An authentic postindustrial economy, in fact, would feature a renaissance of craft expressed in many ways and on different levels. One aspect of dematerialization—a key element of real technological progress—is a trend toward smaller-scale production. The application of eco-design principles provides further possibilities to decentralize. According to John and Nancy Jack Todd (1994: 132):

> Ecological design generates new complexes and systems which make an impact on manufacturing. It has become possible to dovetail new manufacturing into communities and to integrate production, education, food production, waste treatment, housing and the environment into an ecological whole. Almost all the assembly and much of the fabrication that today is done in large plants and factories could be decentralized and transferred to small shops. In recent years sophisticated micro-electronics and machining equipment have transformed manufacturing. Increasingly, many sophisticated machines, computers, airplanes, hang gliders, boats, and even automobiles are micro-manufactured.

Even the use of small robots in home-based shops is not out of the question. Later in this chapter, we'll look at how the ecological redesign of manufacturing to emphasize the service aspect of production also provides opportunities for low-tech, smaller-scale, localized, and craft-oriented work.

This renaissance of many forms of craft work is not a regression to a previous phase of economic development but an advance on the industrial "paleotechnology" that dominated during the era of cog-labor. The well-known work of Piore and Sabel (1984) has highlighted the role of craft within some advanced forms of flexible manufacturing. Narrow forms of specialization seem to be less efficient than work forms that require deeper knowledge, improvisation, and social skills.

Ecological forms of production outside manufacturing clearly put greater emphasis on craft. For example, eco-agriculture must be both an art and a science, and green building demands a recapturing of traditional craft skills while also incorporating new kinds of knowledge, such as building science for carpenters. In manufacturing, new kinds of craft seem to be implicit in advanced production systems, but traditional artisan *handicrafts* may be relevant in goods production for a very different reason—the value placed on creative work and on handcrafted quality.

Here I am not talking simply about "niche markets" for those who can pay big bucks. I mean an end to the *productivist economy-of-labor-time* through the application of a radical end-use approach to needs, goods, time, and life. With the establishment of the postwar waste economy, the relationship between time spent in labor and real qualitative returns grew increasingly irrational. Despite the fact that more and more goods could be produced more cheaply, many of the goods themselves were of questionable value. On one hand, the fabrication of ridiculous alienated "needs" created demand for totally superfluous goods. On the other hand, poor urban and economic design created needs for otherwise unnecessary goods and services.

This is quite obvious in transportation. The fragmentation of urban space made auto-mobility a necessity, especially when workplaces were located so far from home. A vicious cycle was created. The cost of the car, gas, insurance, and maintenance now had to be obtained from the wage, and one needed the car to have the wage. In his classic essay *Energy and Equity,* Ivan Illich (1974) pointed out that the typical American male then devoted more than 1,600 hours a year to his car, driving about 7,500 miles. That works out to 5 miles for each hour, about the same as walking speeds in underdeveloped nations. According to Illich:

> What distinguished the traffic in rich countries from the traffic in poor countries is not more mileage per hour of life-time for the majority, but more hours of compulsory consumption of high doses of energy, packaged and unequally distributed by the transportation industry.

The industrial obsession with producing the greatest volumes of things in the shortest time has little to do with providing use-value, since even consumer needs must be artificially created to make the system work. There are parallels in every sector of the economy. Dominguez and Robin (1992) explore a related theme in *Your Money or Your Life* while showing ways to short-circuit the insanity of needing money to satisfy every need.

The industrial system has become an economy of middlemen and of endless mindless maintenance activities that do an end-run around basic needs. Various writers on economic self-reliance, such as Douthwaite, Roberts and Brandum, Shuman, and Morris, have shown how savings on cheap mass-produced goods are largely false savings, partly because the money usually leaves the community. It doesn't cycle back and provide the spender with employment or demand for his or her own production.

When we are serious about creating qualitative wealth, strict narrow criteria of labor-time in production can no longer be binding. The benefits of craft for the producer, the consumer, and the community may far outweigh the benefits of mass production in many cases.

The productivist economy-of-labor-time is closely connected with industrial capitalism's focus on labor-productivity. A green economy's emphasis on resource-productivity should go a long way to change that, but it is also necessary to explicitly undercut the tyranny of money, that ultimate embodiment of abstract quantity. It is the scarcity of money that, more often than not, will force people both to buy bad quality at an apparently cheap price and to take jobs to do socially destructive work. In a variation on this theme, Michael Rowbotham dramatically illustrates in his book *The Grip of Death* (1998) how institutionalized debt has functioned to drive irrational export war, long-distance trade, and the production of low-quality, rapidly obsolescent goods.

It is possible to create money systems that allow people to put quality first and consider more carefully what they really want and need. In the next chapter, on money, I will look more closely at the role of community currencies—especially post-scarcity account money (like the Local Employment Trading System [LETS])—and their role in facilitating regenerative production of all sorts. When money is not scarce, people's relationship to labor-time is often transformed. They will frequently choose re-creative and aesthetic work over leisure and "free time." And they may choose to pay more to local craftspeople for more beautiful high-quality items.

THE NEW INDUSTRIAL ECO-STRUCTURE

Larger-scale manufacturing certainly has its place in a green economy, but to become regenerative, it must be completely transformed. It has to change both its *purpose* and its organizational *forms*. In this section, I will focus mainly on its form and shape. The most important priority is designing manufacturing systems to work within, or mimic the structure of, natural systems.

In this vein, Robert Frosch (1992: 800) summarizes some of the fundamentals of industrial ecology:

> The idea of an industrial ecology is based upon a straightforward analogy with natural ecological systems. In nature an ecological system operates through a web of connections in which organisms live and consume each other and each other's waste. The system has evolved so that the characteristic of communities of living organisms seems to be that nothing that contains available energy or useful material will be lost. There will evolve some organism that will manage to make its living by dealing with any waste product that provides available energy or usable material. Ecologists talk of a food web: an interconnection of uses of both organisms and their wastes. In the industrial context we may think of this as being use of products and waste products. The system structure of a natural ecology and the structure of an industrial system, or an economic system, are extremely similar.

Industrial ecologists distinguish between the relatively closed systems of nature (like the carbon, nitrogen, and hydrological cycles), which constantly cycle nutrients, and the linear open industrial systems of today, which recycle very little and dispose of much. While some commentators have argued that there can be no such thing as a completely closed industrial system that eliminates all waste (Jackson, 1996), the potential to reduce waste is nevertheless so vast as to create the possibility of a radically different kind of economy.

Many of the ideas about industrial ecology emerged gradually from efforts to find more effective and economical alternatives to conventional "end of pipe" environmental cleanup. "Pollution prevention" (or P2) is the term applied to various preventative or efficiency measures at the level of the firm or individual process. There is a vast and growing literature documenting the big money that many large corporations, such as Dow Chemical, 3M, Dupont, and Chevron, have saved through eco-efficiency and P2 measures, often by soliciting suggestions from the company's workers (Jackson, 1996; Fiksel, 1996; Allenby and Richards, 1994).

Pollution prevention action is reinforced by technological developments that allow smaller scale, greater energy and materials efficiencies, and greater use of recycled materials. Minimills in steel are the best-known example (Kane, 1996).

Infinitely greater efficiencies are possible, however, when whole industries, or networks of firms, are considered. The most well-known examples of industrial ecology or "industrial symbiosis" are industrial park developments like the one in Kalundborg, Denmark. At the Kalundborg development, various producers, including a power plant, a gyproc producer, a fish farm, a pharmaceutical plant, and an oil refinery, are using one another's waste heat and by-products in addition to providing steam for the town's district heating system (Tibbs, 1992). Kalundborg is a spontaneous example, a result of a desire by the various companies to save money and increase efficiency. It stands as an important pioneering effort, but one that can certainly be improved upon through conscious design. Coal-fired power plants and oil refineries hardly rank as ecological forms of production, even when they are embedded in an industrial ecosystem.

Kalundborg has, however, set an important precedent and inspired many other efforts in creating both new (greenfield) parks and abandoned urban (brownfield) sites. In the United States, the President's Council for Sustainable Development has created an Eco-Industrial Park Demonstration Team, which has selected four national demonstration sites, including ones in Chattanooga, Tennessee; Brownsville, Texas; Baltimore, Maryland; and the Tidewater area of Virginia. The city of Chattanooga features four different "eco-industrial parks" connected, directly or indirectly, to its sustainable city initiative. One is called the SMART Park, which intends to

integrate the energy, water, and waste flows of Eureka Foundry, Seaboard Farms, Finley Stadium, the Trade Center expansion, and other businesses in the area, including manufacturers, hotels, restaurants, supermarkets, retailers, and offices. Additional Southside SMART Park components would include a clean fuel ethanol facility, produce greenhouse, tree farm nursery, fish farm, and an eco-block and building products manufacturing facility. Integrating new and renovated Southside housing into the energy and waste flow cycles would also create mutual benefits. (Sustainable Chattanooga, 1997)

Other initiatives have been undertaken in Dartmouth, Nova Scotia (Cote et al., 1994), and South Yorkshire, England. The latter example is a planned "zero discharge" microbrewery/aquaculture/hydroponic horticulture operation in collaboration with England's Earth Centre. A particularly ambitious effort in Japan, scheduled for a year 2000 completion, is the Fujisawa Factory eco-industrial park, in collaboration with the Zero Emissions Research Initiative at the United Nations University and the Japanese Ministry of International Trade and Industry. According to Raymond Cote (1998), it

> will combine industrial, commercial, agricultural, residential and recreational components into a multifaceted community. The Fujisawa Factory park will include technologies and features in energy conservation and cascading, renewable energy, conversion of waste into energy, solar greenhouses, waste water treatment using wetlands, reuse of treated waste water, conversion of ash and other wastes into cement and ceramics, reuse and recycling of materials, etc. The park will be supported by a zero emission center, an environmental clinic and a logistics center.

Cornell University's Work and Environment Initiative (1998) is involved in some cutting-edge projects, including the Baltimore eco-industrial park. Its initiatives are particularly significant because of the efforts to include organized labor into the planning process. (It is, however, important that the union movement makes a concerted effort to develop its own autonomous perspective on eco-industrial development.)

The Cornell project is also unique in being one of the first to advocate expanding the scope of industrial ecology design to *flexible manufacturing networks (FMNs)* for essentially bioregional development. FMNs are networks of companies that combine to produce collaboratively what they cannot produce individually. In the past decade, the FMNs of north-central Italy have captured the attention of development planners and cooperators because of the success of their human-scale enterprises. Many of the Italian examples feature high-tech production for world market niches, but they illustrate the potential of cooperation in even the most advanced forms of manufacturing. This kind of cooperation is essential for the generalization of ecological organization in industry. The creation of an ecological economy is essentially a matter of creating networks of networks, complexes of industrial ecosystems engaged in symbiotic relationships within and without.

Aspects of IE that apply in some way to all levels of production involve improvements in materials efficiency and cleaner process technology; minimizing waste of raw materials; "cascading" the use of materials in reuse; finding good uses for waste products; extending product life in various ways; and using product redesign to facilitate all these goals. Products, materials, and processes must all distinguish between those that are intrinsically dissipative and those that allow recycling. For example, most coatings, pigments, pesticides, fuels, lubricants, and fire retardants fall into the first category, while most structural metals fall into the second category. Substitution of more benign materials, processes, and even end-products is a key strategy of industrial ecology. Later, I will return to product design and materials choice.

Ecological economic design on a grand scale will have to take into account that any industrial system must stay within the capacity of its surrounding natural ecosystem. No matter how tight the industrial system, there will be leaks. Besides spatial linkages, connections between phases within industries must also be considered.

Our existing economy is generally divided into three phases: (1) production of materials (extraction, separation or refining, and physical and chemical preparation to produce finished materials); (2) manufacture of products; and (3) customer product cycle. Our current competitive capitalist economy presents substantial barriers to the cooperation necessary for closing the loops within and between all areas. In particular, the rules of the economic game compel manufacturing and extraction companies to *produce more* in order to survive and prosper. That basic fact must change through new rules for resource and product stewardship. Until that time, new enlightened forms of ecological FMNs can establish relationships that support service-provision (for end-products of the network).

It is certainly true that some of the initiatives for eco-industrial parks and networks thus far lack an authentic ecological vision, and some even support brown industries by making them more efficient. Nevertheless, the whole phenomenon of eco-industrial development is absolutely central to creating green economies. The fact that eventually the profit motive will have to be displaced by a broader range of economic incentives does not mean that we shouldn't seek to make eco-production as profitable as possible in the existing market economy. The Cornell initiative insists that eco-industrial park development should bring returns on assets of 30 to 50 percent above the industry average.

THE CLOSED-LOOP ECONOMY

A groundbreaking book by Robin Murray (1999), *Creating Wealth from Waste*, highlights the clash between two distinct organizational mentalities involved in current struggles over waste. Although focused on possibilities for municipal recycling in England, Murray's analysis and proposals are relevant to most of the industrialized world. His starting point is the well-documented benefits of recycling: environmental, social, and economic. They include the reduction of greenhouse gases, the cutting of toxic pollution, energy conservation (recycling saves three to five times as much energy as does incineration), massive job creation, and reduced materials costs. Murray argues that, even without considering income from the sale of secondary (recycled) materials, a three-stream recycling system is cost-neutral—a sharp contrast to both landfill and incineration. Add to this the reality of a long-term increase in materials prices, and the potential of value-added.

Why then have not all the major capitalist countries moved to take advantage of these benefits? Some—such as Germany and Denmark—have actually begun. But others have not, and in recent years, recycling in many places has come under increasing attack as too expensive and "uneconomic" compared to conventional disposal and incineration. Such defenders of recycling as Canadian Daniel Scott (1999) have pointed out that this attack fails to acknowledge not only the full benefits of recycling but also the full costs of landfill and incineration. Existing markets for resources, waste, and energy, Scott argues, have been deliberately shaped in Canada by the long-time government policy of maintaining resource extraction as the core of the Canadian economy. The entire infrastructure of the economy is biased against secondary materials industry, albeit at great cost.

Murray takes this insight several steps further in his analysis and proposed development strategies. Waste management, he writes, is presently experiencing a conflict between two antithetical forms of "modernization":

1. **The "chemico-energy" mode:** centralized and capital-intensive, its main instrument is incineration, a form of disposal that allows the traditional linear extraction-to-disposal economy to remain intact; and
2. **"Eco-modernization":** the closed-loop economy, featuring more complex flows and simple or specialist treatment. Its key innovations are in collection, not in high-tech plants.

Murray zeroes in on the "perverse markets" where the biggest profits are in the most economically and environmentally destructive modes of waste management. He shows that in the case of England, this is due to skewed and misdirected incentives and bad tax design—policies and mechanisms that also reinforce inefficient monopoly relationships. Murray makes specific proposals for tax redesign that not only readjust incentives but create funds to underwrite secondary materials prices and provide needed stability for local authorities and small collection enterprises. The "problem of markets," he shows convincingly, is financial, not physical. That is, the problem is not capacity of industry to absorb recycled materials, but problems of price and financial planning for the small players who are crucial to the system.

According to Murray, the destructive effects of "perverse markets" are inextricably connected to the power of "perverse institutions." While markets for recycled materials are global and constantly growing, intensive recycling demands a decentralization of collection and a relocalization of many forms of production.

Intensive recycling is labor- and knowledge-intensive and is adapted to the localities involved. It thrives in diversity, and it requires skills in social marketing, household interaction, materials quality control, and sensitivity to the special needs of material processors. The degree of community participation and prosumption involved requires a new kind of eco-citizen culture.

By contrast, the existing waste industry is structured around disposal, which has shaped its institutional and professional culture. As Murray writes, "recycling demands the skills of a modern retailer, not a transporter of aggregates," which in fact is the background of the dominant waste corporations. Many government authorities also tend to prefer dealing with the big disposal companies and their simple yet costly capital-intensive solutions. Lobbyists for the "chemico-energy" solution include former stalwarts of the nuclear industry who have moved into incineration in a big way.

Robin Murray's analysis for the London Planning Advisory Committee, in collaboration with the Demos Working Cities project, culminated in a "Program for Zero Waste." Just a few of its imaginative provisions are a revision of waste taxes; the creation of "zero waste fund" from disposal taxes, which could stabilize secondary material prices; a Green Academy to build relevant skills; a "closed loop industrialisation initiative"; and a Zero Waste Agency. The agency would act as a "system entrepreneur" to catalyze and coordinate cross-boundary relations between the various players in intensive recycling.

Although his focus is on relationships on the first level, Murray emphasizes that "eco-modernization" is a three-level process: (1) recycling, based in four-stream separation at the household/community level; (2) reprocessing of secondary materials; and, ultimately, (3) product design, which intends to make the first two steps easier or even unnecessary. The focus of Murray's study is the first level and collection, which connects the household and the reprocessors. This is the process of creating the secondary materials industry, of displacing the extraction industry with the "mining of the waste stream."

A certain amount of virgin material will always be needed, but in a green economy this amount would be a minuscule fraction of today's extraction industry. Primary industry is disproportionately responsible for pollution and resource use. Worldwatch Institute researchers have called attention to the fact that in the United States, just four primary (extraction and preprocessing) industries account for 71 percent of all toxic emissions: chemicals, metals, paper, and plastics. Five primary industries use 31 percent of energy: paper, steel, aluminium, plastics, and container glass (Young and Sachs, 1994).

A focus on secondary materials would not only create new kinds of work in design and materials handling but also increase the labor-intensity (and knowledge-intensity) of almost all industries. Murray's study estimated that intensive recycling could stimulate the creation of between forty thousand and fifty-five thousand jobs—fifteen thousand of them in collection.

While the work of Murray and others in recycling is important, much of this importance lies in catalyzing a process that should—through reduction and reuse—ultimately make much recycling unnecessary. Mining the waste stream is only a step in the elimination of the concept of waste altogether. Ultimately, the whole concept of "waste management" must be overturned and replaced with one of resource stewardship.

In *The Ecology of Commerce* (1993), Paul Hawken wrote that if all households recycled all their products and materials, the entire economy's waste stream would be reduced only 1 to 2 percent. This is because so much of the waste is generated upstream from final consumption—in extraction and processing. Despite the waste endemic to mass consumption, there has been a tendency throughout this century for the most waste-generating activities to move upstream from household to industry (Brower and Leon, 1999). In *Natural Capitalism* (1999), Hawken, Lovins, and Lovins point out that a single laptop computer generates four thousand times its weight in waste. Economist Robert Ayres estimates that only 6 percent of minerals and renewable resources extracted get embodied in final products, that is, 94 percent is waste (Whitaker, 1994). Hawken, Lovins, and Lovins go farther, arguing that only about 1 percent of all materials mobilized to serve North America is actually made into products and still in use six months after sale. They add that only 2 percent of the total waste stream is recycled.

Reuse plays a special role in the creation of eco-production that is geared to providing such services as nutrition, access, entertainment, and shelter. All "loops" are not the same. Recycling establishes a loop, but it is fairly big and requires a fair amount of energy input. Perhaps most importantly, it leaves intact both traditional capitalist property relationships and incentives for ever-expanding material sales and use. While certainly much more ecological than the extraction industry, recycling is nevertheless consistent with globalization and its long-distance economy.

It is utilization-focused service activities that really begin to create tight loops by extending a product or material's lifetime. "Technological upgrading," "reconditioning and remanufacturing," "repair," and "reuse" form a continuum of decreasing materials and energy intensity, and greater labor-intensity. The continuum corresponds to potentials for decentralization and local production. These reutilization activities also reduce the speed of flow of materials through the economy, something that recycling does not do (Stahel, 1994).

Walter Stahel argues that reuse—that is, selling reutilization—should be a more profitable activity as well. The reason corporations today prefer recycling to reuse, he writes, is that recycling carries a limited product and material lifecycle liability. Selling utilization puts a "cradle to grave" responsibility for the product in the hands of the company. Designing reutilization, and such liability, into the economy would result in new levels of quality and innovation associated with adaptability and durability. An economic focus on reutilization would transform the nature of manufacturing activity into service-oriented production. Operational leasing, rather than outright ownership purchase, would become the predominant form of transaction for a major portion of the economy. Models for this service focus already exist in the marketing strategies of Xerox, Interface Flooring, and others.

PRODUCT DESIGN AND PRODUCT STEWARDSHIP

A focus on reutilization and use-value raises once again the centrality of design. Materials in today's economy are not easily recyclable because they are not designed to be recycled. Closing loops is much easier if products are *designed* to recycle and reuse. Many products today are amalgams or composites of various materials that are difficult, impossible, or expensive to separate. Mixing materials is the big no-no of recycling. As Paul Connett (1993) emphasizes, discarded materials that are mixed are "garbage"; if kept separate, they are "resources." It is not enough to mine the waste stream; it must be transformed into a resource stream.

It is important to recognize that not only are products today designed in ways that make recycling and reuse difficult, but they are typically designed for a scale that is not conducive to closed loops. Many products are designed for long-distance transport, as packaging or to be contained within packaging. They are often designed for world markets and for advertising display. A shift in the predominant scale of economic organization toward the bioregional level would automatically make ecological product design even more sensible and economic. For example, bottle or container reuse is much easier in a local or regional system.

Ecological product design, along with process design, is part of an emergent manufacturing discipline called "design for environment" (DFE). Unlike previous forms of management, DFE must go beyond considerations that affect a company's bottom line. It is, however, consistent with a contemporary trend in industrial design commonly known as "integrated product development," where all aspects of a product's life cycle—including its manufacturability, its distribution and marketing, and its maintenance—are considered from the beginning of product design. Sensible as this sounds, it has not always been the case, because traditional industrial product development usually followed a sequential approach of successive specialists: design, layout, testing, and so on (Fiksel, 1996).

DFE plans for reusability and dismantling, for recyclability, for toxics reduction, for low embodied energy, for durability, and perhaps for disposability/compostability. It must consider both the *source* of its materials and the *impact* of the product's production and use. For this reason, it needs information that goes well beyond normal concerns of the firm.

Design for disassembly is probably the best-known form of DFE and has been used by such companies as Volkswagen, BMW, and NCR Canada. Many of the components of "dying" products can be reincarnated—reused, or resold, or reconditioned. Some products can have their worn parts replaced and themselves find a new lifetime (Papanek, 1995). "Resource cascading," similar to energy cascading in a soft-energy system, attempts to make the most out of products, parts, chemicals, and materials at each level as they degrade. Cascade "chains" can be designed that not only utilize resources in the chain as they degrade but at strategic points can be shifted to other chains where their utility will be greater (Fiksel, 1996).

Numerous criteria are involved in materials selection and product design, and these criteria are somewhat different for different products. "Life Cycle Assessment" (LCA) is a means whereby many of the environmental impacts of a product or material can be evaluated over its entire lifetime. Although the discipline is very young, the procedures not standardized, and the results quite approximate, LCA is being applied to an increasing number of situations as a means to improve production processes (de Oude, 1993; Young and Vanderburg, 1994; Van der Ryn and Cowan, 1996).

Corporate applications of LCA and DFE are certainly commendable if they go beyond public relations, but most well-intended efforts still fall far short of the radical overhaul of industrial production that is required for sustainability. The problem isn't gradualism or incrementalism; it's that the ultimate goals are not qualitative.

William McDonough and Michael Braungart (1998) have called attention to the fact that, if we were truly serious about design for environment, we would have to rule out the use of most of the chemicals currently in commercial use. The partners—one an architect, the other a chemist—were involved in an effort to develop an environmentally benign fabric that could be composted at the end of its life cycle. Of the 8,000 chemicals considered, 7,962 were eliminated. The fabric, and in fact an entire line of fabrics, was created using only 38 chemicals.

Industrial ecologist Hardin Tibbs (1998) sees this extremely selective use of substances as a pattern for eco-manufacturing. The key, he writes,

> would be first to identify a set of materials which have long-term geophysiological compatibility. A fairly small set of acceptable materials could probably be used to supply eighty percent or more of all production needs. The next step would be to devise clusters of production processes which use some or all these materials, and which can be interlocked ecosystem-style. Once this was done, the resulting industrial clusters or industrial ecosystems might stand a reasonable chance of being stable over time.

Braungart, who is a professor for process engineering at Technical University of Northeast Lower Saxony, and McDonough, who was dean of architecture at the University of Virginia, have formed their own design firm, which can help other companies implement more fundamentally ecological production processes. They have devised their own index of sustainability, which includes technical, economic, aesthetic, social justice, and ecological criteria.

Through their consulting company, Braungart and McDonough seem to be taking voluntary product stewardship to a new level, one that incorporates a fairly radical version of the stewardship ethic right into the product design process. This goes well beyond the voluntary stewardship efforts of a number of large corporations, such as Hewlett Packard, AT&T, and the chemical industry through its Responsible Care program. But it seems very unlikely that McDonough and Braungart's kind of stewardship will be generalized through voluntary action. The state must institutionalize new forms of liability that can level the playing field and create appropriate incentives.

Braungart (1994), who in 1982 established Greenpeace Germany's chemistry department, would be aware of this. In the early 1990s, his Environmental Protection Encouragement Agency proposed an economy-scale product stewardship system that has received widespread attention, particularly in writings by Paul Hawken (1993).

Braungart's "Intelligent Product System" is based on the classification of products into three categories:

1. **Consumables** are products that are meant to be completely consumed in one use, such as food or soap powder. They must be completely safe to be absorbed by the natural environment.
2. **Products of service** are items like televisions, cars, and washing machines. The materials in these products might not be so benign in their environmental impacts, but they would be more tightly constrained in terms of disposal. Typically, they would be leased to the customer. At the end of their useful product lives, they would be returned to the producer, where they would be dismantled and recycled back into production in some way. Producers would be responsible for this recycling, and so they would have great incentive to design their products for disassembly.

   Braungart suggests another institution to reinforce patterns of recycling and disassembly: the "waste supermarket," which would be a centralized location where consumers could "de-shop" by returning used service products, including packaging. It would not be a dump site but a source separation depot.
3. **Unmarketables** are products and materials that cannot be consumed or used in any environmentally sound way. They might, for example, be toxic products like used lead-cadmium batteries. Braungart recommends that they be safely stored—at cost to their original producers—in state-owned "waste parking lots" in perpetuity until such time as society found a way to safely dispose of or use the products. This cost to producers would supply some pressure to create products that could either be recycled endlessly or, more likely, be made of more benign materials.

Such a product stewardship system would be part and parcel of a new kind of regulatory framework, which would include other kinds of performance standards and product or material bans. While this may sound as controlling as state socialism, it actually allows a great measure of self-regulation. The focus is on changing the rules of the game, rather than intervening in the details of economic life as Fordist and statist regulation has done. And typically, for every restriction on harmful production, there is an opportunity for regenerative enterprise.

BEYOND PETROCHEMICALS: BENIGN MATERIALS AND THE CARBOHYDRATE ECONOMY

As Tibbs argued above, a focus of green product stewardship would be to get the most out of a relatively small set of benign materials. One important responsibility of the state would be to assist producers in appropriate substitution for toxic materials, substances, and processes.

A major factor in both product and economic design is toxicity. Hazardous waste and toxic pollution are something quite different from questions of efficiency, materials throughput, and even economic growth. Toxicity and pollution are not always simple matters. Toxic substances occur in nature, and supposedly even natural materials can be poisons for humans and other species. But by and large, toxicity in nature is localized. The toxic pollution of our industrial civilization, on the other hand, is vast and endemic. We have created massive amounts of synthetic substances that neither natural systems nor our own immune systems can tolerate.

This has happened in a very short time. According to Tim Jackson (1996), "In 1900, even after 150 years of industrialization, over half of the total materials in use (excluding those used for fuels and for foods) were still provided by agricultural, wildlife and forestry products." The postwar period saw an explosion in the creation of new materials based in petrochemical production. In the United States, the petrochemical industry is responsible for the majority of toxic pollution; only about 1 percent of the industry's hazardous waste is destroyed; and all Superfund sites are petrochemical related. According to Barry Commoner (1990), if all the chemical industry's toxic material could be properly disposed of at the going rate for incineration ($100/ton), the total annual cost of cleaning up this mess would be about $20 billion—or $17.4 billion more than the industry's 1986 after-tax profits! Globally, 40 percent of toxic pollution from manufacturing derives from the chemical industry (Jackson, 1996).

By no means is the chemical industry the only source of hazardous waste and toxic pollution, but it has been more strategic to the capitalist waste economy than any other industry. Besides being a major polluter in its own right, a large portion of its end-products are intrinsically damaging and provide the means of destruction to other industries (for example, agriculture, which is the largest source of nonpoint pollution due to chemical runoff). Its products have been essential in both extending production/consumption loops (plastic packaging, transport fuel) and breaking or distorting natural cycles (nitrate fertilizers).

Petrochemical products certainly have a place in a green economy. Although burning petrochemicals as a transportation fuel is an intrinsically polluting and dissipative use, petrochemicals can be a source of extremely durable and flexible materials—when employed intelligently. This should, however, be only a limited and discriminating use. There are many and growing alternatives to most current uses of petrochemicals.

At the core of the current destructive petrochemical industry is chlorine, widely used as an industrial feedstock in a number of sectors. Chlorinated organic compounds include PCBs, CFCs, dioxins, furans, and other well-known destructive substances (Commoner, 1992; Jackson, 1996; Hawken, 1993). As a class of chemicals, organochlorines pose one of the most dangerous, widespread—and unnecessary—threats to life on the planet (Colburn, Dumanoski, and Myers, 1996). Some of these chemicals are made deliberately, but many—like dioxin—are made spontaneously as a by-product of chlorine use or waste plastics incineration (Gibbs, 1995).

Increasingly, environmentalists and scientists are recognizing that the struggle to ban chlorine is a key to establishing ecological relationships and benign materials production in manufacturing industry. What is in question is not establishing "acceptable" levels of toxins, but whether or not we will be able to create a healthy and ecological basis for production, where "waste equals food."

One fortuitous development for the creation of green industry has been a revolution in biological science over the past couple decades. This is the very same revolution that is bringing us nightmares of imperialistic science in genetic engineering. There are, however, more positive developments, such as biotechnology and its "living machine" natural water treatment and breakthroughs in biochemicals.

Biochemicals are one element of an emerging Carbohydrate Economy, or the industrial use of plant materials. These uses include the use of hemp in textiles, building materials, and industrial products; the use of straw and other agriculture waste products to make building materials; and the use of biochemicals to replace petrochemicals in a growing range of applications.

In the nineteenth century, the first plastics were made from plant materials, for example, celluloid (movie film) and cellophane tape from cellulose. The postwar oil-based economy almost eliminated plant-based chemistry. In recent years, however, technological advances in biological processing have allowed easier separation of plant components and their manufacture into products that can economically compete with fossil fuel–based products. At the same time, petrochemicals are becoming more expensive because environmental regulations are forcing petrochemical producers to internalize their real costs (Morris and Ahmed, 1993).

Biochemical production and use are not intrinsically benign. Biochemicals that are chemically identical to petrochemicals can be made. However, whether substitution is made directly, indirectly (using a functionally but not chemically similar biochemical), or as a whole end product (the most benign substitution), biochemicals typically result in substantially less pollution. Dyes, degradable plastics, inks, paints, detergents, adhesives, cleaners, and plasticizers are examples of bioproducts that are even now found on the market (Morris, Ahmed, and Pettijohn, 1994).

While there is always a danger that agribusiness will attempt to "mine the soil" for biomass, the Institute for Local Self-Reliance estimates that all necessary raw materials for biochemicals production in the United States can come from the 350 million tons of agricultural waste disposed of each year (Morris and Ahmed, 1993).

Biochemicals are just one of the many products that growing sophistication in biomass utilization is making possible. Low-THC hemp is the best known example of a plant material that promises major dividends in displacing more destructive, less versatile and durable products (Hemptech, 1995). Every part of the hemp plant can be used for such applications as building materials (fibreboard and insulation), clothing, food (cooking oils and spreads), and more.

Straw, a major agricultural waste product, is another material that is finding useful applications, particularly in building materials (Lorenz, 1995). Various kinds of sheetgoods are using straw as a key component, and old-fashioned straw-bale construction techniques are being revived as modern builders are finding it cheap, strong, durable, and insulating (Steen et al, 1994). Nontoxic insulation materials are hard to find. Straw has the advantage of being completely benign for both human and environmental health; building with straw also makes good use of a waste product whose annual burning is responsible for high carbon emissions.

The revival of interest in employing plant materials for industrial purposes holds great promise not only for the revival of rural towns but also for more ecological industries in "green cities." Modern industrial capitalism has always valued oil-based materials because of their mobility. Materials could be extracted and processed far away from the point of extraction. A postindustrial green economy puts much more emphasis on regionalism and closing production/consumption loops as tightly as possible.

Hemp, straw, and other biomaterials cannot be transported as easily as oil, but this is not a problem because it is desirable to process them close to where they are grown. Making good use of the natural productivity of the landscape can help create dynamic bioregional economies which employ nature's benign materials in various ways.

One of the most interesting developments emerging from the Carbohydrate Economy is the work of Gunter Pauli (1998) and his colleagues at the Zero Emissions Research Initiative (ZERI), based in the United Nations University in

Tokyo. Pauli was previously founder and president of Ecover, the well-known environmental products company. He was suddenly faced with the realization that the soaps and cleansers his company produced, while slightly reducing pollution of German rivers, generated massive waste in Latin America, the source of Ecover's raw materials. Pauli saw the need—and the possibility—of producing plant-based benign materials through ecological "industrial clusters" that would make productive use of all materials, residues, and by-products. He saw that, by applying an ecosystem approach that generated "value-added" on multiple levels, an "upsizing" process could be initiated that would provide benefits to all stakeholders, and not simply shareholders. ZERI has spawned a number of innovative projects in various parts of the world, including the Fujisawa Factory eco-industrial park described by Raymond Cote above.

Pauli puts great emphasis on making plantations, particularly in the tropics, into "biorefineries." Currently, these plantations are embodiments of monoculture, producing single products with incredible amounts of waste. These same plantations could, however, provide vitamins, adhesives, oils, fibers, food, beer, and much more from symbiotic processes that produce no harmful emissions. At the same time, they can provide much of the planet's necessary cellulose—from fast-growing crops like bamboo, sugar cane, rattan and oil palm—saving the wasteful use of trees like spruce, pine, and fir. From serious carbon dioxide generators, they can become major carbons sinks.

The key to ZERI's methodology is a creative *output-input* visioning process that can complement the traditional P2 input-output methodology. That is, finding safe and productive uses for all outputs of a process can generate unpredictable benefits and "value added" far beyond the efficient use of existing inputs. But this requires broad knowledge and a desire to cooperate with other producers, community stakeholders, and others in order to realize the optimal productivity of not just the firm but also the surrounding community and ecosystem.

COMMUNITY CONSUMERISM AND SHARING

Along with regenerative enterprises and an enlightened state, a third element seems necessary to ensure resource stewardship: new institutions of cooperative consumption and collective consumerism. One of their essential tools is information, and they are closely connected with residential communities moving beyond passive consumption to prosumption, that is, to produce as well as consume, in an increasingly integrated way.

As will be discussed more generally in the final chapter, information in the hands of the community can provide a self-regulatory function. It can have much greater impact than simply individual knowledge can. To achieve transformed relationships to things and resources, "green consumerism," as exercised by informed and ethical *individuals,* certainly has its place. But as a strategy for change in itself, it has major drawbacks. "Shop 'til you drop" is never a solution, no matter how green the products. Creating demand for more environmental products does little to guarantee the overall reduction of materials use. The isolation of consumers and households created by industrialization is itself wasteful and must be overcome. In addition, as Gary Gardner (1999) points out, the trend of corporate capitalism today is toward the concentration of ownership in private hands, and this privatization fuels a drastic polarization of income between rich and poor. In this context, *sharing* can be a crucial means of encouraging social equity as well as ecological efficiency.

Purely individual green consumerism finds its expression in the energy sector as "retail wheeling." In the chapter on energy, I mentioned how this so-called "direct access" of individual consumers to various energy generators has tended to undercut community conservation efforts in many areas. While this ostensibly gives enlightened consumers choice to purchase clean energy, in practice retail wheeling gives *generators* direct access to the *wallets* of isolated, uninformed, and unorganized consumers.

With energy, plugging leaks should be done prior to purchasing energy, and to be most effective, much of this conservation work must be done on the community level as well as in the household or business. It therefore makes sense for the community to do the external energy purchasing, through a kind of "wholesale wheeling," while it coordinates and prioritizes conservation work. A green municipal utility (GMU) is the community vehicle for this, an agent of collective consumerism that has the information and the bargaining power to get the best prices for clean energy. The GMU also has the power to buy external power in ways that can facilitate the development of renewable energy generation *within* the community, also creating long-term benefits in job creation and community empowerment.

The same principle applies to products and materials. Communities can make incredible savings by pooling the use and purchase of many products. Cars are the most obvious examples, and auto sharing co-ops have emerged in many cities throughout the developed world. So-called consumer durables, or what Braungart (1994) calls "products of service," are also used inefficiently. As the Wuppertal Institute's *Sustainable Germany* report (Sachs et al., 1998: 23) says:

> The calculation is simple. A product that is utilized twice as frequently during its lifetime than something comparable reduces the number of goods in circulation by 50 percent. However, washing machines, cars, vacuum cleaners, ladders, lawn-mowers, ski equipment, etc. are usually only used for a few hours or days and then stand around uselessly for most of their lifetime.

The alternative is a range of community co-ops, businesses, and centers that can not only save resources but also provide various other social and economic benefits. Industrial designer Victor Papanek (1973, 1995) has long proposed neighbourhood centers that can double as social centers, laundries, and warehouses for tools and appliances. In chapter 7, we discussed the feminist neighborhood and building designs, which included community kitchens, laundries, and so on in the physical structure of the community (Hayden, 1981, 1984). It is probably the feminist design tradition—dating to the material feminists of the nineteenth century—that supplies the richest body of thinking on prosumption, which fuses individual and social needs. Today, as many people are searching for more fulfilling—and more efficient—models of housing design than the nuclear family detached home that dominated North American development during the twentieth century, more people should be open to the feminist designs. Some cohousing groups, for example, have provided for various forms of collective consumption and facility-sharing in their housing clusters in both Europe and North America.

Local governments as well as community co-ops can potentially exercise a major influence on manufacturing through their procurement policies. Not only can they stimulate demand for reused and reconditioned goods, but they can also support the development of cutting-edge eco-production like biochemicals, hemp, and other plant-based industry (see the next section).

Community retrofit programs, which until now have been largely preoccupied with energy and water conservation, also have great potential as forms of community consumerism. In chapter 7, I surveyed the Ontario Green Communities Initiative (GCI), which attempted to combine "home greenup" inspections with a directory to support local green products and industry. Such creation of demand for green production was premised on the *overall reduction* of materials throughput, implicit in audit recommendations. It provided market power to empower the Green Communities programs to approach manufacturers with recommendations for new (or reconditioned) eco-products, essentially providing guaranteed markets for the producers. The GCI also enlisted the cooperation of local credit unions, which were going to distribute discount cards to their members that could support purchase of certified green materials. There was also some discussion of involving the local LETSystem community currency to further stimulate this regenerative prosumption.

Unfortunately a change in government undermined, or at least delayed, this particular initiative of the GCI, but it nevertheless remains a valid strategy. In fact, it seems very unlikely that a fundamental transformation of manufacturing and resource use can take place without this kind of community-based pressure. Questions of eco-production are ultimately questions of end-use, and community initiatives have the potential to ripple back substantially into manufacturing and extraction.

The development of alternative indicators of regenerative wealth, moreover, must take place at the local and regional levels to best reflect the social and environmental needs of those areas. Forms of cooperative consumerism and community prosumption go hand in hand with participatory planning on the local level. While it is true that the state must play an important role in changing the economic rules, it is unlikely that even many local governments will take such initiatives until community self-organization forces them to do so. And even when the rules are changed, there will still be a need for product-sharing on the community level. Such sharing not only saves material resources but enriches community bonds and quality of life.

ADVANCED TECHNOLOGY AND THE INFORMATION ECONOMY

It should be clear by now that the green economy is not an antitechnology back-to-the-land movement. Technological development has been a crucial factor in the emergence of postindustrial potentials for humanity, but our current stage of development, based in human self-actualization, makes it ever more important to resist seeing technology as a separate thing. The technological extension of our senses and functions has now moved from the extension of our muscles and bodily controls to the extension of our minds and nervous systems through electronic media.

This extension has helped put cultural production at the core of economics, while encouraging a psychological revolution. But human development takes place in all kinds of activities, and green "technologies" are as much low-tech and no-tech as high-tech. Just as a revolution in scientific paradigms is turning the eye of science back on the human subject, so also our technological extension is forcing us to look more closely at the purpose and meaning of what we are producing. The focus of industrial ecology on service and end-use is one way of expressing this. These aspects of context and meaning are, however, antithetical to capitalism, which must put profit first.

Perhaps the greatest intellectual obstacle to our moving on to authentic postindustrial development is the fetishization of "information" by many writers on postindustrialism. The information revolution is certainly important, but this importance is derivative of the new centrality of culture and human development. Human development can never be treated as "neutral," but information can be, and so mainstream academics and ideologists have reified it in the same way that business has commodified it, making it into a "mode of development," in Castells's (1996) terms. One is justified in asking: development for what? Isolated from social and environmental need, Castells's "informational mode of development" is not actually a new "mode of development" but a narrowing and suppression of potentials for human self-actualization. Castells's own description of various impacts of globalization suggests that his "informational mode," which he implies can only be capitalist, could more appropriately be called a "mode of destruction." Information can certainly be treated as neutral, but for it to be considered part of a new mode of development, it must be able to contribute to real or qualitative wealth. A case can be made that earlier capitalist and socialist industrialization—however brutal and unequal—at least spun off significant use-value in the form of food, shelter, clothing, and infrastructure. By contrast, it is difficult to deny that, overall, current capitalist development is destroying more than it creates.

It has become almost dogma among mainstream academics that there is a historical "fit" between the new hypermedia communications environment and corporate globalization (Castells, 1996; Deibert, 1997; Barrett, 1996; Tapscott, 1996). One cannot deny how useful information technology has been in creating new forms of profit-making—like the empty forms of megabyte money in the Casino Economy—and in transcending national regulatory controls that might limit exploitation. But a case can be made that the information economy, unless kept under wraps, threatens many of the most basic aspects of capitalist globalization.

First of all, it would be interesting to see how well globalism and informationalism would "fit" if full-cost accounting was built into market pricing. The wasteful giant loops of global production and consumption are based on cheap dirty energy and undervalued resource extraction. Wayne Roberts and Susan Brandum (1995) go so far as to argue that the global economy would collapse in a day if subsidies for dirty energy alone were suddenly removed.

As noted earlier, corporate globalization is premised on the economically irrational projects of (1) increasing global movement of goods and resources (through free trade), and (2) restricting the free flow of information (through intellectual property rights). The commodification of information considerably restricts it flow. For this reason, corporate capitalism is in something of a bind vis-à-vis information. It needs its free flow to grow and compete. And yet completely free flow would undermine competition and property relations.

As Stewart Brand says, "information wants to be free" (De Kerckhove, 1997). And not only that, it wants to multiply itself. Capitalism, like all class societies, is based in scarcity—in the control of scarce resources—and considerable (wasteful antisocial) effort is taken in capitalism to keep information a scarce resource.

Today, the growth of the Internet coincides with the integration of all the electronic media into "hypermedia"—a digitized multimedia environment where telephones, television, radio, fax machines, movies, CDs, and the Internet are joined into an increasingly seamless interconnected interactive web (DeKerckhove, 1997). (At the moment, this network environment is still forming and far from seamless, but the potential will grow as bandwidth is increased with fiber-optic cable and the like.) Hypermedia may present a significant threat to the very notion of intellectual property rights, not simply because information flows beyond legal jurisdictions, but because the pastiche/montage patterns of hypertext tend to undermine the very notion of discrete authorship. In economies based on commodification and the accumulation of exchange-value, this is a real problem. It would not be a problem for economies geared to create regenerative wealth, just as questions of originality and authorship were never problems for primitive-oral societies.

Informationalism also tends to undermine commodification in other ways, particularly in its capacity for two-way *distributed* communication. The capitalist commodity economy and market sector have always required a Divided Economy—the existence of subordinate nonmarket realms in the home, in village life, or even in whole regions of the world. But information wants to flow everywhere. If allowed to, it can support human potential development and natural systems productivity, both of which demand a reintegration of formal and informal sectors on a whole new basis. Hypermedia are among the tools by which the industrial division of production and consumption can be abolished through postindustrial prosumption. Just as with ecological agriculture or renewable energy or eco-infrastructure, the potential of network economics and hypermedia is to make *every* place a site of regenerative production through a new integration of formal and informal economics. In this sense, hypermedia not only make direct democracy possible, but they require democratic participation for their actualization.

ECO-INFOSTRUCTURE: GAIA'S NERVOUS SYSTEM

It may well be that there is a much *better* fit between this new electronic *planetary nervous system* and the decentralized political and economic forms of the green economy. Bioregional economies, which are both self-reliant and interdependent, can utilize the new media environment to coordinate and cooperate for mutual development. Eco-production in all key sectors is most efficient when distributed, and the new media can service this decentralization.

The capacity of the new technologies to abolish geographical space and to create communities-of-interest in the hypermedia environment does not conflict with place-based economics or identity. The ideal is to *reduce the movement of matter* and *increase the movement of ideas and information.* Planetary culture based simultaneously in universality and specificity is no contradiction, and the grounding of human societies in place-based ecological economies is essential for postcivilizational development.

As Kelly (1994) and various other writers have pointed out, the "network" character of increasingly complex technological and economic systems is *organic,* that is, these systems tend to function a lot like natural systems. At the moment, these quasi-natural technosystems are like cancers, growing at the expense of nonhuman nature. Industrial ecology can help heal the diseased economy by moving to integrate it within ecosystems and to imitate nature's elegance and efficiency. Although this "natural systems" approach can simplify many economic and environmental solutions, the amount and sophistication of information required is much greater than in the capitalist information economy, which is shaped overwhelmingly by dollar-, not resource-, efficiency, let alone ecological balance.

The current information revolution is not simply information acting on material production, but information acting on information (Castells, 1996). Certainly, an eco-economy can employ many of these technologies to useful ends, but the green economy also involves a greater knowledge intensity for most of its *direct* labor, be it with people or resources. This is because it is so decentralized and participatory—with a high "eyes to acres" ratio—and because it deliberately cultivates and employs individual human creativity. Compare, for example, the knowledge required for ecological agriculture, in which delicate balances, biodiversity, and careful observation of microclimates are involved, with the plow-and-spray approach of agribusiness's chemicalized monoculture. The same holds for building, energy production, or any other sector one would care to consider. The green economy needs various levels of specialization, but by and large, the relationship of expertise to ordinary work is different. As such, it is a de-Taylorization of work.

"Living machines," a term coined by designer John Todd, provide a contrast in both work and process. They represent a green alternative to the corporate biotechnology that today represents such a threat to the planet.

John and Nancy Jack Todd (1994: 167) write,

> A living machine is a device made up of living organisms of all types and usually housed within a casing or structure made of extremely lightweight materials. Like a conventional machine, it is comprised of interrelated parts that function together in the performance of some work. Living machines can be designed to produce food or fuels, treat wastes, purify air, regulate climates, or even to do all these things simultaneously. They are designed along the principles evolved by the natural world in building and regulating its great ecologies of forests, lakes, prairies, and estuaries. Their primary energy source is sunlight. Like the planet, living machines have hydrological and mineral cycles.

Some of Todd's machines look like water sculptures—a series of transparent circular tanks that could be (or are) aquaria, which support separate ecosystems. Each ecosystem is engineered for a particular job (for example, absorbing some heavy metal from the water into the plants), but each also has a life and direction of its own, and the engineering process is an open-ended adventure.

Todd sees innumerable benefits, even beyond having sewage plants that look and smell like gardens. Their order of efficiency, he estimates, may be one hundred times greater than that of conventional machines. In addition to helping solve problems of poverty and equity, he also sees such mini-ecosystems allowing humanity to live on much less land. Much of the planet's landscape can regenerate to wilderness, helping protect precious diversity. Today, living machines are being employed on a number of fronts, typically serving to provide alternatives to (chemical) water treatment megaprojects.

Today's capitalist information economy is certainly complex, but it is also excludes large portions of the world, and its goals—for example, to earn lots of money—are certainly not complex. An ecological economy—as we'll see more in the next chapter—has to move from value conveyed by money to value conveyed by social and environmental indicators. This is a much more complex matter. Ecological industry, for example, needs information about the community and environmental impacts not only of their own products and processes—over their entire product life and beyond—but also of impacts of their feedstocks or raw materials in their extraction or production. An eco-industrial park, or green production network, must also have a range of information on materials cycles, energy and water flows, and by-product uses and impacts. While it is true that some advanced forms of (existing) information industry force producers to go beyond a narrow product orientation to provide service, the new ecological forms of liability (which would force a "cradle to reincarnation" responsibility on producers) demand even more comprehensive knowledge. Their emphasis on product leasing rather than ownership will require producers to more rigorously track their product's life cycle, another information-intensive operation.

The new media and information technologies have great potential for conservation. Modeling energy performance and resource flows can save much trial and error. A key element in developing community economic development planning processes will be the accumulation of bioregional resource inventories. Computerized mapping technologies—or geographical information systems (GIS)—will be invaluable in creating these inventories and thus providing an educational function. Various native bands are using GIS to map resources on their lands and land claims (Pearse, 1994; Kemp and Brooke, 1995). Part of architect William McDonough's work, overseeing the design of an eco-village for the Oglala Lakota in South Dakota, included provisions for the native children to do the resource mapping and monitoring via computers (Lazarus, 1993).

The struggle to actualize the authentic developmental potential of our emerging planetary nervous system is absolutely central to establishing green economies. There can be no doubt that the emerging hypermedia web must ultimately be a common carrier, equally accessible to anyone who wants to send or receive. The cost of initially creating the so-called information superhighway, however, presents major obstacles to immediate public control, and it seems clear that whoever gets to build the highway will influence its character for some time to come.

Despite the uncritical optimism of many advocates of the information superhighway, there is no guarantee that it will serve, or be designed to serve, the public interest. The chaotically democratic nature of the Internet was, to a large degree, a fortuitous coincidence. Its originators, the U.S. military, wanted a radically decentralized communications system in case of nuclear war. After university academics inherited the medium, the college counterculture picked up the ball, developing the browser software that made it a *socially* decentralized popular multimedium.

The information highway will likely be much more consciously designed, with large corporate involvement. There is some danger that it will do an end-run around a participatory Internet and be developed as a business and consumer medium.

It may be true that the potential of emerging hypermedia constitutes a great threat to both hierarchical relationships and super-industrial capitalism itself. But these potentials to facilitate regenerative development can only be realized *consciously*. Otherwise, they could suffer the fate of cable television, which has had much greater participatory potential than has been developed by the corporate-consumer culture.

Grassroots media interests have been lobbying governments to guarantee universal access (including a dedicated public "lane" on the highway), affordability, and public consultation on all key design questions. Some questions about work have been raised by organized labor, which is concerned about the abuses of telework. But grassroots forces should also be aware of the potential of the new media to undermine the Divided Economy and to decentralize food, energy, and goods production, along with political and economic power. This vision can and should be considered in the design of the new media because its potential for community self-regulation is one major reason the new hypermedia environment can be considered our "electronic nervous system."

10

True-Value Software:
Regenerative Money and Finance

It may well be in the realm of money and finance that green economies can most dramatically demonstrate that they are the most advanced "information economies." It is *certainly* in the sphere of money that a successful postindustrial redefinition of wealth would be most obvious, since money would be dethroned from its position as god and driving force of the economy to become a humble servant of regenerative human exchange. It is this dethronement that can allow money to achieve its potential as pure information, something that capitalism cannot allow to happen without undermining its fundamental class relationships. For those on the left who really want to go beyond capitalism, they should understand that this will never happen by focusing primarily on controlling money, finance capital, or investment flows, but only by transforming the nature of money altogether.

In this chapter, I will look briefly at this transformed role of money as information-servant, with special attention to how money and finance can serve both as a source of decentralized community planning and as a resource for individual innovation and imagination in the economy. A couple of important subthemes are (1) the role of money and financial systems in helping shape community self-reliance, and (2) how we can fully empower and remunerate all those currently "nonmarket" human activities that are so crucial to developing integrated ecological economies.

To these ends, we have to see how we can both neutralize and eliminate the destructive and totalitarian power of money as it is currently used, and also see how we can design monetary and financial systems to support regenerative production and healthy societies. Consistent with my emphasis throughout this book, I feel that to do the former requires the latter, that it is our positive alternatives that will ultimately create quality and destroy exploitation.

SCARCITY, POWER, AND COMMODITY-MONEY

Conservative writer George Gilder (1989, 1994) waxes sentimental about futuristic possibilities for the economy to transcend matter. He may be on to something, but he will wait a long, long time for global capitalism to be a vehicle for such transcendence, however many computers it produces. Capitalism is based in materiality and scarcity, and it must reproduce both in order to maintain its existence.

This was, of course, a central theme of part 1, where I looked at the Great Depression and the Fordist Waste Economy as responses to potential abundance, abundance that threatened ruling-class control of scarce resources. I discussed how the money system was used, along with waste, to reinforce a scarcity mentality, paradoxically by printing more money, the value of which depreciated. Growth of the money supply offset union wage agreements and provided effective demand for corporate production, while debt was used to chain people to wasteful and unhealthy work, effectively mortgaging the environment and future generations.

In part 1, we also looked at the basic nature of money—as a means of exchange and a store of value—and how it has evolved over time. By and large, there has been a tendency for money to become more a means of exchange and less a store of value (Robertson, 1989; Greco, 1994). Commodity-money has been the typical way to store value, but commodity-money tends not to be flexible enough for complex trading systems. For this reason, hybrid systems have been improvised using credit- or token-money, which is treated much like commodity-money and is partially backed by some commodity like gold.

As economies get more and more complex, commodity-money becomes more and more cumbersome. As a thing-in-itself, it's great at "storing value," but because it's a commodity, it is subject to its own supply-and-demand fluctuations, and there is rarely the right amount of money to facilitate exchange. But because it's so good at storing value, commodity-money is essential to class relationships. As a thing-in-itself, it can be monopolized and controlled—and kept scarce. When money is scarce, people do unnatural things to get it, such as submitting to exploitation, or exploiting others, or destroying the environment.

The forms of credit-money created by the Keynesian Paper Economy were not pure credit-money, or means of exchange. They were hybrid systems that maintained a tenuous, nearly illusory connection to commodity-money. Although created with virtually no backing, they were centrally controlled and treated like commodity-money. While created in copious amounts to stimulate demand, this credit-money's use was subject to either gradual depreciation (in the case of currency) or substantial interest charges (in the case of credit and debt). Interest and debt hooked people into the workaday grind. In this way, (hybrid) credit-money creation has paradoxically been a means of maintaining money-scarcity and the compulsive nature of economic relations.

Today's electronic Megabyte Economy has gone another giant step toward severing the connection between real wealth and money. It seems to have cut money completely away from its material base. Megabyte money is created virtually at will by financial institutions, and currencies are adrift in a sea of floating exchange rates unpegged from gold. Even the stock market today has almost nothing to do with raising capital for corporations, since these needs have been taken care of internally (Henwood, 1997; Dillon, 1996). The growing financial sector is all about speculation.

The ironies are incredible. Speculation is possible only because this money is seen as storing some value in itself, and yet these values are always changing, sometimes drastically, because they really represent nothing in themselves. The Megabyte Economy of Casino Capitalism represents the pure decadence of the commodity relationships on which Marx based his analysis of capitalism. Not only is money the overwhelming end-goal of its economic relationships, but use-values don't even fit into the process, even as a spin-off of money-making, except perhaps to subsidize the gambling.

This subsidization, however, can be substantial. Somebody has to "pay the price for [speculators] feelin' nice." The Casino Economy drains resources from the real economy and, as many critics of globalization have noted, necessarily pumps wealth from the poor to the rich (Dillon, 1996).

This process also trashes the environment. Some commentators have heralded financialization as an evolution of nonmaterial production, but this is an illusion at best. Because the new money is traded as a commodity more feverishly than ever before, money has greater power as a thing-in-itself than it has ever had—even if its commodity status is fictional, and its value depreciates with each passing second. The net effect of this financial trading is greater material waste as valuable resources are drained from the material economy and real resources serve as collateral in a giant crapshoot. As Tim Jackson (1996) writes,

> The economic basis for financial services is mostly speculation about commodity prices and trading in investment capital. Speculating on commodity prices both requires and encourages the flow of material commodities somewhere in the economy, and trading in investment capital is empty if capital is not actually invested—generally in materials-based industries. The financial services sector may appear to reduce the materials intensity of the advanced economies. In fact it serves only to promote material throughput and encourage material consumption.

The commodified credit-money systems of Casino Capitalism are doing tremendous damage to ecological and social life while at the same time concentrating wealth and power on an unprecedented scale. Because the Casino Economy has created such an unhealthy disjunction between the financial and material economies, various commentators have called for measures to reground our money systems in solid commodity backing emphasizing money's role in storing value (Kurtzman, 1993). But the real alternative may lie in the other direction, in the creation of pure credit-money, completing the evolution of money into a pure means of exchange.

GOING LOCAL

The era of globalism and casino economics has witnessed the rise of an important countertrend: the emergence of local currencies. The global "economy without walls" is due primarily to cheap dirty energy, which makes transport costs low or nonexistent. Local currencies are a means of rebuilding the walls or, more accurately, providing a skin for the community economy so that money doesn't just flow out to wherever it gets the most interest. By keeping money flowing internally, these currencies also undercut speculation and support real wealth creation.

The best known local currencies in North America are the Local Employment Trading Systems (LETS), Ithaca Hours, and Time Dollars. [Time Dollars are not actually full-fledged currencies, but service-credit systems that work on similar principles (Cahn and Rowe, 1996)].

LETSystems are pure credit-money systems, which will be described in more detail below. Although initiated in Canada, worldwide there are, at this writing, well over 600 LETSystems, with more than 350 in the UK (Walker and Goldsmith, 1998).

Ithaca Hours, based in Ithaca, New York, is a paper money system, with one hour valued at $10, the average hourly wage in Ithaca. Being centrally issued and limited in quantity, it is not proper account-money, but it has had major impacts in creating jobs and serving needs by stimulating local exchange. Since 1991, more than sixty thousand dollars has been issued to over 1,300 participants, making available a wide range of goods and services. The Ithaca system has been used as the model for many other systems, more than sixty of these in North America alone, including Calgary; Prince George, British Columbia; Cambridge, Massachusetts; Philadelphia; Buffalo; Gainesville, Florida; Madison, Wisconsin; New Orleans; Indianapolis; and San Francisco. Toronto, which has had a LETSystem for years, now has another currency, the Toronto dollar, with major business support in its St. Lawrence area; this new system is loosely modelled on the Ithaca Hour.

The creation of community currencies is an essential support for the development of the closed-loop food, energy, and manufacturing systems that define ecological economies. Closed financial loops, which parallel and facilitate production/consumption loops, are thus created. It is inconceivable that self-reliant bioregional economies, based in natural systems and renewable resources, can be created without postscarcity community currencies.

One reason for this is that, as noted above, these currencies can serve as a kind of organic "skin" for community-based economies, which prevents the leaking of financial resources and keeps them circulating locally. But equally important is the fact that these currencies can help remunerate previously unremunerated and undervalued forms of work that are at the cutting edge of human and ecological development.

Just as feminists have long argued that work at home should not be penalized through its invisibility, greens are emphasizing that we must find ways of properly remunerating food, energy, goods, and service production in and around the home and community. The green economy depends on eliminating the Divided Economy and integrating formal and informal sectors. This is certainly impossible by monetizing (with conventional money) the work that is now unpaid. Conventional money and its market economy require an unpaid sector to subsidize them, and the values intrinsic to the money economy are antithetical to regenerative production.

The integration of formal and informal sectors can happen only by remunerating unpaid work in one (or both) of two ways: (1) through systems of community account-money, and (2) through workers' direct creation of wealth for themselves and their communities.

In the previous chapter, I discussed briefly how the role of craft can and should grow in an economy focused on the direct creation of qualitative wealth. In craft production, part of the wealth creation, or "income," is actually the conditions of creative work established for the workers themselves. The other part of craftspersons' incomes can come from the account-money system, which local customers can afford because they can create this money for themselves.

Many of the most necessary and rewarding activities of a green economy are eco-infrastructure projects like solar energy, food production, and rooftop greening, which happen right in, on, or around people's residences. The remuneration people receive, again, might be derived directly as the product of labor or through some form of accounting. Many of these projects are of direct benefit to whole neighborhoods and communities, and there are any number of ways of sharing and recording this wealth creation.

In our current capitalist economies, volunteerism is being exploited to pick up the slack for undermined public sectors. Community currencies offer a means of providing remuneration for important service work that can avoid the pitfalls of both Welfare State bureaucracy and capitalist volunteerism.

It is by no means necessary to have a single monolithic monetary system. In fact, many alternative-money proponents suggest that different coexisting monetary systems are actually desirable. On one hand, there may be systems for local trade and others for regional, national, or even international trade. On the other hand, various communities of interest—such as craft guilds, student associations, and social movement networks—may find it useful to have their own currencies.

MONEY AS INFORMATION

Local money advocates like Michael Linton (1996), Thomas Greco (1994), and Richard Douthwaite (1996) distinguish between conventional money and regenerative money systems in three key ways:

1. Conventional money is *scarce;* regenerative money is *sufficient.*
2. Conventional money *goes anywhere;* regenerative money *stays local.*
3. Conventional money is *created by institutions* (them); regenerative money is *created by users* (us).

Most of the local money systems being improvised roughly conform to these criteria. Many, however, are basically local versions of national currencies, forms of hybrid commodity/credit money. Their issues are limited, and they are *centrally* issued, albeit by respected community organizations. They don't eliminate the structural problems of money—money scarcity and money being an end in itself—but they contain these problems through local accountability.

There is, however, one form of community money that deals with these problems in a more radical way. Most economists would call it credit-money, but a term that better describes its actual function is "account-money." Through this form, money completes its evolution by becoming pure information. It registers the flows of value between people and organizations as they provide goods and services for one another. In contrast to issued money—which remains to some degree a thing-in-itself—account-money is created anytime there is a need for exchange by the people who need it.

The information function of money is by no means new; it is the essence of money. LETSystem founder Michael Linton is fond of quoting Alan Watts's analysis of the Great Depression. Watts argued that money was only a *measure* of wealth, not wealth itself, and it was insane to think that production and exchange could not take place simply because of a shortage of money. According to Watts, "It was like we were going to build a house, and having all the labor, tools, and materials; but we didn't do it because we didn't have enough *feet or inches.*" Linton (1996) argues that money is not real; it is only information.

Money came about to allow people to carry out exchanges separated in time and space. It allowed more impersonal exchange with people outside one's own village. This character of impersonality has been money's strength and its weakness. Commodity-money was used not just to measure value but to store it so it could be used in another time or place reliably. Whether it was wheat-money, or cattle-money, or tobacco-money, or metal-money, it worked best if the money had some value in itself. In this way, commodity-money systems have functioned as forms of *indirect barter* (Greco, 1994). But, as noted above, commodity-money has never had the appropriate flexibility to facilitate exchanges in complex economies, so various credit-commodity hybrid systems evolved.

Account-money is not new, but the information age increases its potential to function on a large scale at the core of the economy. Account-money is postscarcity money, since it can be created by anyone anytime there is need for an exchange. And because it can be created by anyone, in virtually any amount, it completely undercuts the power of capital accumulation. There is no point in accumulating it for its own sake; the point is to use it. It focuses the entire economy on use-value.

One cannot overestimate the importance of this function. When people can create money anytime they need it, the totalitarian/compulsive power of money evaporates and capitalism loses its most important form of domination. When people know that they can satisfy their most basic survival needs with account-money, they can be choosier about the work they accept and can exercise social and ecological values more easily.

Besides eliminating money's totalitarian power, account-money also undercuts the power of capital as a social force. There is little incentive to accumulate capital for the power it exercises, only for the use-value it creates. Speculation is deflated.

LETS: STORING VALUE IN COMMUNITY

Most new local money systems are geared to providing "interest- and inflation-free" alternatives to conventional money, and virtually all of them are still inventing themselves in response to both community need and practical realities. Some are backed with a commodity like cordwood or energy, and many are issued by some central, albeit local, institution. It is certainly healthy for communities to have a number of forms of money, but it is worthwhile to look more closely at account-money because of the potential it indicates for postindustrial money as well as the depth of the revolution in the ways we must begin to think about value.

The most well-known account-money system is the LETSystem, variously known as either the Local Exchange Trading System or Local Employment Trading System (Linton and Greco, 1987; Greco, 1994; Dauncey 1988; Dobson, 1993). It is basically a debit/credit system of accounting, the unit of account being known as the "green dollar." It is a membership system, with members paying a token membership fee in cash to cover operating costs.

Each person or enterprise has a plus or minus balance of "green dollars," and at any one time half of the system is in debit and half in credit, the system balanced at zero. Thus it is just as respectable to be minus-$500-green as it is to be plus-$500-green. (A plus-$500 individual or business may have contributed something to the community, but a minus-$500 member has created work in the community). The larger the system gets and the more trust grows, the larger the plus or minus limits tend to become. It is thus a self-regulating system, which simply records the "contributions" (credits) made and "commitments" (debits) owed to the community.

Like all local money systems, the currency supplies a "skin" to the economy, preventing leakage of capital, recirculating money and capital, closing production/consumption loops, and optimizing self-reliance. LETS is convenient in that it allows any combination of conventional cash and green dollars for any transaction. This allows the system to grow organically as people are able to buy more and more with green dollars.

LETS, like most local currencies, helps empower informal economic activities. Unlike "basic income" (guaranteed annual income) programs, which also support home-based eco-production, LETS is a self-regulating system, which requires no bureaucracy and little administration, and provides positive feedback for positive action. Very little policing of the system is needed by system administration, since participants in the system can learn (only at the time of a transaction) the balances of people with whom they are considering an exchange. Even if someone exploits the system, purchases a lot, goes heavily into "commitment," and then leaves town, the loss is spread over the entire system and so would not be noticed. The exploiter has simply created a lot of work in the community.

Sometimes the use of green dollars to account for the services in and around the home is misunderstood. The intention is to recognize and support previously unrecognized work, not to quantify all human activity with green dollars or anything else. The "gift economy" will continue in households, neighborhoods, and communities, but there is a whole range of intermediate activities in the community, and even in households, that can be supported with green dollars. All kinds of ecological community projects will be easier when green dollar remuneration is possible. Not only can previously unrecognized skills be acknowledged and employed, but people find all kinds of imaginative ways they can serve others in their community, which would be largely unthinkable in the cash economy.

It must be emphasized that LETS is not a barter system. It is a pure account-money system. Regular commodity-money systems are technically closer to barter systems than are LETSystems; a regular currency is an indirect barter system since the reserve-backed bills function as things-in-themselves, exchanged for the desired product or service. LETSystem "green dollars" are strictly bits of information. The reason why LETSystems are confused with barter systems (which are limited to one-on-one direct exchanges) is because they recapture the *personal* dimension of exchange. This personal dimension is absolutely crucial to new forms of trust and the regrounding of economic relationships in social life.

LETSystems are typically run with computers and have the potential of evolving into sizable systems with a major impact on their local or regional economies. Because of the importance of personal connection and human scale to these community currencies, their growth to large sizes involves the spawning of subsystems. Regional and super-regional systems can be improvised without compromising their local development functions. Percentages for intersystem exchange can be set by each community depending on its economic needs and goals, and separate regional, national, and even global systems can be set up. While some people seem to assume that LETSystem logistics would be too alien to mainstream business, in fact LETS is not all that different in structure from many big-business, for-profit trading networks.

Some account-money systems set the value for their unit of measure in labor-hours. Although people are completely free to set their own prices, a LETS green dollar usually takes the prevailing federal dollar rates. For example, a carpenter getting twenty dollars per hour in Canadian dollars would take approximately the same in green dollars. This system allows maximum flexibility in combining with regular cash, and it provides a framework whereby the community can gradually revalue certain kinds of work if it so chooses. In this sense, the store-of-value function that commodity-money used to take care of is taken over by the community. The green dollar simply registers this community consensus.

Because of our lifelong conditioning about money, it is easy to underestimate the radical implications of this system. Even some analysts who have a fair amount of knowledge about local money systems feel uneasy about the fact that pure account-money like LETS is not a store of value. They feel that some "backing"—be it cordwood or energy—is necessary for value to be acknowledged over a long time period. But the real power of LETS is that it has *no* backing; the value is conveyed by the community.

Obviously, this changes the way we must think about saving and investment. Green dollars are meant to be used, not stored—and used in service to the community. Saving for old age would not be necessary in a green economy because seniors would always have "something to offer" a community and so have no problem in being self-supporting. Even the disabled offer much to those who help them. Green dollars are not used to meticulously quantify all this value but to formally acknowledge this very real energy flow in the economy. Money systems require trust, which might be trust in central banks, in bond issuers, in gold, or some commodity like wheat or solar energy. But the trust upon which our futures hinge is community, and pure account-money systems institutionalize this trust in an unprecedented way, forcing us to reexamine our most basic notions of value.

Obviously, implementing a small LETSystem tomorrow will not automatically eliminate the need for conventional saving and investment. But LETS can be combined in a complementary way with conventional money, with other kinds of local money and community finance. What LETS does is provide simultaneously a vision and experience of regenerative value and a transitional means for this experience to evolve into a larger part of personal and community life.

It will be interesting to see how LETSystems will develop as they grow. They seem to have unlimited potential. LETS founder Michael Linton feels that technological developments like "smart cards" will find their most appropriate use in handling local currencies like LETS. The fact that green dollars are pure information and not a store of value, as well as being local, considerably reduces the security problems associated with electronic money.

One of the main assets of LETSystems is that they can grow organically. Implementing them as a one-shot megaproject, in fact, seems undesirable, even if it were possible. As they grow into formidable economic forces, account-money systems should not need to take over entire local economies in order to substantially transform economic relationships. It seems likely that they would need only to grow to a certain size, *perhaps less than a third of the local economy,* before they would substantially undercut speculation and compulsive labor market relationships.

When people are able to purchase food and shelter with green dollars, the coercive power of private capital and the state will be severely crippled. People can more freely choose their work, their skills, their forms of enterprise. By the same token, speculation in land can be completely undermined when land can be purchased for green dollars. It seems likely that communities would combine such local currencies with land trusts, land banking, and green taxes to transform land tenure. This is an example of how community currencies can be most effective when used as part of overall green community economic development strategies, combining different techniques on various levels—policy, finance, production, and consumption.

MONEY, VALUE, AND PRODUCTION

If there is any general criticism of community currency initiatives so far, it is that many overestimate the importance of monetary change in itself; or conversely, they underestimate the other economic changes necessary for local currencies to survive and achieve their full potential. The most radical aspect of regenerative money systems is how they put *use-value* in command, creating the possibility for quality to displace quantity and helping the ecological service economy, based in human development, to come into existence.

But qualitative production does not emerge spontaneously from monetary change; it must be consciously cultivated. In a green economy, the medium is not the message. The medium is the medium, period. Money, especially regenerative money, is a *means,* which frees us to put our primary attention on the goals of green production. As long as the capitalist economy continues to be focused on production-for-production's-sake and consumption-for-the-sake-of-profit, community currencies will have a tough row to hoe. They will be forced to go against the grain of powerful economic forces. There is also the very real danger that global capitalism will deliberately support the development of small confined local money systems (and community economic development in general) to ease the shock of dismantling vital public services. Local money developers must therefore be very concerned with defining and supporting the long-term goals of green economic development—the *content* of the green economy.

The ideal would be for ecological initiatives in every sector of the economy to look closely at how they can incorporate local currencies into their alternative development strategies. As long as alternatives in energy, manufacturing, the food system, health care, and other areas do not make the most of regenerative money, they will also have to go against the grain of destructive economic powers. No matter how much market prices incorporate full costs, an end-use approach is always compromised to some degree by the profit motive. An end-use approach means that money, matter, and energy are all *means* to an end. Even at a fairly low level of development, community currencies can be a tremendous help in alleviating unhealthy market pressures and helping eco-alternatives to grow. While brown industry and dirty energy still reap subsidies, local money can help level the playing field for retrofit programs, organic agriculture, preventative medicine, and eco-products. It seems best not just to recruit green economic innovators into local money systems but to specifically design alternative projects to utilize local money to support project goals.

Local currencies are means to nurture community culture and solidarity, but they also grow most successfully where cultural bonds are strong. They can perform multidimensional functions for unions, social movement groups, neighborhoods, or any community of interest where there are shared values. Community currencies help to re-embed economic relationships into social and cultural life, so strategies to build the currencies are most effective when organizers place great importance on networking, socials, and celebrations. Account-money systems can evolve into quite complex and sophisticated systems of exchange and investment, but like other aspects of the information age, they can recapture positive elements of village life through a repersonalization of exchange. The importance of this personal element is one big reason why community currencies are (wrongly) characterized as barter systems. Like barter systems, they express and foster personal social bonds.

Although, as mentioned above, community currencies can be employed to nurture and spread the values of any community of interest, all values are not equally regenerative. Local money can put nonmonetary values on (at least) an equal footing with self-aggrandizement, but our development as people and communities depends very much on what these values are. The development of a green economy is, first and foremost, about the development of ourselves as people.

Various writers (Needleman, 1991; Dominguez & Robin, 1992; Crawford, 1994) have written about the individual's relationship to money from a spiritual point of view. They have argued that money has a symbolic significance and a corresponding power over human behavior, which may in fact be far greater than money's strictly economic influence. Authentic personal development, which involves a healthier relationship to money, requires becoming more aware of this symbolic/psychological power.

These writers are certainly correct when they say that it is not enough to change social and economic institutions, especially today when postindustrial productive forces are so connected to culture and human development. This recognition has to be incorporated into the design of new money systems. But the authors also certainly underestimate the importance of social change to individual transformation, at a time when account-money systems can so allow qualitative value to be structured into the economy. Questions of our deeper being cannot be divorced from everyday aspects of giving and taking. Some of the biggest difficulties communities will have in implementing account-money systems at the core of their economies will come from ingrained conditioning about economic life that it is about getting, taking, and storing.

Account-money systems like LETS allow aspects of the gift economies of primitive societies to reemerge (Hyde, 1979). Goods and services would be seen as gifts, not commodities, and the focus would be on *circulating the gift* continuously. This may sound very idealistic, but it is a very practical way of fully utilizing society's creative energy. What is more superstitious is the modern idea that whole populations of people can "provide for the future" by storing money away in pension funds and other financial devices, irrespective of the real social infrastructure that is created. Account-money systems are, in a sense, transitional instruments in the implementation of gift economies. They can account for the value exchanged in a rigorous way, or in a way that simply acknowledges a flow.

While community currencies can undercut the alienated power of the profit motive, they will also magnify both the positive and negative impulses that underlie economic relationships. Regenerative money systems and individual spiritual development are both, in a sense, engaged in the undermining forms of domination. In a green economy, money will serve more transparently not just as a form of information but as energy—human energy expressing our giving to and taking from society and nature. Once money is no longer a thing-in-itself, money systems will act as giant mirrors, reflecting back at us our values and behavior.

INDICATORS: VITAL SIGNS OF REAL WEALTH

By freeing exchange from the tyranny of scarcity and competition, account-money systems open up whole new realms in which market choices and planning interconnect. As social and ecological values become part of everyday exchange, buying and selling become distinctly political acts. Opportunities emerge not only to de-commodify markets but to de-bureaucratize planning.

Quantitative wealth—the exchange-value expressed in conventional money—is very simple and homogeneous. And the more, the better. By contrast, compared to the simple standardized value of material accumulation, *qualitative* value is incredibly complex. Not only must people be aware of their own real needs, but they require much more information about their communities, their environments, and their conceivable futures.

In recent years, a boom in interest in "indicators" of social and environmental welfare has responded to this need for more and better information. This new interest reflects the fact that real wealth bears little relationship to today's capitalist monetary wealth. For a long time, indicators were shaped by and for academics and planners. Today, however, communities are becoming increasingly involved with developing indicators that can help them offset, avoid, or overcome many of the destructive impacts of economic growth and globalization.

There are many kinds of indicators, used for various purposes. If we are to move to regenerative development, almost all of them take on a new importance. The most strategic ones, however, which provide a context for the rest, seem to be emerging from the movement for "healthy city" and "sustainable community" indicators (Hart, 1998; Tyler Norris Associates, 1997; U.S. EPA, 1998). Grassroots indicators are being developed in cities throughout North America, including Seattle, Chattanooga, Toronto, Denver, and Philadelphia.

These community indicators combine grassroots participation and technical information in a unique way. Because the intention is to develop a common language of qualitative value, the process and the content are equally important. The indicators—designed and researched by the community members themselves—are intended not only to monitor change but to make it happen. Indicator development is usually combined with a grassroots process of visioning the future. Key indicators are set to best reflect the goals defined by the community. Not too numerous—generally between twenty and seventy—they can highlight significant relationships between social, economic, environmental, and other factors. They can be listed separately as well as combined in some meaningful index. Some indicators can describe empirical trends; others can register changes in public opinion. The particular combination and often many individual indicators are very specific to the communities in question. They should all be accessible and understandable to all community members. They can be used to educate people about their community and environment, to advocate for sensible planning and development, and to create bonds between different elements in the community.

Here are just a few examples of indicators from the indicator pioneer Sustainable Seattle:

Economy:

- work hours required each month to satisfy basic needs
- house price affordability gap
- income distribution

Environment:

- wild salmon returning to spawn
- wetland water quality vs. urbanization
- percentage of pedestrian-friendly streets

Health and community:

- youth crime
- birth weight by ethnicity
- library circulation rates

Because community indicators express a place's future vision, if truly regenerative communities are to be established, most of the green economic principles described in this book will have to be reflected in the indicators. Because of the emphasis on inclusiveness of most indicator projects to date, there exists in many of them a kind of chamber of commerce mentality that hesitates to fully embrace social and ecological goals. Presumably, this will change as awareness of problems and fundamental solutions slowly grows. But this also suggests a role for more progressive elements of the community to express a more radical vision through their own indicators.

In the mid-1980s, Rodale Press set up a consulting operation called the Regeneration Project (now defunct), which did pioneering work in designing community development processes. One of its most interesting contributions was a set of indices by which communities could assess their level of self-reliance and their relative level of ecological development. This Vitality Index gave a reading of a community's existing situation relative to the "ideal regenerative state." The maximum potential was determined by inventories and assigned the value of 1. If, for example, a region grew 30 percent of its own food but had a potential of 60 percent, it rated a .5 for that part of the economy. Sectors were rated separately but could be combined. The overall Vitality Index combined factors like employment, health, energy, food, shelter, and more.

The project's Regenerative Index quantified the actions, activities, and functions contributing to ecologically regenerative practices. For example, it determined what percentage of farmers used sustainable practices and what businesses produced for local/regional markets. These indices were employed as part of an organic participatory process by which communities could achieve a higher quality of life through greater self-reliance (Rodale Regeneration Project, 1985).

Both the Rodale and current community indicator programs would, of course, be enhanced by more specialized research that could provide data on the state of many aspects of social and economic life. The Regeneration Project put great emphasis on developing regional resource inventories and a detailed understanding of inflows to, and outflows from, a community. A narrow focus on the accumulation of money and material, particularly in the industrialized countries, has created mass ignorance about the social and environmental processes that support society.

Environmentally, we are largely oblivious to the basic biophysical flows that keep us alive. New forms of ecological accounting can help rectify this ignorance. According to Wes Jackson (Van der Ryn and Cowan, 1996: 83), sustainability depends on "our becoming better ecological accountants at the community level. If we must as a future necessity recycle essentially all materials and run on sunlight, then our future will depend on accounting as the most important and interesting discipline."

In the previous chapter, I briefly touched on systems applied to the production process—life cycle assessment (LCA) and the more radical eco-effectiveness evaluation of McDonough and Braungart. But eco-accounting must also be applied to economic development and to individual consumption.

"Ecological footprint" (EF) analysis is a well-known form of eco-accounting that has great potential for both economic policy and education. Basically, it indicates how much territory is needed to support human settlements and activities. This is the territory that is required for both the materials and the energy that a community uses as well as for the "sinks" that nature supplies to absorb our wastes. The EF methodology can provide per capita statistics, such as the fact that the average Canadian requires 4.3 hectares, or three city blocks, to support his or her lifestyle. According to EF developers Wackernagel and Rees (1996), this is more than three times an individual's "fair earthshare" as a citizen of the planet.

Products can also by evaluated and labelled using EF analysis, which seems to have unlimited potential for facilitate regenerative community development. The concept of an ecological footprint lends itself both to popular awareness and to more detailed technical investigation. As its originators argue, it turns problematic concepts like "carrying capacity" (how great a population can an area support) upside-down, focusing more strategically on human responsibility to consume less, and use resources more intelligently.

EF analysis is an instance of the kind of indicators that can emerge from detailed environmental accounts that should be developed in every region. Information on biophysical flows is most important, since it is information that can be used in various ways. Many environmental economists have put a great priority on putting (conventional) monetary values on environmental resources and processes. This practice can sometimes be useful—such as for designing tax systems and calculating externalities—but monetarizing the environment can just as often be a diversion from designing systems that fully respect nature's intrinsic value.

Solid quantitative data is also important to the development of social indicators. Statistics on health, crime, violence against women, racial discrimination, income levels and disparities, and more provide a basis for community understanding and planning. But the qualitative and political dimension in social indicator design is especially crucial.

Of particular importance are indicators designed by women that not only reflect women's status and health in society but also reflect women's perspectives on the entire community. Writers like Marilyn Waring (1988, 1997) and Maria Mies (1986, 1993, 1999) have emphasized not only how traditional social and economic indicators have made women invisible but also how most authentic efforts for development have found that they must make women central because of women's strategic place in society's real-wealth creation. Women's perspectives on the built-environment and spatial design, on social services, on product design, on political decision making, and on much more can be particularly revealing of problems and potentials that most men would be oblivious to. This perspective is especially important in the development of a green economy, where there is such a close relationship between social and environmental forms of regenerative wealth creation and where many of these forms have been so invisible to the industrial economy. Indicators are a means of making important things visible.

An information economy is acceptable only if it is focused on providing useful information about quality. Community indicators are examples of progressive information that can be employed as forms of self-regulation. To date, indicators have been seen as a means to educate and influence policy, but they can be much more. Because account-money systems can begin to undermine the coercive power of money, qualitative value can increasingly act as the driving force of everyday exchange. This is not a simple matter and, even assuming a high degree of social solidarity, it requires lots of information. Indicators therefore represent important distillations of qualitative value that can educate, plan, build community consciousness, and directly support regenerative economic activities.

REGENERATIVE FINANCE AND COMMUNITY SELF-REGULATION

A complete strategy for regenerative finance involves both (1) the creation of local money systems, and (2) establishing community control over conventional financial systems. While only account-money systems can fully transform the alienated nature of exchange, simply exercising democratic control over our own cash incomes and savings can go far to support this transformation. In the developed countries, worker savings and earnings constitute a significant portion of capital on financial markets. Worker pension funds now represent perhaps 40 percent of equity capital (Quarter, 1995; Deaton, 1989).

Conventional economic development tends to assume capital is external to the community, to the region, and to the nation. The focus is on attracting it, usually with subsidies, tax breaks, and the like. Mainstream community economic development (CED), for its part, focuses on filling in gaps and empowering the poorest and most disadvantaged. It may try to plug leaks and to generate some resources internally, but it too puts the emphasis on leveraging external capital

(Perry, 1987). Conventional CED can even be subversive of fundamental change, making possible further abrogation of state responsibility for public welfare.

Green development, by contrast, intends to overhaul the entire economy, so its focus has to be internal. Local and regional development strategies must be developed, and these will have dramatic impacts on international relationships. Depending on the level where change takes place, financing may come from sources either "internal" or "external" to the situation. Nevertheless, what is most needed is a regional financial infrastructure that continually cycles capital internally to needed development.

This is not to discount the major redistribution of resources that will be required to address regional, national, and global inequities. But for this to actually happen, a prerequisite is that each economy possess the capacity to mobilize and recycle home capital. One important key to green development is the reclaiming of our own money for regenerative development. This means making sure our personal money resides within the new financial infrastructure, which includes banks, credit unions, revolving loan funds, pension funds, social collateral and ethical investment funds, and other kinds of progressive investment organizations.

As important as income inequality is to class power, perhaps even more important is that poor people don't have *control* over even the little that they do earn. As writers like Richard Douthwaite (1996) have noted, even poor communities have a considerable amount of money moving in or through them, in the form of bank accounts, pension funds, stocks, bonds, and life insurance. But the poorer a community is, the faster money leaves. In some native reserves and inner-city communities, studies have shown that as much as three-quarters of the money coming into those communities leaves within days and doesn't return.

Mainstream banks are dominant forces in sucking money out of local communities. In the United States, this has been such a problem that it spawned the 1977 Community Reinvestment Act, along with various grassroots organizations across the country being geared to forcing banks to extend credit to poor communities and curtail the banks' "redlining" practices in those communities.

Despite such measures, current trends in the financial industry are aggravating these problems, which are by no means confined to poor communities. Paralleling the rise of the Casino Economy, there is relatively less money going to depositing institutions and more going to mutual funds, trusts, pension funds, stocks, bonds, and other securities. Competition has spurred banks to consolidate and merge, loosening their already thin ties to local communities (Shuman, 1998). Depositor money, used as collateral for global gambling by big institutions, is being used ever more irrationally against the interests of the depositors.

If green economies are to be created, community financial infrastructures will be among the most important means of economic self-regulation. As will be described in the next chapter, the creation of Community, Green City, or Bioregional Development Plans will be essential to guide ecological development.

They will have to be developed in a participatory process, on the basis of substantive information about the existing economy, and in tandem with the creation of community indicators. Community-based financial institutions would be an essential means of exercising benign control of such development, since these institutions would gear their lending to support the objectives of the community plans and indicators.

Clearly, many current laws governing banking and investment would need changing to make this possible, but the ideal would be for the progressive financial institutions to voluntarily strive to direct resources in ways prioritized by the community. For this to happen in the most organic way, it would be desirable that there be a diversity of financial institutions reflecting the various subcultures and communities within the locality or region. The Community Plan would not be a mechanistic blueprint; rather, it would acknowledge various forms of self-activity and innovation within it.

Legislative and institutional obstacles to creating proactive community financial systems are probably less serious than the cultural and political inertia of important players like credit unions, community associations, and trade unions. *Credit unions* will have to be key protagonists in a community financial structure, but very few credit unions today see themselves with any role in commercial lending. Although credit unions in many places were originally spawned by social struggles, they have largely settled into a market niche, limiting themselves to social service and consumer lending.

As community-based prosumption and production grow, however, there should be escalating demands on credit unions to finance ecological development. In addition, credit unions are looking increasingly attractive to the average depositer as the major banks become more and more insensitive to communities. Many credit unions are today becoming increasingly squeezed by financial industry reorganization. On one hand, this makes them particularly disinclined to get into microcredit and small business loans, where administrative costs are high, returns low, and additional expertise is necessary. On the other hand, given public and political dissatisfaction with the big banks, the emergence of a cohesive eco-development movement—featuring Green City Plans, new progress indicators, local currencies, and exciting new enterprises—could easily induce credit unions to explore rewarding new opportunities for expansion.

Ultimately, a community financial infrastructure will have to include the type of banks that are now called *development banks*. These banks are geared not only to providing credit but also to management and development counselling and other technical expertise. In the industrialized world, the most famous of these banks is Chicago's South Shore Bank, which since 1983 has provided hundreds of millions of dollars to renovate low-income housing in its base community, approximately one-third of the housing stock. It not only accepts deposits but leverages funds from other sources because of its social development goals (Taub, 1988). Other examples include the Southern Development Bankcorporation, which Bill Clinton helped South Shore establish in Arkansas, and the Community Capital Bank in Brooklyn, which offers loans for small businesses, nonprofits, and affordable housing (Shuman, 1998). South Shore has also combined with Portland's Ecotrust to establish what they call the first environment bank, Shore-Bank, in the Pacific Northwest. ShoreBank's aim is to "support local businesses such as farmers, fishermen and oyster growers, finding new markets and creating a national identity for local products" (ShoreBank, 1998).

Revolving loan funds, also known as community loan funds, have been a crucial means activists have employed to finance social and environmental investment. They are not-for-profit, usually tax-exempt, organizations that derive their capital from foundations, churches, and individuals, and they tend to lend in small amounts (under ten thousand dollars) for regenerative community-based projects and activities (Nozick, 1992; Gunn and Gunn, 1991; Meeker-Lowry, 1995). Probably the most well-known of these funds in North America are those of the Self-Help Association for a Regional Economy (SHARE) in Massachusetts and the Cascadia Revolving Fund in the Pacific Northwest.

SHARE was founded in 1983, as a means of providing microcredit to people to expand or start small businesses that produce for the local economy in the Great Barrington area. SHARE members authorize local banks to use their savings funds as collateral for loans, all around three thousand dollars. SHARE has also improvised currency issues—"Deli Dollars" to finance a business relocation, and "Berk-Shares," in collaboration with five Berkshire County banks—to provide zero-interest loans to small business.

Cascadia, in a twelve-year period since its founding in 1987, has lent over $7 million to more than 160 businesses. It prioritizes loans to women, minorities, low-income people, and businesses in distressed areas as well as loans for job-creation and environmental production. More than 70 percent of its loans are to low-income people, and it has recovered more than 99 percent of the dollars lent.

Peer lending programs are a way of combining financial support with social support. It uses small groups, or "circles," of four or five peers, who are responsible for one another and who provide advice, support, and counselling for one another. Bangladesh's Grameen Bank popularized the technique, but it is now being used by various kinds of loan programs in the industrialized countries, including Canada's Calmeadow Foundation, which was founded in 1983 to provide microcredit.

Pension funds are among the most strategic targets for people to reclaim control over their own capital. According to Michael Shuman (1998), Americans have roughly $5 trillion in pension assets. Union funds are probably the most strategic, because for unions to put their pension funds to the most progressive use, they will have to reawaken some of their visionary heritage. Over the past decade or so, many unions have moved to reestablish control over their pensions, both because they want to make use of them to bolster declining union employment and because they are worried about the long-term security of their pensions. In the United States, the federal Department of Labor and the AFL-CIO have gotten behind "economically targeted investments" by pension funds (Ellmen, 1998). Because green economic development is by definition labor-intensive, it has great potential to capture union interest. In British Columbia, the Carpentry Workers Pension Plan has taken some innovative steps to simultaneously increase investment returns, provide building trade employment, and finance some interesting eco-development initiatives (Quarter, 1995; Dauncey, 1992).

Ethical investment funds, as currently configured, have to be rated primarily as colossal marketing scams, and yet the potential for individuals to put their individual savings to constructive use seems unlimited. The power of individual investor decisions was obvious in the boycott of apartheid in South Africa. This power has also had its effects on corporate investment in Burma and also, to some extent, on investment in nuclear weapons–connected firms. There are environmental investment programs everywhere, but the whole concept will be next to meaningless until this investment is directed toward building community self-reliance. For this to happen on any significant scale, however, communities themselves must commit to self-reliance and begin to draw up conversion strategies for eco-development.

There are many other forms of regenerative investment possible, including green venture capital funds and community land trusts. Like all of the ones described above, they have their proponents and critics. Unfortunately, most of the discussion revolves around their efficacy as *solutions in themselves.* Like local currencies, eco-efficiency, green consumerism, or reutilization industry, alternative finance is no panacea. Green development is a comprehensive design package, and regenerative development must work on all levels.

A major step for many of the instruments above, particularly pension funds and social investment funds, would be for them to direct their funds to community development. Foundations, credit unions, and even local governments can provide more community development finance. And governments can certainly do a better job of creating incentives, particularly tax incentives, for community investment (Ellmen, 1998).

Clearly, few of us can work on planning or activism that covers all these areas. Most projects, activities, and enterprises, however, provide opportunities to make a number of strategic connections. Local money and community finance can be helpful for many initiatives in community services, health, energy-efficiency, product design, green marketing, and more.

In conclusion, it must be stressed that much green economic development is, in the long run, self-financing. Eco-development—by definition—saves capital, energy, and resources, and these savings can be a major source of financing. Where imagination and ingenuity must take place is at the beginning, where seed-money can make a big difference. The fact that so many green development projects are win/win situations makes investment attractive, the most obvious case being energy retrofit programs, which are paid for via utility-bill monthly deductions. The deduction is a substantial source of income for the investor but is not even noticed by the building owner since the bill is much less than before the retrofit. Seed-money for green development will, therefore, go a long way. The challenge will be to design for the recycling of money as seriously as for the recycling of material resources.

11

The State and Beyond:
Postindustrial Forms of Regulation

A great source of the power of industrial society has been the fundamental antagonism it has structured between the individual and the social, manifest in both the Divided Economy (of paid and unpaid labor) and the separation between politics and economics. This tension has also been a great source of crisis. State socialism attempted to shift the focus—from individual to social—without altering the basic structure; the conflict remained. The entire economy was simply run like a large corporation. A green economy, however, moves to eliminate the split.

In this sense, a radical green perspective shares the concerns of both green capitalists and "left greens." The emphasis of green capitalism is on going with market forces but reshaping them so that prices reflect full social and environmental costs. Left greens, for their part, put their focus on conscious social regulation through a democratized state. Both eco-capitalist and eco-socialist advocates, however, usually underestimate how fundamentally both the state and markets can, and must, be transformed.

The community is the starting point for this transformation. The green perspective is not a mindless localism; rather, it's one of linking scale between levels of community—from neighborhood to planet. A fairly harmonious relationship between these nested hierarchies of regulation is possible only because they are built from the bottom up, with the base being the key level. What's more, this kind of relationship between different levels is possible only because these are relations between wholes, that is, between levels of relative self-reliance.

Clearly this kind of regulation will entail major rearrangement of existing forms of political power. Communities have very little say in many of the areas in which greens advocate new rules, for example, in product stewardship and bans. But laws must be changed, and there are all kinds of ways in which pressure to change the laws can be exerted. In the meantime, existing legal mechanisms (such as taxation) can be used to achieve the same goals.

There is some tendency in capitalist nations for a so-called devolution of certain powers, for example, in Canada, from the federal government to the provinces. This devolution can more accurately be called a *dissolution* of powers, since it is generally part of a trend toward deregulation of big business and dismantling of the national Welfare State. The position of greens, of course, is that any such devolution of power should be opposed unless it results in both a *raising* of social and environmental standards and new forms of grassroots participation in governance.

It is in the community that individual interests and opportunities can be most embedded in social and ecological development. The state here is an instrumental mechanism for community consciousness to operate. In this sense, it goes beyond post-Fordist notions of the "developmental state," which is usually counterposed to the old Fordist "regulatory state." (The term "developmental state" was first used to describe the proactive capitalist states in Japan and Germany, in contrast to the deregulatory neo-Taylorist states of the 1980s U.S. and U.K. regimes [Cohen, 1993]; but it has been expanded slightly to refer to more social-democratic high-wage post-Fordist models advocated by the left [Mackintosh, 1993]. The latter usually point to the small-scale, high-tech, flexible manufacturing networks of north-central Italy as a model for more humane capitalist development.)

Like some of the left's versions of the developmental state, the green community version combines various market strategies with greater levels of democracy. But because greens put a greater emphasis on ecosystem productivity and on production for service (not accumulation), the green perspective must rely more on social organization, especially self-reliance and community processes. This goes hand in hand with a radical redefinition of wealth itself. Left post-Fordism, while emphasizing quality of life more than the old left did, and advocating reduction of paid work time, still stresses distribution, traditional production, the wage relation, and exports. For greens, growing levels of self-reliance mean greater potentials for self-regulation because of the possibility of multiple interacting and complementary forms of mutual benefit and control.

Self-regulation, as I want to show more clearly in this section, does not mean that the economy runs without direct involvement by the state. In fact, the state is, in many respects, *more* involved. But it is involved in a very different way than we are used to; it is involved as a means *to help* the individual to fulfill a social purpose rather than as a policeman or as a substitute for real social bonds. Ethical action would be incorporated into everyday enterprise, not exclusively in private personal life, as it is today, but in the public realm now dominated by competition and self-aggrandizement.

Community-oriented self-regulation would not eliminate the conflict between selfishness and service, which exists even within ourselves. It would, however, work to design social forms to consciously cultivate and support that positive side of the human personality that seeks harmony, growth, and meaning. This does not mean utopia, but it does mean a drastic break with several thousand years of the patriarchal state.

Polanyi (1957) argued that the capitalist market economy severed economic life from its social context. But millennia long before this, the state was organized to shape, suppress, and direct human activity. The state as we know it today is simply the latest model of an institution shaped for domination, which has nevertheless had to accommodate somewhat to changing human potentials and activities. As Mumford, Richardson, Bookchin, Rudhyar, and many others have stressed, class societies have been based on organized violence. For their own survival, they have always had to guard against their own destructive impulses, the very forces of domination they cultivated in their men.

Dominance-based civilization can no longer survive, simply because it now threatens humanity's survival. It would be cynical and stupid to believe that more regenerative forms of social organization are not possible. Such forms of organization have always existed, although increasingly pushed to the margins of power. Our task is to unleash and generalize these relationships on a larger scale. One important key to succeeding at this task is a focus on community.

GREEN COMMUNITY SELF-REGULATION

Throughout part 2, I have called attention to various aspects of self-regulation in a green economy. Unlike capitalist markets, green self-regulation is not driven by the profit motive, by technological change, or by any external force; it is powered by the social and ecological values implicit in human self-actualization. For this reason, there can be no one factor, be it political, economic, monetary, or cultural, that accomplishes such regulation. If one needs to isolate a single thing, let it be the *design perspective,* which attempts to use the most elegant combination of measures to achieve the goal.

The very concept of self-regulation is, of course, something of a myth—in the positive sense of an *archetype* that can never be completely realized but only approximated. Self-regulation here is not meant to suggest a tensionless or frictionless society, but it does point to a society where some of the key oppositions in industrial society, based in institutional domination and alienation, have been resolved. The way these tensions will be resolved is by more fully harnessing human *potentials*—spiritual, political, economic, technological, and cultural.

Contrary to popular intellectual fashion, most greens believe such potentials *do* exist, that they are being suppressed by industrial capitalism, and that it is our responsibility to find appropriate political and economic forms to manifest them. As this book has tried to show, this doesn't mean constructing a detailed blueprint, but instead highlighting a set of principles that can allow people and communities to express their own potentials. From this perspective, self-regulation is simply use of the appropriate forms of human development in their appropriate combination. These forms won't establish Nirvana, but they may turn "development" into something actually regenerative rather than something destructive.

This chapter will review briefly the combination of factors that can approach self-regulation:

- **The scale of the economy:** community and bioregional organization, harnessing technological potentials for decentralization via reutilization industry, distributed energy-generation, eco-infrastructure, local money, co-operative consumption, and so on.
- **Participatory democracy:** green municipalism, participatory Green City plans, community indicators, and pattern-language development.
- **A green regulatory structure:** including community design pattern-languages, performance standards, product stewardship systems, product and substance bans, and other rules that encourage bioregionalism, quality, and community.
- **Green market mechanisms:** ecological tax systems, account-money and other community currencies, and a green financial infrastructure.
- **Knowledge as a regulatory force:** via resource inventories, eco-accounting, product information and labelling, and community indicators.

Again, it must be emphasized that we will need all of these tools if we have any chance of achieving even simple sustainability. It should also be added that all of these factors combined together will still be insufficient if the element of culture is not primary. Real citizenship and community cannot be achieved without a degree of bonding, shared vision, and even celebration. Happily, many of the political and economic aspects listed above—such as pattern-languages, local money, and indicators—can also be *means* of helping achieve this sense of social solidarity.

SCALE AND ACCOUNTABILITY

Critics of technology are justifiably dismissive of the pop/corporate ideology of technological determinism, which goes hand in glove with globalization propaganda. In the process, many of these critics miss understanding that cutting-edge potentials in key areas of technology make possible greater levels of decentralization and democracy. Distributed generation of clean energy; the greater efficiencies resulting from a bioregional organization of reutilization industry and ecological agriculture; the interactive and decentralized nature of hypermedia; and the participatory and distributed nature of eco-infrastructure—all of these and more represent opportunities for community development, *if* we can establish democratic control. That is a big "if," of course, but we are still in a much better position than if technological development were intrinsically centralizing.

The point here is that, if we *could* implement the most efficient economic systems, their very scale of operations would make democratic accountability much more possible. Small is not always necessarily better, but increasingly the most resource-efficient and productive technologies tend to work on a human scale. Writers like Murray Bookchin, Ursula Franklin, Leopold Kohr, Ivan Illich, Jane Jacobs, and E. F. Schumacher, while hardly optimistic about mainstream technological development, have put great emphasis on the conscious use of technology to support human scale. As Illich said in his well-known essay *Energy and Equity* (1974), "free people must travel the road to productive social relations at the speed of a bicycle." For years, mainstream apologists insisted that such dreams were futile since technology required larger scale and centralization. Today, such arguments are still made but seem transparently flimsy and self-serving.

Creating appropriate scale, of course, involves far more than implementing decentralized technologies. Some (non-account-money) local currencies are successful in creating community simply because they make possible more local interdependence and accountability. Forms of cooperative consumption—such as community retrofit programs and neighborhood prosumption centers (where tools and durables are shared)—also entail levels of participation that resist exploitative practices.

The integrated but diverse forms of production and consumption of eco-development are fertile ground for a strong and diverse civil society. Most of the left has been slow to recognize that ecological production provides the decentralized base for the popular democracy long desired by social movements. By the same token, many environmentalists have not yet recognized that thorough-going grassroots participation is essential to establishing ecological relationships. The "eyes to acres" ratio is important when green settlements cultivate so many diversely productive microclimates. Nothing is a panacea, but the complementarity of eco-development and democracy goes far to provide a basis for community self-regulation.

It is not an exaggeration to say that democracy is a tendency of human development, an expression of individual and working-class autonomy. This is not just a theoretical angle on the new productive forces but is attested to by movements all over the world.

For greens, this near identity of democracy and real development is reinforced by the connection, discussed above, between participation and eco-production. There is also, however, a growing recognition, particularly in the cyberculture, that complexity spawns democracy. That is, external forms of hierarchy and control are now too cumbersome to work properly, and various forms of "internal self-regulation" are the only appropriate forms of management. The fall of state socialism is often cited as an example of a dysfunctional form of external management, but we might as well throw in the whole of industrial society. Capitalism has been extremely resilient, but it is also very vulnerable because of the hierarchy and empty forms of wealth endemic to it.

The malaise, decadence, and apathy characterizing electoral politics in the industrialized countries is largely a symptom of the suppression of democratic potentials implicit in globalization and waste. Internal self-regulation on a social scale means *direct democracy,* which is what humanity is, or should be, in the process of transitioning to. This transition is possible only if the community is the base for extended relationships. Direct democracy is not made possible by electronic polling, any more than it is made possible by electronic shopping. It is a possibility because, on the community level, a high level of economic self-reliance can allow politics to be integrated into everyday worklife. Regenerative forms of production demand that democracy can be exercised as much through everyday social and economic relations as in community councils or explicitly political organizations. The local scale allows direct accountability as well as general participation. New information and communications technologies can amplify these capacities like never before, especially by connecting communities into regional, continental, and global networks, but the key relationships remain the mundane, interpersonal connections in the community.

PARTICIPATORY PLANNING AND GREEN MUNICIPALISM

The single most defining characteristic of green, or postindustrial, politics is that it interpenetrates every area of life and is focused on building regenerative alternatives in all those areas. Art, economics, and politics—all lose their autonomy and become part of everyday life.

Even today in the mainstream, we see areas where the boundaries between public, private, and community are blurred. Green politics is directed toward consciously dissolving those boundaries in ways that allow more and more crucial decision making to take place in, or arise from, everyday life. For this to happen, not only must decision making be decentralized, but everyday life must become less fragmented and more related to society's overall goals. Social and ecological vision that can unify means and ends, form and content, must be developed. Again, the strategic level is the local one, the level closest to daily life.

A crucial necessity for green community development is the *Green City (or Community, or Bioregional) Development Plan.* It would not be a blueprint, but it would be comprehensive, in that it would cover all economic sectors and all areas of life that the community valued. It would be drawn up in a participatory manner and would serve as the basis for the development of community indicators. It would set approximate targets, specify certain community guidelines (like design pattern languages) and performance standards, and serve as guidance for community action and lending policies of community financial institutions. It would be based on detailed information, provided by the indicators, eco-accounting, and the Community Resource Inventory (to be discussed later in this chapter).

Although a proper Green City Plan would be done with the broadest possible participation, it is important that visionary perspectives be raised by social movement and community groups for the purpose of discussion and debate. In San Francisco (Berg et al., 1989) and other cities, such prototype Green City Plans have been developed. In Toronto, there is some discussion of collaboration between activist/experts in various sectors—transportation, energy, food system, and housing—to develop this kind of plan, which could be circulated, discussed, and updated every year. Labor councils, women's associations, antipoverty groups, environmental coalitions, and progressive business groups can all be developing their autonomous perspectives on what they think a green development strategy should involve. Educational work based on their research and proposals can contribute to the debate and dialogue essential to a participatory planning process. Meanwhile, the visioning process requisite for community indicator development can be gradually expanding its horizons.

While green politics puts its primary emphasis on the politicization of everyday life through grassroots alternatives, formal political institutions must also be democratized since they play such an important role in determining the overall rules of the game.

In North America, two related strains of grassroots democracy have been proposed by the bioregional and social ecology movements. Both of these models go beyond "democratizing the state" to redesigning it from the ground up. The bioregional model suggests "watershed councils," in line with the notion that, as economies are designed to move with natural processes, both political and economic boundaries will tend to follow ecosystem boundaries.

A more elaborate political vision known as "green municipalism" has emerged from Murray Bookchin's fusion of social anarchism and New England traditions of town councils and citizen assemblies. Green municipalism proposes a political structure of direct democracy based on active and aware citizens in local communities (Bookchin, 1995; Biehl, 1998).

The direct democracy of green municipalism does not mean that all individuals decide on all policy details at all levels. It means the system is designed so that the base level of the "nested hierarchy" of regulation is the most important one— making the "hierarchy" a "lowerarchy" (Brandt, 1995). Representation exists at each higher level, but it is a substantially different kind of representation than we experience today. The representative is not a "leader" making autonomous decisions, but a true representative of his or her community.

The basic unit of a green municipal polity is the citizen assembly, which might encompass a neighborhood or perhaps a dozen or more neighborhoods, depending on the situation and traditions. Citizens would physically meet to discuss and decide on all policy matters. They would elect representatives, who would rotate and could be recalled, and who would simply carry out the mandated decisions. Unlike industrial political structures, where elected politicians have the autonomy to make policy, in a green municipal system, policy and administration would be strictly separated.

Elected representatives would serve on the next higher level of assembly and would strive to express their community's mandate. They would, in turn, elect representatives to the next higher level of assembly, according to the same principles. In this way, communities would be confederated with other communities, institutionalizing interdependence without the coercive hierarchy of the industrial state (McConkey, 1991). Similar to the way that green economic self-reliance does not mean absolute self-sufficiency, so also forms of postindustrial self-regulation would express regional, national, and even planetary interdependence based on relative independence.

Green municipalism builds on the original spirit of green movements that emerged in Europe and Australia in the mid-1970s and defined themselves as "anti-party parties." Most of the radical elements in these parties left as these green parties gradually became seduced by conventional mass voter appeal and by preoccupation with specific legislation.

Green municipalists put priority on long-term structural change. Bookchin (1991) suggests that, until such time as assemblies can be officially chartered by local government, they can still form and grow based on their moral and educational power. They can also run candidates for existing city councils, who would be required to represent the citizen assemblies in ways described above.

A key to the creation of real democracy is the *de-professionalization of politics*. Individuals would not nominate themselves to run for office, but they would be selected by their communities and would be subject to recall at any time. Green municipalists argue that conventional political parties, even on the local level, are fundamentally antidemocratic since they mirror the hierarchy of the industrial state and there must be a strong relationship between means and ends.

Green municipal networks have been suggested as nonparty means to create broader networks of community groups committed to green development. These networks might at first simply endorse candidates from established parties in regular municipal elections. Further on, they would nominate their own candidates to run. (Individuals could not propose themselves as network candidates.) Simultaneously, the network could facilitate the gradual emergence of parallel systems of neighborhood governance, such as assemblies.

This would not have to be an adversarial development if it evolved organically. Various forms of community self-governance should in any case emerge from various economic initiatives: retrofit programs, ecological restoration projects, community gardening and community-supported agriculture, and so on. The local state and local utilities would be involved in these programs, and it is possible that much of the administration of these programs would devolve to the neighborhood activists and experts. In this sense, (successful) green economic development would absorb the state into the community in a positive sense. These organic activities could provide a base for full-fledged green municipal political structures.

While there are few examples of actual green municipal citizen assemblies in operation, the philosophical influence of green municipalism has been great. This is partly due to the way Murray Bookchin has embedded this perspective in the philosophy of Social Ecology, but it is also because of a popular sense of untapped democratic potentials. It is to be expected that concerns with political alternatives will grow as green economic alternatives mature.

NEW RULES AND REGULATION

Participatory planning and democratized political structures provide a foundation for new forms of regulation that set out rules of the game, which mandate regenerative activities, provide incentives and coordination for them, and support innovation and experimentation. The Green City, or Community Development, Plan would lay out the vision upon which the rules are revised.

As with the previous two elements—scale and participation—important changes in law and administration would have to take place to implement new rules. To argue that regional product stewardship, for example, is impossible because only the federal government now has jurisdiction under existing law misses the point of this book. As mentioned earlier in this chapter, laws can be changed, and as long as a political movement is strong, it can always find ways to make progress toward its goals until the laws are changed.

All economies are based on certain rules that define how things should work. The new rules upon which a green economy is based differ from those of the industrial economy in several ways. First, they are explicit and are based on a definite vision of society's goals. Second, they try to simplify regulation and build regenerative activity into people's everyday activities. One way they do this is by emphasizing *performance* standards (for example, a certain degree of overall energy efficiency for new buildings), which focus on results, rather than mandating particular means of meeting those standards (for example, a prescribed amount of a particular wall insulation). A similar principle applies to architectural pattern languages, which would give lots of flexibility regarding how and which patterns would be applied. Finally, the new rules would try as much as possible to build in incentives for excellence, rather than just minimum standards.

New rules based on a general vision but that encourage flexibility and excellence might seem somewhat paradoxical. Measures like product bans and architectural pattern languages might, on one hand, appear even more draconian than state-socialist "command-and-control" measures, and yet, on the other hand, simultaneously be much less interventionist than Western capitalist "end-of-pipe/back-seat-driver" style regulation. The rest of this section will discuss just a few of the many kinds of rules that can be used.

Among the most important new rules in a green economy are those that most define society's relationship to material resources. As discussed earlier, the core paradigm of authentic postindustrialism is that of the *ecological service economy,* where the focus of the economy is on providing for human needs and doing this in the most efficient way possible. New rules are required to provide both incentives for an end-use approach and disincentives for resource use. At the core of this new regulatory paradigm is a radical new concept of producer liability, expressed in *product stewardship rules.* In the chapter on manufacturing, we looked at an example of such rules—the proposal for an "intelligent product system"— and how such systems can catalyze resource-efficiencies, improve human health, reduce pollution, and create local high-skilled work by closing loops.

In that chapter, we also saw that some industrial ecologists recommend a fairly small set of benign substances as the basis for most industrial production. Placing limits on the number of chemicals and materials used would be one of the more radical aspects of state action. Initially, this would mean product bans or, more accurately, phase-outs to limit the set of approved substances to those that would not damage the environment or human health. Eventually, with the phase-outs completed, it would simply mean the application of the "precautionary principle" to the approval of all new chemicals and substances.

Although this may sound quite draconian, product bans—and product stewardship liability in general—simplify state activities. Fordist end-of-pipe regulation, by contrast, requires giant bureaucracies to monitor and limit dangerous substances. Banning these substances outright is a much simpler task, and producers easily adjust to the new rules if the phase-out time is adequate. In their emphasis on zero-discharge, the rules are straightforward and positive. Some monitoring would, of course, be necessary during the phasing-out period, but generally bans eliminate bureaucracy. In an economy where only benign materials are used, the need for environmental monitoring is much reduced, or it can take other, more constructive forms. In essence, bans are a form of regulation that have an effect similar to incentives.

Product and material bans can be a useful tool, not simply in saving vast amounts in cleanup and health costs but also in stimulating the creation of bioregional economies. Substitution is a process that is deep and multidimensional. In most cases, it is not simply a substitution of a particular chemical for another. Plastics, for example, have made possible a vast transport-based food industry. The ban of a toxic chemical might be one more economic incentive to create a regionally based food system of fresh healthy foods, which also create lots of local employment. Such bans might also encourage experimentation with "solar cooling" and refrigeration, with greenhouse technology and production, or with vegetation that might be used both for water purification and as an industrial feedstock.

Material and substance phase-outs would be part of an overall eco-economic strategy to create healthy local industry based on principles of industrial ecology. The creation of secondary materials industry could be designed with reference to existing local and regional waste streams. Disposal and other green taxes could be used to gradually turn waste streams into resource streams. All this would, of course, be based on detailed knowledge of the bioregion and technical possibilities for economic conversion.

Architectural and community design pattern languages are means by which communities can express relatedness (Alexander, 1977, 1979). Today, our cities and communities express the chaos and fragmentation of private-property relations. Existing zoning and building bylaws typically enforce the wrong kind of standardization and the wrong kind of diversity. These rules need to change to encourage ecological mixed-use development, which emphasizes *access,* rather than mobility, and the natural productivity of the landscape. Just as important as these laws are the pattern languages that communities should develop to provide guidelines for the incremental piecemeal acts of building that can create a feeling of wholeness. These pattern languages were discussed in chapter 7, but they should be mentioned here in connection with community self-regulation because, like community indicators, they would express a community's vision and consciousness. Clearly, various communities or even neighborhoods in the city would have their own pattern languages. Some would be more rigorous than others, and some might be mandatory, some voluntary, and so on. They would, in almost all cases, seem desirable.

Green economies would be created and perpetuated by a whole range of incentives and disincentives, in addition to those mentioned above. The New Rules Project of the Institute for Local Self-Reliance (ILSR; based in Minneapolis and Washington, D.C.) is geared to preempting retrogressive laws, reexamining long-standing policy, and proposing action on new rules that can build self-reliant economies. The ILSR points out that the postwar Waste Economy in the United States was based on mechanisms like the Highway Trust Fund, the oil depletion allowance, and massive subsidies for suburban sprawl with its expensive dispersed infrastructure. The ILSR has been calling attention to a number of measures—local, state, and federal—that can assist in the development of local economies. These measures include green taxes to incorporate the full cost of long-distance transport and trade; appropriate taxation of electronic commerce; discouragement of absentee ownership; renewable energy portfolio standards for utilities; and the abolition of garbage exports. These measures are suggestive of a whole range of areas where green economic design can be applied (Institute for Local Self-Reliance, 1997).

DESIGNING MARKETS FOR REGENERATIVE EXCHANGE

A major focus of the green economy's new rules would be to shape market mechanisms to encourage regenerative production. Product stewardship systems certainly rearrange the boundaries within which markets work. More often than not, market mechanisms are thought of as those things that affect the direction of the profit motive, usually by forcing previously external social and environmental costs to be incorporated into market prices.

Many social movement activists are skeptical of market-oriented approaches, usually for good reason. Markets often cannot touch whole realms of economic life that are crucial to green production and human development. Also, the concept of "making the polluter pay" seems to imply that, if the polluter pays, he is entitled to pollute. For this reason, many on the left put the emphasis of new rules on constraining profit-making enterprise. This is certainly justified; product stewardship is, after all, one kind of constraint.

But, as emphasized in the previous chapter on money, truly regenerative economic activity depends ultimately on dethroning the profit motive as the primary driving force of the economy. In this sense, there are certain kinds of market mechanisms, such as account-money systems, that completely redefine the basic incentives of the economy. Markets are turned into places for exchange of use-value, not places to accumulate exchange-value.

This kind of local money system is particularly appropriate to the decentralized forms of production characteristic of a green economy. Murray Bookchin (1995) feels that green municipalism requires municipal ownership of the primary means of production. He argues that worker co-ops, for example, are capable of acting just as selfishly as capitalist firms. That is certainly true, of course, in an economy driven by the profit motive. But if the profit motive is undercut by account-money and reinforced in the transition with land taxes, a community plan, and other nonmaterial and nonmonetary incentives, such complete community ownership might be seen as an unnecessary and cumbersome option.

Municipalization of production ultimately presents most of the same problems as nationalization. It's a collectivization that is primarily defensive in nature and that restricts flexibility and feedback in individual activity. Society does not really need to be protected from the selfish individual; it simply needs rules that do not constantly reward the selfish individual. Most people will choose regenerative activity if given half a chance. There is certainly a role for community or public ownership, but this role should be determined by appropriate function rather than as a defense against egoistic individualism.

Given the goal and possibility of freeing the economy from the profit motive, conventional market mechanisms can nevertheless play a useful transitional role without their having complete responsibility for creating an ecological economy by themselves. Account-money systems will take some time to develop, and in any case, it is essential that we be forcing prices to reflect real costs. Since our goal is to increasingly employ social and environmental indicators as the most appropriate measures of value, we need not be obsessed with getting exact dollar figures about costs. The main purpose of eco-accounting is not always to translate environmental costs into exact dollar figures; it is also to force the market to reflect real value. The emphasis should be to constantly create pressure on business to engage in less destructive and more regenerative production.

While it is true that the profit motive can never establish fully ecological relationships, it is nevertheless desirable for private producers to have some financial stake in eco-production. For those corporate producers who truly commit themselves to regenerative production, there should be tangible rewards. The main point, however, is that market mechanisms are not a *substitute* for conscious design of the economy; rather, they are an *instrument* of such design.

ECOLOGICAL TAX REFORM

Green taxes are probably the most important mechanism for, as von Weiszacker (1994: 117-28) puts it, "making prices tell the ecological truth." Environmental taxes can be used for any number of purposes: to discourage pollution, to raise revenue, to change consumer behavior, and so on. They are currently being used around the world in various ways, and a number of U.S. states, including Oregon, Maine, Vermont, and Minnesota, have major ecological tax reforms on the table (Morris, 1998).

Our particular concern here is how green taxes can act as tools to help create an ecological service economy. Market mechanisms are incapable of doing this themselves. Fundamental regulatory changes like product stewardship systems are perhaps most important, but green taxation can be very helpful, particularly in reversing the relationship between materials and labor. In the industrialized countries, labor is relatively more expensive and more highly taxed; materials are cheap and lightly taxed. Green taxation can level the playing field for eco-materials vis-à-vis nonecological products, it can discourage waste, and it can help create an economy that is more people-intensive than capital-intensive.

Because of the unpopularity of taxes, green tax advocates have stressed the notion of ecological tax reform, or "tax shifting," which would make the reforms revenue-neutral. That is, no more revenue would be required; it would just be derived from different sources. The idea is to tax "bads" like pollution and resource extraction rather than "goods" like income and investment (Roodman, 1998; Friends of the Earth, 1998; Jackson, 1996; Cobb, Halstead, and Rowe, 1995; Roberts and Brandum, 1995; von Weizsacker, 1994; Hawken, 1993; von Weizsacker and Jesinghaus, 1992; Michael Jacobs, 1991).

While some mainstream tax shift proposals put equal emphasis on shifting away from labor and capital, it's clear the top priority must be a shift from labor. On one hand, it is a way to rearrange the labor/materials relationship, conserving resources while making labor more attractive to employ. On the other hand, it is a means of reversing the regressive trend from taxes on profit and capital to taxes on labor and individuals. In fact, the payroll tax is the fastest growing of all major taxes (Friends of the Earth, 1998), now comprising almost 30 percent of U.S. tax revenues. With personal income taxes amounting to 30 percent and corporate income taxes at a mere 6.3 percent, it's clear the average working stiff is getting stiffed. A number of proponents have argued that, even without a focus on capital, alleviating the tax burden on labor would not only reduce unemployment but be a tremendous stimulus for the entire economy (Tindale and Holtham, 1996).

There is some debate whether a major move to green taxation would mean an eventual end to income tax altogether. Some advocates of income tax abolition argue that a tax on net worth (a "wealth tax") could actually be more effective than an income tax in controlling inequality. Nevertheless, the idea of everyone supporting government with a portion of one's earnings seems fair, particularly if society can eliminate radical inequality and government can become an instrument of participatory democracy. Eventually, people should be able to pay taxes at least partly in local currencies.

In any case, the transition away from labor and income taxes would be gradual. For a complete elimination of income tax, the Wuppertal Institute's von Weiszacker (1992, 1994) recommends a forty-year transition, while Paul Hawken (1993) suggests twenty years.

An ecological tax system would have to begin by eliminating all subsidies to brown industry, a major impact in itself. The Worldwatch Institute estimates annual subsidies to polluting and extraction industry at over $650 billion worldwide (Roodman, 1998), while Friends of the Earth (1998) cites $22 billion in tax breaks for corporate polluters and brown industry in the United States. Although national governments are the source of most of these subsidies, local and regional governments have been falling all over themselves in recent years to entice any and all investment.

A 5- to 10-percent tax on energy and other selected items could be implemented and increased 5 to 10 percent a year. The highest priority would be an energy or carbon tax. A tax on energy affects virtually all areas of production, especially energy-intensive manufacturing and extraction industry.

Other taxed items could be raw materials (both metals and renewables), emissions, toxic emissions and toxic substances, extractive industry, water, and land used for building. Disposal taxes could also be useful in reducing waste and supporting product stewardship.

Land taxes, or ground rent, are a fairly progressive means of reducing speculation in land while dissipating pressures for suburban sprawl. They focus development on the *use* of land, not its "spec" value. Today, property taxes tend to lump together taxes on buildings and taxes on land. Critics argue they really must be separated since they have drastically different effects. The major portion of taxation should be on land, with very little, if any, on buildings. While land taxes must be consciously designed to protect and encourage green space in cities, as well as to protect small homeowners, seniors, and other groups, they can complement the development of local currencies, land trusts, and ecological land-use planning.

The specific impact of taxation is much more difficult to gauge than the impact of regulations (Michael Jacobs, 1991; Roodman, 1996), and this impact would be exaggerated in such a comprehensive overhaul. Within a short time, however, patterns would be visible, and taxes would be adjusted to make the transition as smooth and effective as possible. While taxes on the selected "bads" would rise from year to year, eventually the tax system would have to be adjusted to reassess the baddest of the bad. While green taxes ostensibly undercut their own sources of revenue by forcing these sources to clean up, there will always be room for improvement, and it is likely that making the economy healthier and more efficient would reduce health costs and many other expenses of the state. A regenerative system, therefore, would be less expensive.

Taxes would be selected to be reasonably easy to administer. The cost of evaluating new products, processes, and materials would be paid for by the producers. Where possible, it would be desirable to harmonize the taxes with other regions and nations. But von Weizsacker (1994) writes that this is less necessary than with conventional regulatory pollution-control measures since many industries will be forced into efficiencies that make them more competitive. In any case, problems of international competition are much less a factor in designing bioregional systems.

Questions of equity must be central in designing green tax systems. Many environmental taxes, by themselves, are regressive in that they are kinds of consumption taxes that affect the poor comparatively more than the rich (Morris, 1998). Energy costs, for example, make up a larger portion of poor people's income. Nevertheless, these issues can be dealt with in many different ways. On one hand, community currencies may be able to provide for many basic needs. On the other hand, self-financing community retrofit programs can cut energy expenses in housing, and these programs can also prioritize training for lower-income people in building retrofit skills, so jobs would be available. Needless to say, an energy tax would make building-retrofit a growth industry. Equivalent alternative transport programs could be devised to offset transportation expenses. Tax regimes could be "terraced" so that the tax only applies to consumption over a certain level (Roodman, 1998). If necessary, lump sum rebates could be made to lower-income people, as provided by Greenpeace Germany's 1994 Energy Tax proposal, which has garnered broad public support (Roodman, 1996, 1998).

Green tax proponents in England have even suggested the possibility of using environmental taxes to finance *basic income* (guaranteed annual income) schemes (Tindale and Holtham, 1996)—something that would have the effect of supporting eco-production in and around the home and community. While basic income programs would require more state involvement than do local account-money systems, they would have a similar effect of breaking down formal/informal economic divisions. As long as the dividend was large enough to properly cover people's basic needs, these programs would be a substantial improvement over current capitalist state welfare systems since they could incorporate many support programs into one simple program (Van Parijs, 1992). People would be free to earn more on top of the dividend. Possible abuses of the program would be greatly reduced in a community-based economy, where basic incomes could be combined with training in food growing, energy retrofit, solar and wind power, preventive health care, and other skills needed in the community. Basic income is not as intrinsically self-regulating as an account-money system nor as transforming of capitalist market relationships, nevertheless communities might consider basic income programs as a transitional support for community development, at least until such time as community currencies were sufficiently developed.

Finally, a tax on one significant "bad" must be mentioned. This is a tax on financial transactions, what has, on the international level, been called a "Tobin tax." Ross Gelbspan (1997) has been the most well-known advocate of linking a financial tax with positive environmental measures. This tax is normally seen as a measure to decrease the volatility of the Casino Economy's speculative markets, but different advocates argue for different uses of the tax revenue. Gelbspan suggests a .25 percent (that is, one-quarter of 1 percent) tax on all international financial transactions (which total $1.3 trillion a day), with the revenue—amounting to $200 billion a year—going to renewable energy development around the world. He sees it as a way to jump-start the clean power industry without unduly burdening the fossil fuel industry.

My feeling is that a Tobin tax, or even its equivalent on a national or regional level, might certainly be a useful tool—as part of a comprehensive overhaul of the economy's basic incentives and disincentives. But as a panacea itself, it would certainly be a failure since it could not deal with the fundamental systemic problems.

In summary, ecological tax reform is a positive measure that involves major state intervention in the economy, but impact of which is to enhance the self-regulating character of the economy. While taxing the bads, the net effect is to reward the goods and create a win/win scenario for all but the worst offenders. Like other green economic mechanisms, it creates space in the economy for social and ecological purposes, especially when combined with some of these other mechanisms.

KNOWLEDGE AND SELF-REGULATION

It has become a hackneyed cliché of the Microsoft generation that information is power. The happy reality is that information *can* provide power—if social and ecological values can turn it into practical knowledge that is useful for regenerative activity.

Knowledge is necessary for the community to realize its potential for self-reliance and independence. In previous chapters, I have referred to important forms of information to be used in community development. The community indicators discussed in the previous chapter are one of the most important expressions of overall community values. But these indicators are based on a wealth of other information, some of it very specialized—about the community; about the region and environment; about material resources, products, and processes; about the cultures and subcultures of the area; and about neighboring communities and the rest of the world.

Despite the fact that we supposedly now live in an information society, most of us are hopelessly lacking in basic essential information about our communities, about our environment, and about regenerative forms of production. We are also lacking in knowledge about regenerative forms of consumption.

According to community developer and political theorist Robin Murray (1993), the Fordist state was just as effective in de-skilling users and consumers of social services as Fordist mass production was in de-skilling line workers. Public ignorance puts many responsibilities in the lap of the state that don't need to be there. Information in the hands of the community can provide a self-regulatory function.

Every sector of a green economy must focus on the knowledge-building required to be successful, be it in agriculture, manufacturing, building, communications, health, or social services. For enlightened consumption, communities can exercise substantial control over their development simply by supporting ecological producers in their region, but this support requires product evaluation and labelling using locally developed criteria.

For this and for all aspects of planning and decision making, there must be an easily available information utility that contains basic information about the bioregion. The Rodale Regeneration Project described earlier put great emphasis on the notion of a regional resource inventory that would provide not only basic information about physical resources but also demographic, economic, and social statistics. This type of information is particularly important in developing import substitution strategies for selecting priorities to make the economic conversion to self-reliance as painless as possible.

Local universities can be a great resource in developing appropriate databases and geographical information (mapping) systems that can make the development of both community indicators and strategic planning easier. Schools, colleges, and universities can also be training and education centers for eco-development. Implementing a community development focus can help universities gradually free themselves from the government-cutback and corporate-prostitution mentality that currently grips many institutions of ostensibly higher learning.

In the long run, it is crucial that communities make good use of electronic communications technology. Substantial portions of available bandwidth should be devoted to relevant community information, education, discussion, and visioning. The current wasteland of brainwashing and escapism that dominates television represents massive waste of human potential. It seems inconceivable that green alternatives could make much of an impact on society without simultaneously transforming major portions of the consciousness industry. Especially today, when media is in such a transition, it is important that social and community movements engage in struggle for the design and progressive utilization of media.

BEYOND THE BIOREGION: PLANETARY TRANSFORMATION

As stated in the introduction, the focus of this book has been ecological transformation in the industrialized countries. This focus is because, on one hand, the comparatively rich countries of the North are the main source of global problems and the chief obstacles to their resolution, and on the other hand, although the principles of green economics can be applied universally, they must be applied in different ways in less "developed" countries.

My focus on the local is not because global relationships should be ignored or postponed (Shiva, 1989). Alternatives are developing on the international level as well as on the local and national levels. However, for international alternatives to deal with fundamental long-term relationships, they must be able to create space for ecological economies at a regional level. In a sense, global cooperation is creating a level of community. But ultimately, our global initiatives, even strictly oppositional ones, will be more successful when they are more organically connected to community power at the local level.

There is an international aspect even to green municipalism, as expressed in "confederalism." Confederalism is not just a structure of network organization but a philosophy of interdependence. Green municipal confederations can, in fact, begin with groups and individuals from a certain area that subscribe to green municipalist principles. Eventually, green confederations would comprise citizen or municipal or regional assemblies, but, whether in nascent or mature form, the communities would be bound by their responsibility to the larger, even global, community. Green municipalists and bioregionalists acknowledge that international communication and support are necessary for regenerative development.

International solidarity has always played a crucial role in social movement development in all countries. Pressure to establish human rights, democracy, and fair trade practices can create space for greater gains, besides simply giving essential help to those in need. None of these important activities is seen to be exclusive of the local economic development work emphasized in this book. In fact, it is fairly important that community developers be aware of, and engaged with, what is happening elsewhere for many reasons. One important reason is the fundamental moral responsibility that Northerners have because the North's development has taken place on the backs of the "less developed" nations. Neocolonial relationships may have succeeded colonial ones in modern capitalism, but the responsibilities of citizens in the developed world have not decreased. In fact, they have increased.

It is crucial, of course, that the North reduce its consumption and help facilitate a massive global redistribution of wealth. But, as this book has emphasized, the nature of "wealth" is changing, and real development is not simply a matter of shipping money or resources to needy countries. This is not to say that major transfers of material resources or capital are not warranted. As I mentioned above, much of the North's development has been financed by theft, in one form or another, from the South. But the key factor has to be a basic redistribution of *power*. This must be a shift of power to the *grassroots level*, and not simply to the corrupt elites, of underdeveloped nations. How we build power at the grassroots level is one question; how we help this happen in other places is another question altogether. The nature of global green economic cooperation and development could easily be the topic of another book.

With this understood, it is nevertheless important to say something about the relationship of trade and investment to green development. As Herman Daly (1996) has argued, intelligent economic policy today should entail (1) putting more restrictions on the wasteful long-distance flow of material goods and resources, and (2) decreasing restrictions of the flow of information. He points out that current trends in capitalist globalization are moving in precisely the opposite direction: toward decreasing restrictions on goods through free trade, and toward growing restrictions on the flow of information through intellectual property rights. The new economic constitutions that corporate globalization is trying to push through—like the Multinational Agreement on Investment—are essentially corporate versions of "new rules" that tie economies to purely quantitative economics and money-making for its own sake. Even worse, it is money-making that is prejudiced against local capitalists.

Various critics of these trade and investment agreements have suggested measures like capital controls and global (Tobin) taxes on speculative financial transactions. These certainly might be useful tools, but the only reliable protection from exploitative capital is a regenerative economic order, created by the application of the green economic principles discussed in this book. There are any number of political and economic ways to support regenerative trade and international development, but a few very general principles bear emphasizing:

1. Regenerative trade policy should *discourage* most external trade and direct investment and *encourage* the flow of information, especially that which helps communities and regions generate and recycle their own capital while cultivating their natural and social productivity.
2. Ending subsidies to brown industry, and particularly cheap energy, must be a prerequisite for any and all external trade. Most global trade is possible only because of dirty energy and minimal transport costs.
3. External trade incentives and disincentives should be based on eco-indicators, full-cost accounting, and real social need. They also should prioritize regenerative development in the Third World.

BUSINESS, LABOR, AND THE STATE

The major players in the industrial economy have been business, labor, and the state. At different times, one or another of these players has supplied the initiative to create strategic change. In the postindustrial context, it seems unrealistic to depend on any of these players to be the source of major structural change. Green business advocates may champion enlightened business and the left may have high hopes for a state run by more progressive parties or for a revitalized labor movement, but it seems that, in most cases, it will take community or social movement forces (or perhaps a crisis) to spark big business, unions, and the state into regenerative action. Nevertheless, neither business nor labor nor the state is a monolithic entity. Within the federal state, for example, there are people within environment or energy ministries who are doing cutting-edge work in their areas: from eco-industrial park development, to indicators, to advanced houses. The same is true within corporate culture and the labor movement. While, at the moment, they are still voices crying out in the wilderness, circumstances could provide a breakthrough.

Small business probably has the largest scope for movement of all sectors, but what I am calling "small business" is an arena in which many kinds of social forces meet. There is traditional small business and microbusiness, ecopreneurial private enterprise, nonprofit enterprise, for-profit co-operatives, and more. Green construction, community-shared agriculture, auto share networks, and so on are all included here. This is the place where social and community movements develop their economic activities and is therefore closely connected with civil society. Fortunately, many regenerative forms of production do not require large capital outlays for start-up, but this sector nevertheless tends to lack sufficient resources, and it certainly lacks the power to change the prevailing rules of the game, which favor large corporate enterprise. Nevertheless, it is an area which has tremendous potential to marshal greater resources when communities become more serious about prioritizing eco-development. Even without this help, ecopreneurialism and green community economic development (CED) is a crucial force in raising community consciousness and vision.

Large corporations have great resources, but they benefit the most from the industrial system, which is essentially theirs. Even manufacturing corporations (for example, General Motors) are now primarily financial entities and therefore are totally hooked into the Casino Economy. Most will vociferously resist strict new forms of liability, bioregional scale, community accountability, and worker participation. Despite the restrictiveness of the corporate milieu, there are people within large corporations doing important work, in such areas as industrial ecology and appropriate technology. Growing pressures on companies to change could enhance these people's influence. Given enough demand, many companies could profit greatly from providing eco-products and services, and some companies may even welcome liability legislation that supports what they are already doing to some degree, such as design for disassembly and operational leasing.

Communities may be well served by cultivating alliances with some of these more progressive producers. Once major rule changes can be incorporated into law, the number of potential corporate allies should grow substantially, especially if the rules reward excellence and innovation and not simply minimum standards. Unlike small business, large corporations will not change for ethical reasons, no matter how well-intentioned their management is. The rules must be changed or communities must provide them opportunities for profit from regenerative production (for example, community retrofit programs that provide markets for eco-materials producers).

Earlier in this chapter, I summarized aspects of the postindustrial state, but the existing industrial *state* is a very different entity. It is important to recognize that the state in modern industrial society is a complex institution and is difficult to stereotype. There are many people within the state doing interesting work. Nevertheless, one of the most dangerous attitudes activists can have is to expect substantial regenerative initiatives to emerge from the state. We have to work to create conditions where the state has no choice but to involve itself in community-initiated activities and on community terms.

The greatest potential, of course, is in local government, which is closest to the community. In areas where social and community movements can establish substantial alternatives, or even create adequate pressure for change, local governments can be transformed quickly. Moreover, even before these governments can be transformed, they can be pressured to implement progressive action. We can already see this all over the world: from municipal PVC bans in Germany, to Chattanooga's sustainable city initiative, to Toronto's Better Buildings program. Municipal politics is clearly a strategic arena for green economic alternatives and community development.

Organized labor is unlikely to be a pacesetter in a green transformation. Nevertheless, the role of unions is particularly important in the conversion process. To play an effective role, labor must relinquish its status as "cog in the machine." It must move proactively to redefine and reorient wealth production and to revive traditions of worker-control and self-management, while extending its long-time concern with the fair distribution of wealth.

Unions have been integrated into the system of both unlimited material growth and the Waste Economy by the union contract, which is overwhelmingly focused on the wage relationship. Organized labor will have to build its concerns with community welfare so that it can support more direct forms of remuneration, wealth creation, and quality of life. It will have to become a more proactive force in CED far beyond a simple concern with job-creation.

The reduction of work time (O'Hara, 1993; Anders Hayden, 1999) can be an important strategic tool for many unions, but it should not be an end in itself. As an end in itself, shorter work hours are an escape from social responsibility. There is no shortage of work to be done in society—just a shortage of paid work. Unions must work with communities in finding ways to make sure needed work gets done. This may mean finding ways to remunerate work done in the informal economy, or it could entail (paid) work-sharing. But unions should be working with communities, while employing community currencies and other methods, in devising their overall strategies.

Union initiatives in the ecological conversion of production may influence desired work time. By and large, eco-production is more labor-intensive. If the purpose of reduction of paid work time is simply to make jobs available to other workers, eco-production may make this reduction unnecessary, especially if efforts to make work more fulfilling pay off. If the purpose of work-time reduction is to increase quality free time, this is another matter.

The point is that unions must examine the sector they're in and determine how to make it fully ecological. Manufacturing workers, for example, should be introducing industrial ecology to companies and putting a labor slant on it that emphasizes regenerative work.

Unions will be in a much better position vis-à-vis "tech change" if they are well-informed concerning applications of eco-technology. Unions can also be working with the community in providing guaranteed markets for socially useful production, giving them more influence on management.

The model of the Lucas Aerospace Workers, a pioneering attempt at converting production to social uses more than twenty years ago, is still relevant (McRobie, 1981), but it needs to be generalized as a major focus of union activity. It cannot be limited to sunset industries and unprofitable companies, but labor will have to cultivate more political power to make this happen. Unions need systematic research into ecological technology and conversion strategies, and they need to be working with communities to implement regional development strategies. Every labor council should have a green think tank at work on these concerns and collaborating with progressive universities on relevant research.

Organized labor must also get more imaginative in organizing the vast and growing sectors of McJobs. This requires close community connections. In many cases, owners of small exploitative businesses can be allies in a community context if they are willing to change and benefit from CED. Ways can be worked out to use community currencies to pay decent wages and provide demand for responsible local businesses. If and when strikes are necessary in this sector, community support is essential for workers to have a chance.

Developing a labor-oriented regional green economic development program is a long-term process, but a visionary labor movement will win allies in the community and even with progressive business. Moving on a broad social front will provide a better base for increasing worker power in production and for worker ownership. Again, this needs to happen in healthy industries and companies, not just as the typical scenario of a worker buyout of a dying enterprise (Quarter,

1995). Labor expertise in the area of green development not only will enable unions to develop progressive new forms of eco-skills training but will provide guidance for the optimal utilization of labor investment and pension funds.

In the long run, only green development provides an effective alternative to neo-Taylorism, technological change, the hourglass economy, declining social services, and the crippling of collective bargaining.

ECONOMIC CONVERSION AND (R)EVOLUTIONARY STRATEGY

The purpose of this book has been to highlight general tendencies of economic development that go well beyond economics. This has been the focus because basic changes in our productive forces are transforming the very nature of wealth away from material things to quality of life and being. Great numbers of people are suffering material depravation, ironically because the industrial system blocks any efforts to move beyond material production to *production for human development*. Another apparent paradox is that to move to unbridled production for human development we must reawaken an ancient reverence for the material world—but as a living organism, not a dead thing.

The connection between the new wealth and human development makes the project of revolutionary change take on much greater *evolutionary* implications than did the old Marxist notion, because we have to be creating a new, more whole, human being. This need demands a basic change in the nature of revolutionary strategy: from a focus on *opposition* to an emphasis on *alternatives*. As discussed in chapter 5, during an earlier stage of capitalism, the enlightened proletariat and its allies sought to make the revolution in order to gradually establish direct democracy and the New Human Being. Today, it's the other way around: we must create direct democracy and the New Human Being in order to achieve the revolution.

This goal requires big changes in the process of making change because, unlike the old form of revolution, direct democracy and new ways of being cannot be achieved overnight, with a sudden top-down transformation. It has to be an incremental organic process, very much like, as Robert Rodale (1985) wrote, ecological plant succession.

New dangers, of course, arise from this process, since incremental change more often than not results in co-optation and marginal reform that simply reinforces the status quo. This is the great problem of our era: how do we implement gradual organic change that is also radical and qualitative? The modest answer this book proposes is simply grassroots alternatives guided by large social visions.

This answer will not be a popular one in academic circles, which these days are more divorced than ever from practical activism and are immersed in a decadent form of intellectualistic liberalism called postmodernism, which is suspicious of any large social or political vision. Fortunately, cutting-edge elements of all the new social movements are becoming more engaged in developing vision in tandem with practical alternatives. My hope is that this book can contribute in some way to discussion about the form and content of some of these alternatives.

One of the biggest problems of focusing on the creation of grassroots alternatives is that they appear to skeptics to be so *utopian*. To the impatient realist, it might seem more reasonable to tinker with, or add some controls on, the existing system. In fact, the main reason a green economy sounds so utopian is that the existing system is so incredibly irrational, unjust, and inefficient. What some might consider utopian is simply a common-sense orientation to serve basic human needs in a relatively efficient way.

The simple directness of green economic alternatives is one big reason why their appeal is potentially so great. A major portion of green change is a "no regrets/win-win" proposition. Properly designed initiatives can provide dollar savings or profits, higher quality of life, and tremendously interesting work. There may be some self-indulgence to be sacrificed, but even here we can appeal to self-interest of a different sort—the attraction to a higher, more fulfilling quality of life. People can truly "Get a Life" (Roberts and Brandum, 1995) by looking to serve society and the planet.

The "ecotopian" aspect of green development—the fact that it deals with real needs, real efficiencies, and qualitative factors—may actually be its most powerful source of magnetic appeal. By contrast, the sad compromises proposed by some elements of the left (Lipietz, 1995, 1992)—involving "managed" global trade, marginal state democratization, new wage pacts, and international environmental regulations—may be more unattainable than alternatives that involve many people on a much deeper level. Besides not dealing with the fundamental problems, these compromises provide no substance to resonate with people's real needs and hopes.

A grassroots green economic perspective toes the line between positive and critical consciousness. Green solutions are economic solutions that, as permaculturalist Bill Mollison (1983) argues, always bring real returns. They're such a good deal, claims Amory Lovins, that they amount to not just a "free lunch" but a "lunch you get paid to eat." Greens will, therefore, often be working with business (or, increasingly, *be* business). As greens work with market forces, they should appreciate the limits of markets and be able to go beyond narrow green capitalism with an authentic community vision.

By the same token, CED is sometimes being used by governments as a means to abrogate their responsibilities while the Welfare State is being dismantled. It is a way to "keep the little people busy" with marginal self-employment while bolstering corporate competitiveness in world markets. Authentic community economic development means nothing less than CED's becoming the basis for all economic activity, mainstream or otherwise. Greens can contribute an ecological perspective to demonstrate how this can happen.

As alternatives are being improvised, it is important to be realistic about how change is made. There will be tremendous systemic resistance to many initiatives, however sensible and even profitable they may be. "Institutional inefficiency" is the term Lovins (1993) uses for organizations constantly working against their own best interests.

Having 51-percent support for green alternatives may not be necessary to have major impacts. It is very likely that a major sea-change in developed countries may require some form of catastrophe, be it an economic or ecological crash, urban social collapse, a health crisis, or whatever. The majority of people may not be willing to seriously look at alternatives until then. The important point is that our alternatives must be functioning well by the time that crisis occurs, and they must begin to penetrate the mainstream and not just the fringe as proven examples of another way of doing things. If they aren't functioning at this level when a collapse does come, many people will more likely opt for ethnic cleansing or survivalism than for ecological community. In short, our alternatives need to be much more developed than they are today. Today, our actions are as "seed groups," planting kernels that may bloom fabulously someday. If not, then we have still opted for a life more full of joy and depth.

This work has tried mainly to convey an approach, a strategic perspective based on current trends and emerging potentials. Current trends in capitalism, particularly the polarization of rich and poor and the financialization of production, make it essential that we recapture a radicalism that truly goes "to the roots" of our problems. We must come up with alternative development plans that not only serve social and environmental needs but unleash human potentials.

It's time to get more ecotopian and more practical at the same time. We need to get more projects and enterprises going in every sector of the economy. It's something we can begin in our own job, profession, or neighborhood. Everything worth doing can be done in a green way.

Our social movement activity has to continue getting more positive—opposing poverty, homelessness, exploitation, racism, and other injustices with grassroots alternatives as well as oppositional activity. We can defend hard-won gains by opposing cutbacks to the Welfare State while upping the ante by planning even more comprehensive community-based welfare services. Our work against corporate trade agreements needs to support the alternative economic development going on right in our own bioregions. Truly radical solutions are by no means extremist, but centered and organic. Our oppositionalism should be like that of the Tai Chi master who can blend with, and divert, an attack while transmuting the negative into positive.

A great benefit of green activism, based in alternatives, is that, even against great odds, it can provide tremendous personal fulfilment. There is great satisfaction in making community gardens, in building ecological structures, in providing regenerative human services—a real contrast to the rapid burnout that often comes with oppositional activity and old-line movement organizing. Today, even old-style organizing can be enriched by the practical gains accompanying green economic development.

The social movements of today are still quite young. We are in the process of developing a common language to define our historical situation. Unfortunately, we don't have a lot of time to refine it, but we will have to do our best, even while recognizing that each of our perspectives is limited. In recent years, there has been a virtual explosion of interest and writing on green economics, in tandem with growing popular disillusionment concerning corporate globalization. And yet awareness of alternatives to globalization is still quite dim. My hope is that this book can contribute to such awareness, and provide some context for the development of strategies which can deal with our fundamental problems.

Works Cited

Allenby, Braden R., and Deanna J. Richards, eds. 1994. *The Greening of Industrial Ecosystems*. Washington D.C.: National Academy Press.

Alexander, Christopher. 1979. *The Timeless Way of Building*. New York: Oxford University Press.

Alexander, Christopher, Hajo Neis, Artemis Anninou, and Ingrid King. 1987. *A New Theory of Urban Design*. New York: Oxford University Press.

Alexander, Christopher, Murray Silverstein, Shlomo Angel, Sara Ishikawa, and Denny Abrams. 1975. *The Oregon Experiment*. New York: Oxford University Press.

Alexander, Christopher, Sara Iskikawa, Murray Silverstein, with Max Jacobson, Ingrid Fiksdahl-King, and Shlomo Angel. 1977. *A Pattern Language: Towns, Buildings, Construction*. New York: Oxford University Press.

Alexander, Christopher, with Howard Davis, Julio Martinez, and Don Corner. 1985. *The Production of Houses*. New York: Oxford University Press.

Amott, Teresa. 1993. *Caught in a Crisis: Women and the U.S. Economy Today*. New York: Monthly Review.

Armstrong, Pat, and Hugh Armstrong. 1990. *Theorizing Women's Work*. Toronto: Garamond.

Arrighi, Giovanni. 1994. *The Long Twentieth Century: Money, Power and the Origins of Our Times*. London: Verso.

Ayres, Ed. 1996. "The Expanding Shadow Economy." *World Watch* 9:4 (July/August): 10–23.

Ayres, Robert U. 1993. "Industrial Metabolism—Closing the Materials Cycle." In *Clean Production Strategies*, edited by Tim Jackson. Boca Raton, Fla.: Lewis.

———. 1998. *Turning Point: The End of the Growth Paradigm*. London: Earthscan.

Bahro, Rudolf. 1994. *Avoiding Social & Ecological Disaster: The Politics of World Transformation*. Bath, U.K.: Gateway.

———. 1986. *Building the Green Movement*. Philadelphia: New Society.

———. 1982. *Socialism and Survival*. London: Heretic.

Baran, Paul A., and Paul M. Sweezy. 1966. *Monopoly Capital*. New York: Monthly Review.

Barnet, Richard J., and John Cavanagh. 1994. *Global Dreams: Imperial Corporations and the New World Order*. New York: Touchstone.

Barrett, Neil. 1996. *The State of the Cybernation: Cultural, Political and Economic Implications of the Internet*. London: Kogan Page.

Bazelon, David. 1963. *The Paper Economy*. New York: Vintage.

Bennis, Warren. 1966. *Beyond Bureaucracy: Essays on the Development and Evolution of Human Organization*. New York: McGraw-Hill.

Berg, Peter, Beryl Magilavy and Seth Zukerman. 1989. *A Green City Program for San Francisco Bay Area Cities and Towns*. San Francisco: Planet Drum Books.

Berman, Daniel M., and John T. O'Connor. 1996. *Who Owns the Sun? People, Politics, and the Struggle for a Solar Economy*. White River Junction, Vt.: Chelsea Green.

Berman, Morris. 1989. *Coming to Our Senses: Body and Spirit in the Hidden History of the West*. New York: Simon and Schuster.

———. 1981. *The Reenchantment of the World*. Ithaca: Cornell University Press.

Berry, Thomas. 1988. *The Dream of the Earth*. San Francisco: Sierra Club Books.

Berry, Wendell. 1987. *Home Economics: 14 Essays*. San Francisco: North Point.

———. 1990. *What Are People For?: Essays by Wendell Berry*. San Francisco: North Point.

Biehl, Janet. 1998. *The Politics of Social Ecology: Libertarian Municipalism*. Montreal: Black Rose.

Block, Fred L. 1977. *The Origins of International Economic Disorder: A Study of International Monetary Policy from World War II to the Present*. Berkeley: University of California Press.

———. 1987. *Revising State Theory: Essays in Politics and Postindustrialism*. Philadelphia: Temple University Press.

Block, Fred, and Larry Hirschhorn. 1979. "New Productive Forces and the Contradictions of Contemporary Capitalism: A Postindustrial Perspective." *Theory and Society* 7 (May–June): 363–90.

Bonefeld, Werner. 1995. "Monetarism and Crisis." In *Global Capital, National State and the Politics of Money*, edited by Werber Bonefeld and John Holloway. New York: St. Martin's.

Bookchin, Murray. 1995. *From Urbanization to Cities*. London: Cassell.

———. 1991. "Libertarian Municipalism: An Overview." *Green Perspectives: A Social Ecology Publication* 24 (October): 1–6.

———. 1989. *Remaking Society*. Montreal: Black Rose.

Brand, Stewart. 1994. *How Buildings Learn: What Happens after They're Built*. New York: Viking/Penguin.

Brandt, Barbara. 1995. *Whole Life Economics: Revaluing Daily Life*. Philadelphia: New Society.

Braungart, Michael. 1994. "Product Life-Cycle Management to Replace Waste Management." In *Industrial Ecology and Global Change*, edited by Socolow, Andrews, Berkhout, and Thomas, 335–37. New York: Cambridge University Press.

Braverman, Harvey. 1974. *Labour and Monopoly Capitalism*. New York: Monthly Review.

Brecher, Jeremy, and Tim Costello. 1994. *Global Village or Global Pillage: Economic Reconstruction from the Bottom Up*. Boston: South End.

Brody, David. 1980. *Workers in Industrial America: Essays on the 20th Century Struggle*. New York: Oxford University Press.

Brower, Michael and Warren Leon. 1999. *The Consumer's Guide to Effective Environmental Choices: Practical Advice from the Union of Concerned Scientists*. New York: Three Rivers Press.

Burns, Scott. 1975. *The Household Economy: Its Shape, Origins and Future*. Boston: Beacon.

Cahn, Edgar, and Jonathan Rowe. 1992. *Time Dollars*. Emmaus, Pa.: Rodale.

Calthorpe, Peter. 1993. *The Next American Metropolis: Ecology, Community and the American Dream*. New York: Princeton Architectural Press.

Castells, Manuel. 1989. *The Informational City: Information Technology, Economic Restructuring and the Urban-Regional Process*. Oxford: Basil Blackwell.

———. 1996. *The Rise of the Network Society*. Oxford: Basil Blackwell.

Chandler, Alfred. 1977. *The Visible Hand: The Managerial Revolution in American Business*. Cambridge, Mass.: Belknap.

Cobb, Clifford, Ted Halstead, and Jonathan Rowe. 1995. "If the GDP is Up, Why is America Down?" *Atlantic Monthly* (October): 60.

———. 1995. *The Genuine Progress Indicator: Summary of Data and Methodology*. San Francisco: Redefining Progress.

Cohen, Stephen S. 1993. "Geo-Economics: Lessons from America's Mistakes." In *The New Global Economy in the Information Age: Reflections on Our Changing World*, edited by Martin Carnoy, Manuel Castells, Stephen S. Cohen, and Fernando Henrique Cardoso, 97–148. University Park, Pa.: Penn State University Press.

Colburn, Theo, Dianne Dumanoski, and John P. Myers. 1996. *Our Stolen Future*. New York: Plume/Penguin.

Cole, Nancy, and P. J. Skerrett. 1995. *Renewables Are Ready: People Creating Renewable Energy Solutions*. White River Junction, Vt.: Real Goods/Chelsea Green.

Commoner, Barry. 1992. "Breaking the Chlorine Trap." Audiotape of lecture presented at Chlorine-Free Great Lakes conference (December).

———. 1971. *The Closing Circle: Nature, Man, and Technology*. New York: Knopf, 1971.

———. 1990. *Making Peace With the Planet*. New York: Pantheon.

Connett, Paul. 1993. "Waste Management as if the Future Mattered." Film.

Cornell Work and Environment Initiative. 1998. Web site, <http://www.cfe.cornell.edu/wei/eid.html>.

Cote, Raymond P., and E. Cohen-Rosenthal. 1998. "Designing Eco-Industrial Parks: A Synthesis of Some Experiences." Web site, <http://www.cfe.cornell.edu/wei/design.doc.htm>.

Cote, Raymond P., Robert Ellison, Jill Grant, Jeremy Hall, Peter Klynstra, Michael Martin, and Peter Wade. 1994. "Designing and Operating Industrial Parks as Ecosystems." Halifax, N.S.: Dalhousie University's School for Resource and Environmental Studies.

Cowan, Ruth Schwartz. 1983. *More Work For Mother: The Ironies of Household Technology from the Open Hearth to the Microwave*. New York: Basic.

Crawford, Tad. 1994. *The Secret Life of Money: How Money Can Be Food for the Soul*. New York: Allworth.

Dalla Costa, Mariarosa, and Selma James. 1975. *The Power of Women and the Subversion of the Community*. Bristol: Falling Wall.

Daly, Herman E. 1996. *Beyond Growth: The Economics of Sustainable Development*. Boston: Beacon.

Daly, Herman E., and John B. Cobb. 1989. *For the Common Good: Redirecting the Economy Toward Community, the Environment, and a Sustainable Future*. Boston: Beacon.

Dauncey, Guy. 1988. *After the Crash: The Emergence of the Rainbow Economy*. Bosingstake, Hants, Eng.: Green Print.

———. 1993. "Eco-Community Design," *In Context* 35 (spring).

Deaton, Richard. 1989. *The Political Economy of Pensions: Power, Politics and Social Change in Canada, Britain and the U.S.* Vancouver: University of British Columbia Press.

Deibert, Ronald J. 1997. *Parchment, Printing, and Hypermedia: Communication in World Order Transformation*. New York: Columbia University Press.

DeKerckhove, Derrick. 1997. *Connected Intelligence: The Arrival of the Web Society*. Toronto: Somerville House.

——. 1995. *The Skin of Culture: Investigating the New Electronic Reality*. Toronto: Somerville House.

De Oude, N. 1993. "Product Life Cycle Analysis—Developing a Methodology." In *Clean Production Strategies: Developing Preventive Environmental Management in the Industrial Economy*, edited by Tim Jackson. Boca Raton, Fla.: Lewis.

Dillon, John. 1996. *Turning the Tide: Confronting the Money Traders*. Ottawa: Canadian Centre for Policy Alternatives.

Dobson, Ross V. G. 1993. *Bringing the Economy Home from the Market*. Montreal: Black Rose.

Dominguez, Joseph R., and Vicki Robin. 1991 (reprinted 1999). *The Growth Illusion: How Economic Growth has Enriched the Few, Impoverished the Many and Endangered the Planet*. Gabriola Island, B.C.: New Society Publishers.

——. 1996. *Short-Circuit: Strengthening Local Economies for Security in an Unstable World*. Dublin: Lilliput.

——. 1992. *Your Money or Your Life: Transforming Your Relationship with Money and Achieving Financial Independence*. New York: Viking.

Dubofsky, Melvyn. 1987. "Technological Change and American Worker Movements, 1870–1970." In *Technology, the Economy and Society: The American Experience*, edited by Joel Colton and Stuart Bruchey, 162–85. New York: Columbia University Press.

Dunn, Seth. 1997. "Power of Choice." *World Watch* (September/October): 30–35.

Eichler, Margrit, ed. 1995. *Change of Plans: Towards a Non-Sexist Sustainable City*. Toronto: Garamond.

Ellmen, Eugene. 1998. "Community-Supported Financing of Small Business and Microenterprise." Research report for Industry Canada (June). Canadian Community Investment web site, <http://www.web.net/~invest/papers.html>.

Fiksel, Joseph et al. 1996. *Design for Environment: Creating Eco-Efficient Products and Processes*. New York: McGraw-Hill.

Flavin, Christopher, and Nicholas Lenssen. 1994. *Power Surge: Guide to the Coming Energy Revolution*. New York: Worldwatch/Norton.

Fowler, Edmund D. 1992. *Building Cities That Work*. Montreal: McGill-Queen's University Press.

Foster, John Bellamy. 1994. *The Vulnerable Planet: A Short Economic History of the Environment*. New York: Cornerstone/MR.

Franklin, Ursula. 1990. *The Real World of Technology*, The Massey Lectures. Montreal: CBC Enterprises.

Friedman, John. 1994. "Where We Stand: A Decade of World City Research." In *World Cities in a World-System*, edited by Paul L. Knox and Peter J. Taylor. New York: Cambridge University Press.

Friends of the Earth. 1998. *Citizens' Guide to Environmental Tax Shifting*. Washington, D.C.: Friends of the Earth.

Frosch, Robert A. 1992. "Industrial Ecology: A Philosophical Introduction." *Proceedings of the National Academy of Sciences* 89 (February): 800–803.

Fuller, R. Buckminster. 1969. *Utopia or Oblivion: The Prospects for Humanity*. New York: Bantam.

Galbraith, John Kenneth. 1973. *Economics and the Public Purpose*. Boston: Houghton Mifflin.

——. 1975. *Money: Whence It Came, Where It Went*. Boston: Houghton Mifflin.

Gamble, Andrew. 1988. *The Free Economy and the Strong State: The Politics of Thatcherism*. London: MacMillan Education.

Gardner, Gary. 1999. "Our Shared Future." *World Watch* 12:4 (July/August).

Garreau, Joel. 1991. *Edge City: Life on the New Frontier*. New York: Doubleday.

Geddes, Patrick. 1915. *Cities in Evolution*. New York: Harper & Row.

Gehl, Jan. 1987. *Life between Buildings: Using Public Space*. New York: Van Nostrand Reinold.

Gelbspan, Ross. 1997. *The Heat Is On: The High Stakes Battle over Earth's Threatened Climate*. Reading, Mass.: Addison-Wesley.

Gibbs, Lois Marie, and the Citizens Clearinghouse for Hazardous Waste. 1995. *Dying from Dioxin: A Citizen's Guide to Reclaiming Our Health and Rebuilding Democracy*. Boston: South End.

Gilder, George. 1994. *Life after Television*. New York: Norton.

——. 1989. *Microcosm: The Quantum Revolution in Economics and Technology*. New York: Simon & Schuster.

Gordon, David M., Richard Edwards, and Michael Reich. 1982. *Segmented Work, Divided Workers: The Historical Transformation of Labor in the United States*. Cambridge: Cambridge University Press.

Gorz, Andre. 1980. *Farewell to the Working Class: An Essay on Post-Industrial Socialism*. Boston: South End.

——. 1983. *Paths to Paradise*. Boston: South End.

Greco, Thomas A. 1994. *New Money for Healthy Communities*. Tucson: Greco.

Grossman, Richard. 1978. "Energy and Jobs." In *Sun: A Handbook for the Solar Decade*, ed. Stephen Lyons. San Francisco: Friends of the Earth.

Gunn, Christopher, and Hazel Dayton Gunn. 1991. *Reclaiming Capital: Democratic Initiatives and Community Development*. Ithaca: Cornell University Press.

Guttman, Robert. 1994. *How Credit-Money Shapes the Economy: The United States in a Global System*. Armonk, N.Y.: Sharpe.

Harrison, Bennett. 1994. *Lean and Mean: The Changing Landscape of Corporate Power in the Age of Flexibility*. New York: Basic.

Harrison, Bennett, and Barry Bluestone. 1988. *The Great U-Turn: Corporate Restructuring and the Polarizing of America*. New York: Basic.

Hart, Maureen. 1998. Sustainable Community Indicators web site, <http://www.subjectmatters.com/indicators>.

Harvey, David. 1989. *The Urban Experience*. Baltimore: Johns Hopkins University Press.

Hawken, Paul. 1993. *The Ecology of Commerce: A Declaration of Sustainability*. New York: Harper Business.

——. 1996. "Natural Capitalism." 1996. Presentation given to Ontario Hydro central headquarters, Toronto (June 6).

Hawken, Paul, Amory Lovins, and L. Hunter Lovins. 1999. *Natural Capitalism: Creating the Next Industrial Revolution*. Boston: Little, Brown.

Hayden, Anders. 1999. *Sharing the Work, Sparing the Planet: Work Time, Consumption and Ecology*. London and New York: Zed; Toronto: Between the Lines; Sydney: Pluto Press Australia.

Hayden, Delores. 1981. *The Grand Domestic Revolution: A History of Feminist Designs for Homes, Neighborhoods and Cities*. Boston: MIT Press.

――. 1984. *Redesigning the American Dream: The Future of Housing, Work and Family Life*. New York: Norton.

Hemptech. 1995. *Industrial Hemp: Practical Products—Paper to Fabric to Cosmetics*. Booklet. Ojai, Calif.: Hemptech.

Henderson, Hazel. 1978 (reprinted 1996). *Creating Alternative Futures: The End of Economics*. West Hartford, Conn.: Kumarian.

――. 1991 (reprinted 1995). *Paradigms in Progress: Life Beyond Economics*. San Francisco: Berrett-Koehler.

――. 1981. *The Politics of the Solar Age: Alternatives to Economics*. New York: Doubleday; New York: TOES Books (1988).

Henwood, Doug. 1997. *Wall Street: How It Works and for Whom*. London: Verso.

Hirschhorn, Larry. 1984. *Beyond Mechanization: Work and Technology in a Postindustrial Age*. Cambridge, Mass.: MIT Press.

Hoffman, W. G. 1958. *The Growth of Industrial Economies*. Manchester: Manchester University Press.

Hough, Michael. 1995. *Cities and Natural Process*. New York: Routledge.

Hunnicutt, Benjamin Kline. 1988. *Work without End: Abandoning Shorter Hours for the Right to Work*. Philadelphia: Temple University Press.

Hyde, Lewis. 1979. *The Gift: Imagination and the Erotic Life of Property*. New York: Vintage.

Illich, Ivan. 1974. *Energy and Equity*. London: Calder & Boyars.

Institute for Community Economics. 1982. *The Community Land Trust Handbook*. Emmaus, Pa.: Rodale.

Institute for Local Self-Reliance. 1997. *The New Rules Project: Designing Rules as if Community Matters*. Minneapolis: Institute for Local Self-Reliance.

Jackson, Tim. 1961. *The Death and Life of Great American Cities*. New York: Random House.

――. 1970. *The Economy of Cities*. New York: Random House.

――. 1996. *Material Concerns: Pollution, Profit and Quality of Life*. London: Routledge.

――. 1992. *Systems of Survival*. New York: Random House.

Jacobs, Michael. 1991. *The Green Economy: Environment, Sustainable Development and the Politics of the Future*. London: Pluto.

Jessup, Phil. 1992. "Energy and Cities." International Congress on Local Environmental Initiatives presentation to Energy Action Council of Toronto forum, Urban Environment Centre (spring).

Kane, Hal. 1996. "Shifting to Sustainable Industries." In *State of the World 1996*, edited by Lester Brown et al. New York: Worldwatch/Norton.

Kats, Gregory H., Arthur H. Rosenfeld, and Scott A. McGaraghan. 1998. "Energy Retrofits: History and Future of ESCOs in the Age of Deregulation: A $100 Billion US Market." E-Design Online web site, <http://www.fcn.state.fl.us/fdi/e-design/online/9706/retro.htm>.

Kelly, Kevin. 1994. *Out of Control: The New Biology of Machines, Social Systems and the Economic World*. Reading, Mass.: Addison-Wesley.

Kemp, William B., and Lorraine F. Brooke. 1995. "Toward Information Self-Sufficiency: The Nunavik Inuit Gather Information on Ecology and Land Use." *Cultural Survival Quarterly* (winter): 25–28.

Kennedy, Margrit. 1995. *Interest and Inflation-Free Money: Creating an Exchange Medium That Works for Everybody and Protects the Earth*. Philadelphia: New Society.

Kessler-Harris, Alice. 1982. *Out to Work: A History of Wage-Earning Women in the United States*. New York: Oxford University Press.

Kindleberger, Charles. 1978. *Manias, Panics, and Crashes*. New York: Basic Books.

King, Stanley, with Merinda Conley, Bill Latimer, and Drew Ferrari. 1989. *Co-Design: A Process of Design Participation*. New York: Van Nostrand Reinhold.

Kneen, Brewster. 1995. "CSA Roots in Japan." *In Context* 42 (fall): 30.

Knox, Paul, and John Agnew. 1989. *The Geography of the World Economy*. London: Edward Arnold.

Korten, David. 1999. *The Post-Corporate World: Life after Capitalism*. San Francisco: Berrett-Koehler.

Kurtzman, Joel. 1993. *The Death of Money: How the Electronic Economy Has Destabilized the World's Markets and Created Financial Chaos*. New York: Little, Brown.

Laitner, Skip. 1995. "Energy Efficiency Investments as a Productivity Strategy for the United States: An Overview." Report for Economic Research Associates (June).

Lazarus, Chris. 1993. "Working Gently with the Genius of Place: An Interview with William McDonough on the Relevance of Indigenous Architecture." *Earthword* 5 (fall).

Leonard, George. 1972. *The Transformation: A Guide to the Inevitable Changes in Humankind*. New York: Delta.

Linton, Michael. 1996. "Money and the Sustainable Economy," in *LETSystems - New Money: An overview of LETSystems, local currencies and the future of money*. LETSystem web site, <http://www.gmlets.u-net.com/explore/sustain.html>.

———. 1996. "Money Is Information," in *LETSystems - New Money: An overview of LETSystems, local currencies and the future of money*. LETSystem web site, <http://www.gmlets.u-net.com/explore/minfo.html>.

Linton, Michael, and Thomas Greco. 1987. "The Local Employment Trading System." *Whole Earth Review* (summer).

Lipietz, Alain. 1995. *Green Hopes: The Future of Political Ecology*. Cambridge: Polity.

———. 1992. *Towards a New Economic Order: Post-Fordism, Ecology and Democracy*. Cambridge: Polity.

Lorenz, David. 1995. *A New Industry Emerges: Making Construction Materials from Cellulosic Wastes*. Washington, D.C.: Institute for Local Self-Reliance.

Lovins, Amory. 1989. "Energy, People, and Industrialization." Paper commissioned for the Hoover Institution conference "Human Demography and Natural Resources," Stanford University (February 1–3).

———. 1993. "Institutional Inefficiency: Guidelines for Overcoming the Market Failure That Is Now Causing Widespread Energy Waste." *In Context* 35: 16–17.

———. 1986. "Negawatts—Rx for Megagoofs." *Public Power* (March–April): 10–16.

———. 1977. *Soft Energy Paths*. New York: Harper Colophon.

Lyle, John Tillman. 1994. *Regenerative Design for Sustainable Development*. New York: John Wiley.

Mackintosh, Maureen. 1993. "Creating the Developmental State: Reflections on Policy As a Process." In *A Different Kind of State? Popular Power and Democratic Administration*, edited by Greg Albo, David Languille, and Leo Panitch, 36–50. Toronto: Oxford University Press.

Mandel, Ernest. 1962. *Marxist Economic Theory*. London: Merlin.

Mander, Jerry, and Edward Goldsmith. 1996. *The Case Against the Global Economy, and for a Turn Toward the Local*. San Francisco: Sierra Club Books.

Marx, Karl. 1961. *Capital*, vol. 1 (1887). Moscow: Foreign Languages Publishing House.

———. 1962. "Preface to Contribution to the Critique of Political Economy" (1859). In *Karl Marx and Frederick Engels: Selected Works*, vol. 1, 361–65. Moscow: Foreign Languages Publishing House.

Mattera, Philip. 1985. *Off the Books: The Rise of the Underground Economy*. London: Pluto.

Matthaei, Julie A. 1982. *An Economic History of Women in America: Women's Work, the Sexual Division of Labour, and the Development of Capitalism*. New York: Schocken.

McCamant, Kathryn. 1988. *Cohousing: A Contemporary Approach to Housing Ourselves*. Berkeley, Calif.: Habitat.

McConkey, Mike. 1991. "Green Municipal Democracy." In *Towards a Toronto Green City Program*. Toronto: Green City Programme Project.

McDonough, William, and Michael Braungart. 1998. "The Next Industrial Revolution." *Atlantic Monthly* (October).

McLuhan, Marshall. 1964. *Understanding Media: The Extensions of Man*. New York: Mentor.

McMurtry, John. 1999. *The Cancer Stage of Capitalism*. London: Pluto.

———. 1998. *Unequal Freedoms: the Global Market as an Ethical System*. Toronto: Garamond Press.

McQuaig, Linda. 1998. *The Cult of Impotence: Selling the Myth of Powerlessness in the Global Economy*. Toronto: Viking.

———. 1995. *Shooting the Hippo: Death by Deficit and Other Canadian Myths*. Toronto: Penguin.

McRobie, George. 1981. *Small Is Possible*. New York: Harper & Row.

Meeker-Lowry, Susan. 1995. *Invested in the Common Good*. Gabriola Island, B.C.: New Society.

Melman, Seymour. 1987. *Profits Without Production*. Philadelphia: University of Pennsylvania Press.

Mies, Maria. 1986. *Patriarchy and Accumulation on a World Scale: Women in the International Division of Labour*. London: Zed.

Mies, Maria, and Vandana Shiva. 1993. *Ecofeminism*. London: Zed.

Mies, Maria and Veronika Bennholdt-Thomsen. 1999. *The Subsistence Perspective: Beyond The Globalized Economy*. London, New York: Zed Books; Victoria, Australia: Spinifex Press.

Miles, Angela R. 1996. *Integrative Feminisms: Building Global Visions, 1960s–1990s*. New York: Routledge.

———. 1979. "The Politics of Feminist Radicalism: A Study in Integrative Feminism." Unpublished Ph.D. diss., University of Toronto.

Mollison, Bill. 1990. *Permaculture*. New York: Island.

———. 1983. "Principles of Permaculture Design." Audiotape of workshop given at Chinook Learning Community Planetary Village Conference (June).

Montgomery, David. 1993. *Citizen Worker: The Experience of Workers in the U.S. with Democracy and the Free Market*. Cambridge: Cambridge University Press.

———. 1979. *Workers' Control in America: Studies in the History of Work, Technology and Labor Struggles*. Cambridge: Cambridge University Press.

Morris, David. 1998. "Mapping Environmental Taxes: Obstacles and Opportunities." Keynote address given to Greening State Taxes: National Conference on State Tax Reform for a Sustainable Economy, Seattle (December).

Morris, David, and Irshad Ahmed. 1993. *The Carbohydrate Economy: Making Chemicals and Industrial Materials from Plant Matter*. Washington, D.C.: Institute for Local Self-Reliance.

Morris, David, Irshad Ahmed, and David Pettijohn. 1994. *Replacing Petrochemicals with Biochemicals: A Pollution Prevention Strategy for the Great Lakes Region*. Washington, D.C.: Institute for Local Self-Reliance.

Mumford, Lewis. 1967. *The Myth of the Machine: Technics and Human Development*. New York: Harcourt, Brace and World.

Murray, Robin. 1988. *Breaking with Bureaucracy: Ownership, Control and Nationalization*. Manchester: Center for Local Economic Strategies.

———. 1999. *Creating Wealth from Waste*. London: Demos.

———. 1993. "Transforming the 'Fordist' State." In *A Different Kind of State?* edited by Greg Albo, David Languille, and Leo Panitch, 51–65. Toronto: Oxford University Press.

Naisbitt, John. 1982. *Megatrends: Ten New Directions Transforming Our Lives*. New York: Warner Books.

Needleman, Jacob. 1991. *Money and the Meaning of Life*. New York: Doubleday/Currency.

Noble, David. 1977. *America By Design: Science, Technology and the Rise of Corporate Capitalism*. New York: Oxford University Press.

———. 1984. *Forces of Production: A Social History of Industrial Automation*. New York: Oxford University Press.

Nozick, Marcia. 1992. *No Place like Home: Building Sustainable Communities*. Ottawa: Canadian Council on Social Development.

O'Connor, James. 1973. *The Fiscal Crisis of the State*. New York: St. Martin's.

———. 1998. *Natural Causes: Essays in Ecological Marxism*. New York: Guilford.

O'Hara, Bruce. 1993. *Working Harder Isn't Working: How We Can Save the Environment, the Economy, and Our Sanity by Working Less and Enjoying Life More*. Vancouver: New Star.

O'Sullivan, Edmund. 1999. *Transformative Learning: Educational Vision for the 21ˢᵗ Century*. London: Zed.

Paehlke, Robert C. 1989. *Environmentalism and the Future of Progressive Politics*. New Haven, Conn.: Yale University Press.

Papanek, Victor. 1973. *Design for the Real World*. New York: Bantam.

———. 1995. *The Green Imperative: Natural Design for the Real World*. New York: Thames and Hudson.

Pauli, Gunter. 1998. *Upsizing: The Road to Zero Emissions, More Jobs, More Income, No Pollution*. Sheffield, U.K.: Greenleaf.

Pearse, Tony. 1994. "Tradition Plus High-Tech: A First Nations Example." In *Futures By Design: The Practice of Ecological Planning*, edited by Doug Aberley, 112–19. Gabriola Island, B.C.: New Society.

Perry, Stewart E. 1987. *Communities on the Way: Rebuilding Local Economies in the United States and Canada*. Albany: State University of New York Press.

Pietila, Hilkka. 1993. "A New Picture of Human Economy—A Woman's Perspective." Paper presented to International Interdisciplinary Congress on Women, San Jose, Costa Rica (February 22–26).

Piore, Michael, and Charles Sabel. 1984. *The Second Industrial Divide*. New York: Basic.

Polanyi, Karl. 1957. *The Great Transformation*. New York: Beacon.

———. 1968. *Primitive, Archaic and Modern Economies*, edited by George Dalton. New York: Beacon.

Pollard, Sidney. 1990. *Typology of Industrialization Processes in the 19th Century*. London: Harwood.

Quarter, Jack. 1992. *Canada's Social Economy: Cooperatives, Non-Profits and Other Community Enterprises*. Toronto: James Lorimer.

———. 1995. *Crossing the Line: Unionized Employee Ownership and Investment Funds*. Toronto: James Lorimer.

Rees, William E. 1995. "More Jobs, Less Damage: A Framework for Sustainability, Growth and Employment," *Alternatives Journal* 21: 4 (Oct./Nov.): 24–30.

Ribeiro, Darcy. 1968. *The Civilizational Process*. Washington, D.C.: Smithsonian Institution Press.

Richardson, Herbert W. 1971. *Nun, Witch, Playmate: The Americanization of Sex*. New York: Harper & Row.

Richta, Radovan, et al. 1969. *Civilization at the Crossroads: Social and Human Implications of the Scientific and Technological Revolution*. Prague: International Arts and Sciences.

Rifkin, Jeremy. 1995. *The End of Work: The Decline of the Global Labor Force and the Dawn of the Post-Market Era*. New York: Tarcher/Putnam.

Roberts, Wayne, and Susan Brandum. 1995. *Get a Life! How to Make a Good Buck, Dance Around the Dinosaurs, and Save the World While You're at It*. Toronto: Get a Life Publishers.

Roberts, Wayne, Rod MacRae, and Lori Stahlbrand. 1999. *Real Food for a Change*. Toronto: Random House.

Robertson, James. 1989. *Future Wealth: New Economics for the 21st Century*. London: Cassel.

———. 1985. *Future Work: Jobs, Self-Employment and Leisure after the Industrial Age*. Aldershot, Hants, Eng.: Gower.

Rodale Regeneration Project. 1985. *Regenerating America: A Grassroots Plan for Helping Local Economies to Thrive*. Booklet. Emmaus, Pa.: Rodale.

Rodale, Robert. 1985. "Pioneer Enterprises in Regeneration Zones," *Whole Earth Review*, no. 47 (July): 34-38; originally printed as a pamphlet by Rodale Regeneration Project, Emmaus, Pa.

Roodman, David M. 1995. "Harnessing the Market for the Environment." In Lester Brown et al., *State of the World 1996*. New York: Worldwatch/Norton.

———. 1998. *The Natural Wealth of Nations: Harnessing the Market for the Environment*. New York: Norton.

Roodman, David Malin, and Nicholas Lenssen. 1995. *A Building Revolution: How Ecology and Health Concerns Are Transforming Construction*. Worldwatch Paper 124 (March).

Roseland, Mark. 1998. *Towards Sustainable Communities: Resources for Citizens and their Governments*. Gabriola Island, B.C.: New Society.

Ross, David P., and Peter J. Usher. 1986. *From the Roots Up: Economic Development as if Community Mattered*. Croton-on-Hudson, N.Y.: Bootstrap.

Rowbotham, Michael. 1998. *The Grip of Death: A Study of Modern Money, Debt Slavery and Destructive Economics*. Charlbury, Oxfordshire, U.K.: Jon Carpenter.

Rowthorn, Bob. 1980. *Capitalism, Conflict and Inflation*. London: Lawrence and Wishart.

Rudhyar, Dane. 1979. *Beyond Individualism: The Psychology of Transformation*. London: Quest.

———. 1974. *We Can Begin Again Together*. Tucson: Omen.

Rybczynski, Witold. 1986. *Home: A Short History of an Idea*, New York: Viking Penguin.

Sabel, Charles. 1987. "The Re-Emergence of Regional Economies: Changes in the Scale of Production." In *Experimenting with Scale*, Social Science Research Council, Western European committee (August): 20–21.

Sachs, Wolfgang, Reinhard Loske, Manfred Linz, and other researchers of the Wuppertal Institute for Climate, Environment and Energy. 1998. *Greening the North: A Post-Industrial Blueprint for Ecology and Equity*. London: Zed.

Sassen, Saskia. 1994. *Cities in a World Economy*. Thousand Oaks, Calif.: Pine Forge.

———. 1991. *The Global City: New York, London, Tokyo*. Princeton: Princeton University Press.

Schor, Juliet B. 1992. *The Overworked American: The Unexpected Decline of Leisure*. New York: Basic.

Scott, Daniel. 1999. "Redeeming the Blue Box." *Alternatives Journal* 25:4 (fall).

Seabrook, Jeremy. 1991. *The Myth of the Market: Promises and Illusions*. Montreal: Black Rose Books.

Seccombe, Wally. 1993. *Weathering the Storm: Working-Class Families from the Industrial Revolution to the Fertility Decline*. London: Verso.

Shiva, Vandana. 1989. *Staying Alive: Women, Ecology and Development*. London: Zed.

Shorebank. 1998. Eco-bank web site, <http://www.eco-bank.com/index.html>.

Shuman, Michael H. 1998. *Going Local: Creating Self-Reliant Communities in a Global Age*. New York: Free.

Sklar, Holly. 1995. *Chaos or Community? Seeking Solutions, Not Scapegoats for Bad Economics*. Boston: South End.

Sklar, Martin J. 1969. "On the Proletarian Revolution and the End of Political-Economic Society." *Radical America* (May–June).

Smeloff, Ed, and Peter Asmus. 1997. *Reinventing Electric Utilities: Competition, Citizen Action, and Clean Power*. Washington, D.C.: Island.

Snooks, Graeme Donald. 1994. "Great Waves of Economic Change: The Industrial Revolution in Historical Perspective, 1000 to 2000." In *Was the Industrial Revolution Necessary?*, edited by Graeme Donald Snooks. New York: Routledge.

Sorkin, Michael, ed. 1992. *Variations on a Theme Park: The New American City and the End of Public Space*. New York: Noonday.

Sprague, Joan Forrester. 1991. *More Than Housing: Lifeboats for Women and Children*. Boston: Butterworth Architecture.

Stahel, Walter R. 1994. "The Utilization-Focused Service Economy: Resource Efficiency and Product-Life Extension." In *The Greening of Industrial Ecosystems*, edited by Braden R. Allenby and Deanna Richards, 178–90. Washington, D.C.: National Academy.

Steen, Athena Swentzell, Bill Steen, and David Bainbridge, with David Eisenberg. 1994. *The Strawbale House*. White River Junction, Vt.: Chelsea Green.

Stone, Michael Eric. 1993. *Shelter Poverty: New Ideas on Housing Affordability*. Philadelphia: Temple University Press.

Strange, Susan. 1986. *Casino Capitalism*. Oxford: Basil Blackwell.

———. 1998. *Mad Money: When Markets Outgrow Governments*. Ann Arbor: University of Michigan Press.

Sustainable Chattanooga. 1997. "'SMART Park' Eco-Industrial Initiative Announced For Chattanooga's Southside." Press release (November 19). Web site, <http://www.chattanooga.net/chamber/smartpart.html>.

Tapscott, Don. 1996. *The Digital Economy: Promise and Peril in the Age of Networked Intelligence*. New York: McGraw-Hill.

Taub, Richard P. 1988. *Community Capitalism*. Boston: Harvard Business School Press.

Tibbs, Hardin B. C. 1998. "Humane Ecostructure: Can Industry Become Gaia's Friend?" *Whole Earth Review* (summer): 61-63.

———. 1992. "Industrial Ecology: An Environmental Agenda for Industry." *Whole Earth Review* (winter): 4–19.

Tindale, Stephen, and Gerald Holtham. 1996. *Green Tax Reform: Pollution Payments and Labour Tax Cuts*. London: Institute for Public Policy Research.

Todd, Nancy Jack, and John Todd. 1994. *From Eco-Cities to Living Machines: Principles of Ecological Design*. Berkeley, Calif.: North Atlantic.

Toffler, Alvin. 1972. *Future Shock*. New York: Bantam.

———. 1980. *The Third Wave*. New York: Bantam.

Tomaney, John. 1994. "A New Paradigm of Work Organization and Technology?" In *Post-Fordism: A Reader*, edited by Ash Amin. Cambridge, Mass.: Basil Blackwell.

Tyler Norris Associates, Redefining Progress, and Sustainable Seattle. 1997. *Community Indicators Handbook*. San Francisco: Redefining Progess.

U.S. EPA. 1998. "Green Community Indicators." U.S. EPA Green Communities home page. Web site, <http://www.epa.gov/region03/greenkit/indicato.htm>.

Van der Ryn, Sim, and Stuart Cowan. 1996. *Ecological Design*. Washington, D.C.: Island.

Van En, Robyn. 1995. "Eating for Your Community: Towards Agriculture Supported Community." *In Context* 42 (fall).

Van Parijs, Philippe. 1992. *Arguing for Basic Income: Ethical Foundation for a Radical Reform*. London: Verso.

Von Weizsacker, Ernst Ulrich. 1994. *Earth Politics*. London: Zed.

Von Weizsacker, Ernst U., and Jochen Jesinghaus. 1992. *Ecological Tax Reform: A Policy Proposal for Sustainable Development*. London: Zed.

Wackernagel, Mathis, and William Rees. 1996. *Our Ecological Footprint: Reducing Human Impact on the Earth*. Gabriola Island, B.C.: New Society.

Walker, Perry, and Edward Goldsmith. 1998. "A Currency for Every Community." *Ecologist* 28:4 (July/August).

Wallerstein, Immanuel. 1979. *The Capitalist World-Economy*. Cambridge: Cambridge University Press.

Wann, David. 1996. *Deep Design: Pathways to a Livable Future*. Washington, D.C.: Island.

Waring, Marilyn. 1988. *If Women Counted: A New Feminist Economics*. San Francisco: Harper & Row.

———. 1997. *Three Masquerades: Essays on Equality, Work and Hu(man) Rights*. Toronto: University of Toronto Press.

Warshall, Peter. 1998. "Modern Landscape Ecology: Patterns of Infrastructure, Patterns of Ecostructure, Visions of a Gentler Way." *Whole Earth Review* (summer).

Watts, Alan W. 1967. "Instinct, Intelligence and Anxiety." In Watts, *This Is It! and Other Essays*, 41–58. New York: Collier-Macmillan.

Wekerle, Gerda R., Rebecca Peterson, and David Morley. 1980. *New Space for Women.* Boulder, Colo.: Westview.

WELD (West Enders for Local Democracy, Toronto). 1997. "Draft Proposal to Establish Ward-Based Citizens' Assemblies." (August.)

Whitaker, Jennifer Seymour. 1994. *Salvaging the Land of Plenty: Garbage and the American Dream*. New York: William Morrow.

Whyte, William H. 1988. *City: Rediscovering the Center*. New York: Anchor/Doubleday.

Wriggley, E.A. 1994. "The Classical Economists, the Stationary State, and the Industrial Revolution." In *Was the Industrial Revolution Necessary?*, edited by Graeme Donald Snooks. New York: Routledge.

Young, John E., and Aaron Sachs. 1994. *The Next Efficiency Revolution: Creating a Sustainable Materials Economy*. Worldwatch Paper 121 (September).

Young, Steven B., and Willem H. Vanderburg. 1994. "An Overview of Life Cycle Assessment (LCA) and Industrial Materials." Paper for Centre for Technology and Society, University of Toronto.

Zielinski, Sue. 1995. "Transporting Ourselves to Sustainable Economic Growth." Paper submitted to the International Institute for Sustainable Development meeting, Winnipeg, Manitoba, Canada (June 23–25).

Index

About the Author

Brian Milani is coordinator of Toronto's Eco-Materials Project, an ecological building materials information and advocacy group. He also teaches courses on green political-economy and ecological economics at the Metro Labour Education Centre, OISE/UT's Transformative Learning Centre, and York University's Faculty of Environmental Studies. A former carpenter and builder, he was a partner and co-founder of Toronto's Green City Construction. A longtime labor, community, and environmental activist, he has been active with Carpenters locals 27 and 452, the Green Work Alliance, Environmentalists Plan Toronto, the BC and Ontario Greens, and Citizens for Local Democracy. For the last eight years, he has been involved with the Coalition for a Green Economy in Toronto.

MUHLENBERG COLLEGE LIBRARY

3 1542 00201 4599

338.9 M637d
Milani, Brian, 1948–
Designing the green economy
: the postindustrial
alternative to corporate
globalization

DATE DUE

WITHDRAWN

Trexler Library
Muhlenberg College
Allentown, PA 18104